OBJECTIVE MORALITY WITHOUT GOD?

OBJECTIVE MORALITY WITHOUT GOD?

A Friendly Debate Between an Atheist and a Christian

Tom Jump and Rick Mattson
Forward by David K. Clark, PhD

Objective Morality Without God?
A Friendly Debate Between an Atheist and a Christian

ISBN 978-0-9997740-2-1

Contents

Foreword by David K. Clark, PhD

P EOPLE WITH CONFLICTING views don't talk with each other today. Some actually move to states where the local politics are to their liking so they don't have to live next to neighbors who think differently. When opponents are forced to share spaces, say, on a university campus, their interactions often quickly descend into shouting matches.

But in a free democracy, better ideas emerge in an evolutionary manner—the fittest survive. The best ideas are tested in the wild, not coddled in hothouses. Any idea, even a crazy conspiracy theory, can survive in the perfect growing environment that carefully eliminates any contrary evidence. But a vibrant society seeks better ways of thinking by fostering open discussion that challenges every claim and tests every idea.

The book you hold in your hands seeks to do just this. It's an example of an illuminating conversation between two people who couldn't disagree more. Their dialogue is civil even though their chosen topics are contentious. They actively dig into substantive topics that, in other contexts, often lead to shouting matches. But instead of allowing their lower brains to hijack their thinking processes, they calm their emotions, engage their thinking brains, and honestly engage each other's points.

So my most basic reason for valuing this conversation is that as a Christian, I find this mutual commitment to conversation most commendable. Dialogue demonstrates a mutual respect, an appreciation, a due regard for another person regardless of that person's ideas. Respect for others should depend on their status as human beings, not on common intellectual commitments or shared tribal membership.

Tom Jump is an atheist who holds extended conversations with Christians. He wants to know what Christians think. He seeks to answer their questions and rebut their critiques. He invites Christians to evaluate his views. He doesn't want his dialogue partner to abandon his faith simply because some Christians are hypocrites—which, sadly, they are. Tom invites him to consider atheism because he thinks his thought processes and life choices make the most sense of real life and the real world.

Rick Mattson is a Christian who listens carefully to atheists. Unlike believers who think you have to shut down your mind to find faith in Christ, he looks to ground his faith in real history and genuine philosophy. He seeks to offer a reasonable case for his faith. He doesn't want Tom to follow Jesus simply because faith leads to the most joy-filled life—although demonstrably it does. He also wants Tom to follow Jesus because good evidence suggests that Jesus is the Truth.

I appreciate both authors for this combination of passion and restraint. They're willing and able to engage each other seriously in a rare kind of discussion that is neither blasé nor belligerent. I'm convinced we need more of this kind of exchange in our time, whether the topic is religion or ethics, politics or science.

I have a further reason for welcoming this volume. I'm grateful that the authors agree that thinking is relevant to faith. We live in a day when people believe that religious faith is a private, subjective, non-rational affair. On this view, faith is about emotions and relationships, but not about objective reality.

If this were right, then people with contradictory religious views can both be in good standing, rationally speaking. I might believe that Jesus is the Son of God, for example, and you might think that Jesus is not the Son of God but only a great religious teacher. According to this privatized view of religion, we could both be right. Even though we contradict each other, both our views would be considered completely legitimate. Usually, this way of thinking is connected to an attitude in which religion is relegated to the world of feelings or emotions.

As a Christian, I do believe that a relationally healthy and emotionally satisfying intimacy with our Creator is the whole point of faith. But this subjectivized view of faith is wrong-headed. If our deepest life convictions aren't true or false in any sense, this disconnects our personal lives from reality. This is extremely hazardous.

Let me give a specific example. The Christian faith says that an intimate attachment to God is the antidote to a lonely, disconnected, depressed, or narcissistic life. This intimate connection to God is called "salvation." Christians say that salvation is the path to joyful life.

But if the teachings of the Christian faith make no real claim to being true, then the Good News that Jesus taught us has no power to make any practical difference in life. If this message is to make a real difference, the convictions of faith should be seen as true claims about the world. In this case, if they are in fact true, they lead to abundant living. If they are in fact false, then they lead nowhere. The actual truth of the Christian message is therefore critically important. What's great about this volume is that Christian claims are treated with the seriousness they deserve.

A final reason for commending this conversation is simple: it reveals the inner logic of the two very prominent perspectives Tom and Rick hold regarding faith and morality. It's instructive to observe an atheist seeking to frame a reasonable ground for his moral convictions. Great thinkers have long struggled with the basic dilemma: If there is no God, what then grounds morality? Either there is a God whose will and purposes for human life ground the distinction between right and wrong, or there is no God and therefore no "right" or "good" way to live, and life becomes whatever the powerful wish it to be.

Now, of course, some people willingly dispense with morality. Nietzsche was famous for saying that morality is but herd instinct, that it has no objective character, and that it is rooted in power.

But this move exacts a price. If there is no moral duty in our universe—if we as humans do not in any sense have an obligation to live in certain ways and guard against certain behaviors—then what happens when I'm under threat? Yes, if I wish to steal your inheritance, then being without any moral duties will work to my advantage. But on the other hand, if someone is trying to steal my inheritance, the moral duty to respect the property of others protects me. Nietzsche's philosophy may benefit the powerful, but it terrorizes the underprivileged.

If Nietzsche's option is not reasonable, then what? I appreciate Tom and Rick for truly digging into the questions around the fundamentally moral nature of human existence on Earth. Neither skirts the issue. It's front and center, as it should be. It forms the structure within which individuals find the meaning of existence and communities shape their common life.

For these reasons, I commend this dialogue as a prompt for the kind of serious reflection that you as a reader may find helpful in your quest to live a well-reasoned life.

David K. Clark is Theology Professor Emeritus at Bethel Seminary in St. Paul, MN, and author of *To Know and Love God.*

Introduction

By Rick Mattson

IN 1895 THE iconic American philosopher, William James, in his address to the Harvard Young Men's Christian Association, talked about two groups of people who tend to be pessimistic about spiritual matters. "Pessimism is essentially a religious disease," James said. The first of the two groups resolves their pessimism through spiritual contemplation, which comes naturally as they "wing their way to . . . a better world." They find solace in religion. The second group, however, cannot get past what James calls the "hard facts" of the visible world and thus they remain skeptical about religion. They are "positively shocked" at the ease with which the first group moves into the realm of the spirit.

I'm a member of the group that chooses religion, what James elsewhere calls a believer in "masses and holy water." Many religious skeptics (James's second group) view people like me as engaged in an act of blind faith – a leap in the dark. You want something such as religion to be true, so you make it so, at least in your mind. This is sometimes called "fideism" (faith without reason).

However, James also hints at a third way, something different than either fideism or skepticism. If the first group embraces religion without reason and the skeptical group rejects religion because of the hard facts of reality, the third group is positively inspired by these facts. For them, study of the natural world *inspires* religious trust toward a "better world." I hope to be in this third category – a person who looks at nature and is inspired toward God. My friend Tom Jump does not join me on this path. He identifies more with the religiously skeptical group and thinks nature itself has its own integrity. In Tom's view, we can learn much from the natural world, including how to live our lives ethically. To my thinking, nature points toward a law-giver (God). But to Tom, nature itself is the law-giver. Hence this book. Tom and I are debating in these pages the most probable source of objective morality: is it God? Or nature?

Two principles. I'm grateful to Tom for trusting me to write this introduction. Such charity demonstrates at least two important principles we're trying to model for the larger atheist and Christian communities (and other readers). The first is teamwork in seeking for truth. Steel sharpens steel, and there are few more effective cutting tools than a partner who scrutinizes your every utterance as you craft a worldview that corresponds, you hope, to reality. Thus you'll see Tom and I cutting sharply into each other's positions to challenge various lines of argumentation. We trust this exercise will help readers examine their own positions more critically.

The second principle is about attitude and tone of voice. We're trying to model deep disagreement respectfully. I find such considerate treatment of an opponent, whether philosophical or political, rare in the contemporary scene. Even in the university world where I work, where healthy public and private debate was once valued and practiced (to the great benefit of society), respectful disagreement has devolved into intransigent dogma and a sense of infallibility on all sides. We don't talk anymore, we simply cancel. University culture has become a war of fundamentalisms which, by definition, don't listen to each other. Here, steel doesn't sharpen steel because there is little openness to correction from an opponent. The pursuit of truth has been replaced by the pursuit of power – not the visionary, generous power to host liberal discourse, but the power to indoctrinate. In that sense, Tom and I are a throwback to the former days when neighboring parties could disagree *constructively.* A philosophy professor at a private college said to me recently, "We've become *illiberal.*" I took that to mean that we're no longer liberal in the classic sense, welcoming of opposing voices, no longer thinking of ourselves as humble truth-seekers but merely as ideologues entrenched in our insular tribal communities. Myself, I value Tom's friendship and I'm not going to let a "little thing" like opposing worldviews get in the way. It takes effort to maintain friendship amidst decisive disagreement. But so what? To me, Tom is worth it.

An important thing to know as you read the material is that Tom's and my debate unfolded sequentially. We didn't fully understand each other's positions until we wrote back and forth several times. Thus, we don't feign ignorance of each other to carry the reader along. Rather, the book is a live debate between two people who are gradually learning what the other thinks. I'm still not positive I understand all of Tom's positions. In any case, certainly, I've learned much from Tom (and about him), sharp thinker that he is.

The last word. Since this book was originally Tom's idea, he gets the last word. About ten years ago I received an email from a young atheist who'd heard there was a campus apologist living in St. Paul, MN – me. Soon after, Tom and I met for lunch and engaged in a friendly debate about the existence of God and the viability of Christianity. Subsequently, I appeared on his popular YouTube channel a couple of times. When he suggested writing a book together on the topic of ethics, I agreed right away. Tom never demanded that he get the last word in the book but it only seemed appropriate since the idea of the book was his. Thus, I will say here: I believe there are reasonable responses to Tom's final chapter that I'm not able to share.

The one thing Tom and I do agree on is that morality is objective. Neither of us thinks morality is based on the subjective opinions of human beings, but is grounded in a higher reality: nature (Tom) or God (me). So, philosophically, we both stand against relativistic conceptions of morality that are dependent on the shifting sands of cultural context. On this common ground, we find footing for what we hope is a helpful debate about objective morality.

OBJECTIVE MORALITY WITHOUT GOD?

Rick's Case for Theistic Morality

TO BEGIN, I'D like to offer a specific example of an ethical dilemma in hopes of finding a source of guidance for resolving it. Perhaps this source will be found within my own experience, or in my community, or in a majority vote, or in God. Whatever the source of morality, I'd want it to be an "objective" standard – that is, unchanging and universally true rather than representing mere subjective human opinion. More on that later.

For now, here is the ethical dilemma: Should I rob old man Biggie to support an orphanage?

Biggie made his money in oil and has a reputation for shady dealings. The orphans in question are suffering and are in need of an upgraded facility in which to grow and become productive citizens. I have the ability to embezzle funds from Biggie and funnel the money to do good. Biggie would never miss the stolen funds. He is greedy but slothful and disorganized. As I try to make the right decision about whether to victimize Biggie for a supposed greater good, here are some (but perhaps not all) options available to me:

I could look within. I could consult my conscience and experience and decide on my own whether or not to steal from Biggie. This would place me and my subjective opinions in the driver's seat. But who am I as a person? Am I humble or arrogant? Motivated by feelings or mainly by logic? A lot of the decision about whether to steal from Biggie depends on the quality of the decision-maker, and maybe even the person's current mood. Let's just say that I am both arrogant and feelings-oriented; thus I'm highly confident in myself, and I trust my heart to speak the truth in all situations (feelings are a reliable guide). So I decide to steal the money and help the underprivileged.

On the other hand, if I were humble and more logical, I might have made the opposite decision. It's hard to say. Either way, when the self is in charge of morality and only the self is consulted, morality seems very unstable.

I could consult my community. Morality in this case would be a group decision. This seems more reliable than just deciding on my own. As good as group decision-making sounds, I'd be worried about the quality of the group. If it were comprised mainly of any of these diverse categories: university professors, welders, daycare providers, single moms, or church elders, the advice I received would likely vary widely. Plato thought that philosophers should be in charge of society and morality; I doubt this would be a popular choice these days. In any case, the variable perspectives and character of the chosen community would be quite a wildcard in the Biggie decision-making process.

And how would I choose the community? I could recruit from any of the groups just mentioned (or many others), or I could default to one or more of my current communities, such as relatives, golfers, or clergy. In any case, a community-based decision defaults at least to some extent back to *my* choices. Yes, the community is giving its input, but the choice is still mine about which community to listen to. I can imagine the conflicting advice I'd receive from, say, ten police officers versus ten former orphans. So it seems I'm still placing myself and my opinions as the main arbiter of the moral dilemma of stealing from Biggie.

I could say, "majority rules." This method is similar to the community-based approach just mentioned but I'm trying to broaden it a bit by assuming I could poll hundreds, perhaps thousands of people to help with my decision. Practically speaking, during the polling process I'd have to hide my identity or change the details of the problem to protect myself from possible arrest for threatening to commit a crime against Biggie.

I'd also like to ask, Would a simple majority be sufficient? What if 51% voted to rob Biggie and 49% said no? That's a pretty close call. I'd have to be very committed to the idea of a simple majority to follow its rule. But again, this looks as though the standard of right and wrong is me and my judgment about whether to believe in the wisdom of a simple majority. Perhaps I'd make a slightly different rule for myself in advance: I won't commit the crime unless the majority in favor is at least 70%. This seems more reasonable, considering the risks involved. But more reasonable to whom? To me.

And is it really true that my adjusted rule of 70% majority is more important than the welfare of the orphans? Every illustration has its limits, and one could argue that there are other practical ways of helping the orphans, such as legitimate fundraising efforts. This I grant. But let's say the situation is pretty desperate and I don't have other means at my disposal. Old Biggie is the only possible solution. One could easily question my judgment that a 70% majority is the proper threshold for taking positive action against Biggie.

I could simply obey the law of the land. The law forbids stealing, case closed. The orphans continue to suffer, Biggie lives an indulgent and careless life (in my opinion), and I remain on the high ground of morality as decided by law.

In the backdrop of the laws of the land are the constitution and jurisprudence, which are themselves the product of democratically elected officials – roughly, the rule of majority. So, in deciding to obey the law, I'm holding to a more general principle of voluntary submission to the rules of society as negotiated and handed down by its elected leaders. This sounds very upright and respectable but it assumes I live in a just society. Robin Hood, by contrast, believed himself to be living in an *un*just society (Nottinghamshire), so he stole from the rich for the sake of the poor and felt justified in doing so. But let's say I give my country the benefit of the doubt and think quite highly of the rule of law, so I normally obey it. But is the present predicament an exception? Do the destitute orphans demand a crime of mercy at Biggie's expense, one that he'll never even notice? Do I become Robin Hood for a day? Once again, I am the standard of morality as I weigh the factors. I'm the one who ultimately decides right from wrong.

I could follow the rule of "consent." Biggie in this case has not given his consent to be robbed, so I'd refrain from doing so.

As in the rule of majority, I'd have to be very committed to a rule of consent to be guided by it in every situation. But is my commitment to consent more important than the well-being of orphans? Consent is a concept. Orphans are flesh-and-blood kids with real needs. It seems cold and uncaring to elevate a concept above human need. And who's to say that the rule of consent is always to be obeyed? What if I consult my feelings, my rationality, my community, and a given majority (if available), and all signs point to robbing Biggie without his consent? As important as consent is (between sexual partners, for example), it's hard to see how it should be an overriding ethic that prevents me from pilfering a low-life like Biggie for the sake of my beloved kids in the orphanage.

I could follow democratic liberalism in the West. This is a broad concept that I mention for its foundational role in ethics (in at least one part of the world). It may not give specific guidance. Lindsay and Pluckrose write, "Liberalism is thus best thought of as a shared common ground, providing a framework for conflict resolution and one within which people with a variety of views on political, economic, and social questions can rationally debate the options for public policy."[1] The authors seem to think that reasoned-based negotiation is the way society moves forward. They point to democratic countries in the West as examples of proper progression toward an overall just and flourishing world, despite setbacks and imperfections along the way. They criticize religion as often holding back progress, yet give grudging respect for its ethical standards which have helped shape the West.

Myself, I'm a big-picture thinker, so I find grand visions of justice helpful in framing ethical questions. It seems to me that in the kind of democratic liberalism Lindsay and Pluckrose are describing, I could go either way. I could be a radical Robin Hood and take from Biggie what he (perhaps) gained unjustly, and give to a good cause. Or I could take the long view and say that

---

1   Helen Pluckrose and James Lindsay, *Cynical Theories: How Activist Scholarship Made Everything about Race, Gender, and Identity – and Why This Harms Everybody* (Pitchstone Publishing, Kindle Ed.), p11.

if society was filled with people who, like Robin Hood, viewed themselves as above the law, anarchy would ensue. Thus, at least in one time and place, orphans will suffer. Yet, the preservation of a lawful society is an overriding concern, and I'd leave Biggie's bank accounts untouched.

So it seems democratic liberalism doesn't provide specific enough advice to make my decision either way.

I could consult a broad consensus of morality (if it exists) of history/culture. I like this idea because it relies on the wisdom of the ages, and I tend to trust tradition. In *The Abolition of Man,* C.S. Lewis refers to the great traditions of "truth" – whether Platonic, Aristotelian, Stoic, Christian, Oriental – as the *Tao.* The *Tao* is "Nature. . . the Way, the Road. It is the way in which the universe goes on."[2] Thus the *Tao* correlates with nature, with how things are. Lewis makes no attempt to prove the *Tao,* only to suggest it as a source of reliable wisdom compiled, as it is, from a variety of traditions that have served humankind.

Yet, when one steps out of this pluralistic religious mix and consults *non*-religious sources, differences become apparent. Egoism, for example, seeks the good of the self as its main goal. This may entail care for others but the endpoint is still self-serving. A version of egoism that I've heard in atheist circles is "enlightened self-interest," where serving others is a positive way to serve oneself. That sounds contrary to the principle of self-sacrifice put forth by Jesus. So while religious sources might agree on at least some general ethical principles, consensus breaks down when secular voices are included. And as appealing as a "broad consensus through history" sounds, I am doubtful it can be established.

A further thorny problem is that consensus doesn't always represent truth or reality. 51% or 70% or 95% of people can still be wrong about something. Let's say, for instance, that all religion is false and there is no afterlife. That would mean the vast majority of people in history (maybe 90%) are sadly mistaken about these matters, including me. Atheists, of course, make this claim. So, if and when atheists base an ethical or epistemological claim on a broad consensus, they should qualify the claim as evidential and not take it as any kind of proof or ultimate statement of truth.

---

2   C.S. Lewis, *The Abolition of Man* (MacMillan paperback ed., 1965), p28.

I could appeal to God. This approach would finally get me out of being in charge (though the appeal to liberalism, in general, accomplishes this to some extent. But I'd still have to decide whether liberalism was a worthy guide) of ethics. And while theism doesn't necessarily provide chapter and verse about whether to rob Biggie, various theistic religions would certainly provide input that is thought authoritative by many.

A couple of problems here. One is deciding which theism is preferable. How would one make the decision, say, between Christianity and Islam? A second issue is whether the ethics of Jehovah or Allah or another deity are, in fact, *just*. This is known as the Euthyphro problem, from the writings of Plato. It asks the question of whether something is just (good) because God wills it, or if God wills it because it is just. In other words, is true morality found in the will of God or someplace outside of God by which God can be measured?

Personally, I've never struggled much with the Euthyphro dilemma. I've always thought that God as creator was the proper author of moral values, whether I liked them or not, and that his values are rooted in his eternal nature and character. Tom will disagree with me on this. He thinks there are objective moral values without God.

An important point to make here is that I hold to a robust definition of God as "creator." That is, God invented the cosmos and brought it into being. There was no world, no empty space, no energy, no electrons or atoms, no consciousness aside from God's, before God created the universe. The God I'm positing is not part of the universe, just as an author is not inside his own book. I have written a couple of books and I can tell you that no matter what my characters seem to think or say, there is no part of their reality I did not create. If you interpret them differently than I wrote them – if you think there is something in my book that *they* actually created or discovered apart from me, I will think you are mistaken. The theism I have in mind makes something from – literally – nothing, so the "something" (the world), including all its ethics and moral values, issues from the creator. There was no bigger moral system in place outside of God before God created the universe. And there certainly is no bigger moral system than God's morality *inside* the universe, the universe God himself created.

The claim I'm making for objective morality, then, is that it is found in this God. By "objective" I mean actual and true, not merely a function of human opinion. God is the eternal, unchanging standard of right and wrong, good and evil. I can't imagine an alternative source of objective morality aside from God, so I look forward to hearing Tom's ideas on the topic.

Now if a critic wishes to attack my definition of God and cosmology (origin of the universe), we will step for the moment away from ethics and into metaphysics. A critic may wish to chip away at the idea of God as eternal and self-existent, or the idea of God creating a universe wholly outside himself, or the definition of "nothingness" just mentioned. These are all common strategies of atheists and other critics, and I understand their importance. But this is not really a book about metaphysics per se. We're asking the question of whether there is "objective morality" outside of God, so in the way I'm defining God, I believe the answer is no.

In the chapters to come, I am glad to defend this understanding of God. But I do wish to be taken as one who holds to a robust version of "creation *ex nihilo*" – that is, creation out of nothing. Without that beginning, it's hard to see why there should be any ultimate basis for morality, whether theistic or naturalistic.

To summarize, I am arguing that in real-life situations such as Biggie and the orphans, we need specific moral guidance – or at least I do. Who and where this guidance comes from is an unavoidable question. Let's say for the moment that objective morality exists somewhere and is unrelated to God. Maybe God doesn't exist at all. In that case, I'd need to know *where* to find this objective morality, what its basis is, and who authorizes it or at least commends it. And I'd need to know whether it is binding or optional, and if binding – says who? Enforced by whom?

Former Yale law professor Allen Leff offered the "says who?" principle. Leff was not a theist but wrote that if we believe in true morality, the source of this morality will always be in question. As soon as someone (or some group, tribe, government, etc.) says, "Do x," the response can always be, "Says who?"[3]

Perhaps there is no enforcement of objective morality without God. People could disobey it with impunity. Perhaps compliance with the rules is simply voluntary. But in that case, a strong dissenter, whether individual, group,

---

3   Quoted in Douglas Groothuis, *Christian Apologetics: A Comprehensive Case for Biblical Faith* (IVP Academic, 2011), Kindle location 3706-26.

nation, etc., could merely dismiss the ethic and create its own ethic instead. The defenders of objective morality (without God) would have little recourse against a strong dissenter, aside from the satisfaction of thinking themselves right and the strong dissenter dead wrong.

Put more bluntly, the biggest bully in the room will get his way whether he is objectively "right" or not. And if he has ten other bullies to assist, no tribe of morally upright persons will prevail. Tom may point out that according to a secular objective standard, the bullies are just wrong, to which I reply with Leff, "says who?" Who makes this decision? And is it binding for everyone? Is it enforceable?

As a theist myself, many questions about morality are answerable. If God exists and has disclosed himself, say, in Scripture and tradition, I can access God's wisdom about any ethical question. The available advice may be more general than the question itself, but in community, with other interpreters (contemporary and in tradition), I can discern a general methodology of social ethics and come down to a solid conclusion on most issues. In the case of whether to rob Biggie for a payoff to the orphans, Christian morality would forbid it. The eighth commandment given in the Old Testament prohibits stealing, and the Bible overall frowns on the idea of dishonest gain, even for supposed noble ends. Robin Hood, as appealing as he is to my pop-culture sensibilities, probably wouldn't be commended by the Bible, at least as a model for my decision about Biggie.

To answer the "says who?" question for the theist, the answer is God, the author of all morality. Are ethics enforceable? Ultimately, yes. God will eventually prevail. But in this life, enforcement will only occur if the powers-that-be adopt a Christian ethic – not in a theocracy, but in a free pluralistic society.

A formal argument

Here is a more formal way of stating what I've said above.

Premise 1: In order for something to qualify as "objective morality," it needs to have the following properties:

- True in a "mind-independent" way. That is, moral principles which are true whether any person or group (or culture or nation) thinks so or not. In philosophy this is referred to as "ontological" truth – something that really is the case. I offer this mind-independent property as "objective" because it goes beyond mere human opinion which is always subject to the "says who?" objection.

- Unchanging and universally valid for all time and place. Moral standards that shift with the times and the supposed progress of society would not be objective, in my view.
- Discoverable. We'd need some way to access these moral principles. Otherwise, we'd have no way of knowing they're objective.

Premise 2: God provides the properties just mentioned.

I'm thinking here of God as revealed in the Judeo-Christian tradition, the one who created the universe from nothing and revealed himself to Israel and through Jesus Christ. Again, it's the prerogative of the creator to set the standards for creation, much the same as an author sets the standards for his or her work of fiction.

Conclusion

Therefore, God is the basis of objective morality. Later, I will put this a different way – I'll actually *start* with God. But for now, I'll move from objective morality to God.

Tom and readers, I guess what I'm saying is that true moral principles need to come from outside the system, outside the imagination (and negotiations) of fallible human beings. By contrast, within the system of human interactions, I doubt we'd ever know whose claim to believe regarding morality. To any claimant I'd always be asking, "Says who?" But with God, there is an *absolute* sense in which moral principles are given, and this by a being who, by definition, is all-wise, all-powerful, and the author of all that is. What could be more objective than that?

But of course, this assumes such a being exists. As a Christian theist, I do believe in this being, so it's difficult to see how objective morality could lie outside God's purview or exist at all if God is a fiction. Without God, the law of the jungle prevails. Might makes right, whether in the form of military or voting blocs or the wealthy or the decrees of the elite. Whoever is strongest sets the table for everyone else. That's how kingdoms and governments, schools and businesses, homes and individuals have always operated. Those that appealed to God along the way (and did not abuse his laws, as many surely have) were on the right track. Others who obeyed the laws of God without intentionally doing so were also correct, though accidentally so.

Tom, I'm not a professional philosopher (though I read them, including a variety of perspectives) so I will have trouble teasing out the technicalities of exactly what "objective morality" really is. But I offer the plainer treatment stated in this chapter and turn things over to you, my friend.

CHAPTER 1.2

Tom's Response to Rick's Case for Theistic Morality

I MAGINE WE ARE in a boat in the middle of the ocean, we both agree there is a tide or current which objectively exists whether we like it or not, and we want to know which way the current or tide is carrying us. You have several options:

1. I could look within. What direction do I feel I am moving? Which direction is the easiest to paddle or that I have the least resistance, most movement etc.? This is some evidence—not great but it's something.

2. I could consult my community. I could look around at the direction other ships around me are floating and what they are experiencing. This is not a bad idea could give us some insight.

3. I could simply obey the law of the land. Maybe there is some law in this ocean to always paddle left. In other words, one culture with one pattern of how they interact with the current. It's not great—similar to consulting a community.

4. I could follow democratic liberalism in the West. I can see a very large, successful ship which I know is a product of thousands of years of

shipping technologies. It seems to be able to tell which way the current is going. Maybe we should follow their example? This is also not a bad starting point, It's just a single culture/community but a strong contender for one which may have more insight into the current.

5. I could say, "Majority rules." The direction most people seem to be floating is a good indicator of which direction the current is going. Combining all the cultures instead of looking at only one is also not a bad idea. It seems like a reasonable way to try and increase the odds of following the current.

6. If it exists, I could consult a broad consensus of ships across history/ culture. We could look at the pattern of ships across time. Which way the ships tended to move? How have their movements changed? Are there any overriding patterns? Given shipping technology has progressed, maybe there are certain shipping lanes which are far faster, and better than others, because they are following the currents? Maybe the speed of the ships has been increased with time, and we can see a clear and consistent pattern of how ships have been moving? This is a phenomenal idea that would give us a very good base of evidence to try to figure out which way the current is moving. I believe this is the best method presented so far.

7. I could follow the pattern "[Whatever we want to name it.]" If the above methods provide a clear pattern in the majority/consensus across history of ships and patterns they have traversed, it seems rational that we should follow the direction of that pattern if we want to follow the current. This seems like a very good idea to me.

All of these seem like decent arguments to increase the probability of us following the direction of the current. Also, I've attempted to order them from the weakest to the strongest method. This last one I'm not so sure about. Where should it be placed on the list?

8. I could appeal to the tide spirits. Two thousand years ago, my ancestors wrote a book which states the currents were created by the All-Powerful tide spirits and they made the current go left. The book says this is

correct because tide spirits created everything and are All-Powerful and All-Knowing.

This argument seems essentially like taking a specific cultures interpretation of the current, (from far in the past, mind you), and basing your conclusion on that culture alone—ignoring all the other evidence. This is essentially no different from argument #2 or #3 other than being from an ancient culture. Which makes this argument slightly less reliable, if we believe modern societies have a slightly better understanding of reality than those of the ancient past. From my perspective, it seems this argument should be placed between #1 and #2 on the hierarchy of reliability. Therefore, making it not a particularly good argument to rely upon for decision-making.

There was one other option from a little later in Rick's opening I also wanted to include:

9. In community with other [religious] interpreters (contemporary and in tradition) I can discern a general methodology of social ethics and come down to a solid conclusion on most issues.

Rick presents this as a seemingly a better option, however I'm not sure how. This seems identical to #2, #3, or maybe #4, depending on how it is interpreted. Something along the lines of using a combination of Christian cultures' interpretations of the currents. So, I do not follow how this is supposed to be a better solution to the problem, as it seems identical to the ones he has already provided.

From my analogy, the tide/current would be objective morality. If it exists, I believe it would have an impact on moral beings, (the ships), and their behaviors over time, (the direction they are floating), and if so, we should see some consistent pattern in the way moral behaviors are altered—making it a very good basis of evidence to know about the moral law.

From here there are several approaches the tide spirit believer can take:

1. They can argue the current doesn't have any discernable pattern/effect on the ships, so looking for patterns in the ships' trajectory is pointless and not evidence.

It seems when we use the word morality, we are referring to the actions of people, (the movement of those ships). Therefore, if we are looking for objective morality, we should look at the patterns in the behaviors of people and which actions we tend to label moral and immoral. If you disagree, where else should be we looking for evidence of patterns in morality other than the patterns in things to which moral language refer?

Until such time as we have a better basis of evidence about morality to work off of, looking in patterns of moral behaviors seems like the best place to start. If there is a better alternative to look for evidence of morality, please present it as I know of none.

2. They can argue only certain patterns in the ships matter, and so we need to filter out which patterns are actually representative of the current. (Fair enough I agree, how do you do this?)
3. There is independent evidence of the tide spirits by which we can show they exist, and if we already know they exist then they are a plausible cause for morality by extension.

But then, you admit just going by the evidence of morality cannot lead us to the tide spirits, and you need these external bases independent of morality, meaning morality on its own doesn't indicate them, which would be conceding the topic of this book. Suffice to say I believe all evidence best indicates naturalism and atheism but that would be a more general God debate which is outside of the purview of this book.

4. They can argue they have received a message directly from the tide spirits about morality which is an independent source of evidence about morality.

Most cultures tend to make similar claims. The way we would test this would be the same as how we would test to see if it is scientifically accurate. We would test if the revelation from the tide spirits corresponds to the patterns in the evidence we observe. I do not think any revelation-based texts are able to answer any of the moral dilemmas or philosophical problems in morality, and they seem to directly contradict our moral intuitions, and do not in any way accurately map onto the moral progress we have seen throughout the improvement through cultures. Using the Bible as a guide to morality seems as effective as using it as a science text, which is to say it is as effective as any man written text from an ancient society lacking the knowledge of modern progress in the field.

5.   Additional justification claims/arguments are what really matter.

This seems to be the path most theists take. They provide a list of alternative justifications/arguments and say these alternatives are what really matter to providing a basis of morality.

Let us look at the alternative arguments Rick has provided, (pp. 1-11), to see if any give us insight into morality and help us delineate between possible sources of morality. (Some of the quotes I use here may not have that purpose in Rick's opening, and so might be out of context.)

Circular Reasoning

1.   True in a "mind-independent" way. That is, moral principles which are true whether any person or group, (or culture or nation), thinks so or not.
2.   Unchanging and universally valid for all time and place. Moral standards that shift with the times and the supposed progress of society would not be objective in my view.
3.   Discoverable. We'd need some way to access these moral principles. Otherwise, we'd have no way of knowing they're objective.
4.   With theism, many questions about morality are answerable. If God exists, and has disclosed himself, say, in Scripture and tradition, I can access God's wisdom about any ethical question.

I agree morality is mind-independent, unchanging, and discoverable, but it seems God is none of those things, disqualifying him from being a basis of objective morality. More importantly, saying that for objective morality to exist it must have these properties is not actually evidence morality has any of those properties. We need something we see, in reality, when exploring the evidence of morality that leads us to the conclusion that morality actually has these properties. Whereas it seems Rick's argument is more something like:

P1, I believe morality is objective
P2, Objective morality requires these properties
P3, God provides these
C, Therefore God is the basis of objective morality

Rick seems to have skipped the first step of providing some evidence that morality has any of these properties. So, we would first need independent evidence morality actually has these properties. Otherwise, it tells us nothing about reality. It's just giving us a preference about what Rick would like to be the case. I am not sure I saw any such reason provided in the opening.

I don't think discoverability is required for objective morality. It could be true, even if we couldn't discover it. But I definitely don't think "the Bible says so" or "God revealed it to us" counts as discoverability. Whereas, following the evidence such as in the ship analogy seems to do so far better. I would definitely be interested to know how God-based morality is discoverable/which pattern in evidence leads to it. I believe that is the key piece in the puzzle I am not seeing from the theist perspective.

Asserting a hypothesis that provides the desired answers isn't evidence. Anyone can make up infinitely many hypotheses that can provide desired answers. What we need is evidence that indicates one over the rest. Even if you were to say ONLY God can provide these things, that would simply be demonstrably false. To give rudimentary examples; a law of physics can be unchanging, discoverable, and mind-independent. Also, a Platonic object, a priori abstract, supernatural field, higher order emergent property, etc. All of these seem far more mind-independent, unchanging, and potentially discoverable than God. Maybe if the remaining arguments Rick provided could eliminate some of these, that might be good evidence. Unfortunately, I don't think any of the remaining points are relevant to morality at all.

Can only imagine God can do it/argument from ignorance?

If it didn't come from God I'd need to know:

5. Where to find this objective morality
6. What its basis is
7. As a Christian theist, I do believe in this being, so it's difficult to see how objective morality could lie outside God's purview or exist at all if God is a fiction.

Obviously, I believe I have answers to what morality's basis is, and where to find objective morality. But even if I didn't, this would not be evidence of God. Even if I said, "I don't know," to both of these questions that wouldn't make God a better answer by virtue of the fact someone imagined it. That would be akin to saying, "What caused the earthquake? Oh, you don't know? Then, Thor did it!" So, the real question is, "what evidence indicates the God answer?" If there is none that indicates a God, then the God hypothesis is eliminated, even if no other explanations were provided.

I can understand that from the theist perspective, for someone who believes in a triple omni being, it can be difficult to think of something lesser than God as objective. However, the fundamental nature of reality, whatever it is, is objective. So, even if the fundamental nature of reality is just naturalism or materialism, it would be the objective standard. And so, if there is some undiscovered law of physics governing morality, then it is objective. You do not need a triple omni being for things to be objective.

None of these points provide any independent basis for knowledge about morality.

Says Who/Authoritative

8. Who authorizes it or at least commends it.
9. Without God, the law of the jungle prevails. Might makes right, whether in the form of military or voting blocs or the wealthy or the decrees of the elite. Whoever is strongest sets the table for everyone else. That's how kingdoms and governments, schools and businesses, homes and individuals have always operated. Those that appealed to God, (and not abused his laws, as slave owners surely did), were on the

right track. Others who obeyed the laws of God without intentionally doing so were also correct, though accidentally so.

10. A strong dissenter, whether individual, group, nation, etc., could simply dismiss the ethic and create its own ethic instead. The defenders of objective morality would have little recourse against a strong dissenter, aside from the satisfaction of thinking themselves right and the strong dissenter dead wrong.

11. And, I'd need to know whether it is binding or optional, and if binding – says who? Enforced by whom?

12. To answer the "says who?" question for the theists, the answer is God, the author of all morality. Are ethics enforceable? Ultimately, yes. God will eventually prevail. But in this life, enforcement will only occur if the powers-that-be adopt a Christian ethic – not in a theocracy, but in a free pluralistic society.

13. True moral principles need to come from outside the system, outside the imagination, (and negotiations), of fallible human beings. By contrast, within the system of human interactions I doubt we'd ever know whose claim to believe regarding morality. To any claimant I'd always be asking, "Says who?" But with God, there is an *absolute* sense in which moral principles are given, and this by a being who, by definition, is all-wise, all-powerful, and the author of all that is. What could be more objective than that? But of course, this assumes such a being exists.

It's not a who, it's a what: Reality. Reality is the ultimate authority, (if it is the case in reality that is the highest authority and supersedes any commands). You can't get more objective than "it is Reality." There is this tendency for theists to want to say you need a "command" —as in a dictate from a conscious entity—though, I know not why. I have not seen any argument that this would add to morality, or why morality would require it. It just seems like a personal preference that some people would like it if morality had this, but that isn't evidence morality actually does have such a property, and I would like to know if any such evidence exists.

The same would apply to enforcement. I don't understand why theists bring this up, as if it's relevant to the morality debate?

My best guess is that it feels to many like it would be nice if there was some compelling force to convince people to do the right thing. Yes, I agree. But, that has absolutely nothing to do with what objective morality is.

The argument would be something like:

P1, I would like it better if the basis of objective morality enforced morality.

P2, The morality I like better is the correct one.

C, Therefore the basis of objective morality has enforcement.

Unless you can explain how enforcement matters to the truth of morality, simply having a preference isn't relevant, and I don't know why theists continually bring this up.

Saying that, without God, "might makes right" is a false dichotomy/fallacy. It is perfectly possible to have an afterlife and/or judgment and enforcement of morality without a God, such as in the case of Karma or a moral force of nature which exacts justice. Or, a natural afterlife without a God which gives people justice. A karmic like field would be one such example. And, this example has equally as much evidence as a God—that is to say "someone imagined it." So, asking for enforcement doesn't really pose a challenge to a non-god-based morality. More importantly, you don't need enforcement for morality to be objective in the first place. If something is factually immoral, even if nothing enforces it, that doesn't somehow stop it from being immoral. So, enforcement seems entirely irrelevant to whether morality is objective or not, unless someone is making the argument you NEED enforcement or it's not real, (morality/enforcement is somehow a required property of morality). This seems incoherent to me as facts don't suddenly stop being true when they are not enforced. Enforcement never makes a fact true. That wouldn't even make sense.

So, this "Says who?" question is answered by reality. And, whether or not dissenters are convinced to act in accordance with reality, or if there is enforcement, leads to the question, "How is this relevant to the topic?" As far as I can tell, neither of these properties have anything to do with what is moral, unless Rick has an argument for why these would be required.

So, as with the last set of points, none of these seem relevant to giving us insights into the nature of morality.

CHAPTER 1.3

Rick

TOM OFFERS AN interesting analogy against my assertion in 1.1 that God can be the only true basis for objective morality. Tom asks us to imagine being adrift on a boat in the ocean, trying to figure out which way the current is flowing.

This is a physical analogy, and I wonder if it applies to the spiritual framework in which I speak about morality. Embedded in Tom's analogy is an appeal to natural causes, which automatically rules out theism. For example, the act of observing other physical phenomena in the ocean, such as the direction of neighboring ships (in order to discern the direction of the current) seems to assume that ethical properties would, in some way, be *physical*. Tom says, "We need something we see, in reality, when exploring the evidence of morality." That sounds very physical/material to me.

Perhaps a better analogy would be that of a household. Children need guidance, and parents provide it. Children don't merely look around the house and see "physical" morality. Rather, they receive instruction from their parents in the form of verbal rules and guidance. Good parents also model an upright moral life (imperfectly, I'm sure), which kids can observe physically.

But even then they need to interpret the behavior of their parents with some sort of self-talk such as, "follow that example of kindness," or, more negatively, "avoid that example of dishonesty," etc. My point is that the theistic morality I'm suggesting is given in language and can't be observed physically until it's modeled, and even then requires interpretation.

Second, I am sympathetic to Tom's objection that if one just makes up an ancient God and calls it a Trinity (or whatever), that would count as a basis for ethics. Tom puts my argument this way:

P1, I believe morality is objective

P2, Objective morality requires these properties

P3, God provides these

C, Therefore God is the basis of objective morality

That's a good summary of my position thus far. It requires that I'm able to observe certain moral principles in the world that are objective, such as evils that are objectively wrong. Rape and torturing babies are two examples. All of us tend to believe prohibitions on these horrible acts go beyond personal or cultural preferences and are simply wrong – universally so.

There's also another piece to the puzzle that I bring to the idea of objective morality that Tom's summary doesn't mention: I actually start with God, not just the data of moral behavior. More on this idea below.

Third, Tom says, "I agree morality is mind-independent, unchanging, and discoverable but it seems God is none of those things, disqualifying him from being a basis of objective morality."

Tom is into a theological judgment here – that God is *not* mind-independent, not unchanging, and not discoverable. This is an odd objection indeed. On naturalistic premises, God is none of these because God doesn't exist. But on theistic premises, why not? On theistic premises, God is, in fact, mind-independent because God creates all minds. And in Judeo-Christian theology, God is, in a sense, unchanging – that is, he maintains a constant eternal disposition toward good and evil. And of course, God is discoverable not because human beings are able on their own to find God, but because God has graciously revealed himself to us.

Now if we wish to debate whether God exists and has revealed himself to humanity, that is probably a different book.

Fourth, Tom thinks enforcement a weak criterion for morality, and, for the moment, I agree. Again, just because objective morality is not enforceable doesn't mean it doesn't exist. I think we agree on this.

Fifth, Tom responds to my "Says who?" objection by saying, in essence, that "reality" says so. You don't need a "who." My original objection was that as soon as some citizen or tribe or country (or whomever) declares something to be the case, a dissenter could object with, "Says who? What gives you the right to impose your understanding of objective morality on the rest of us?" But again, Tom thinks there needn't be a who. "Reality" is the who (or the what) that "says so," and that is enough.

But I wonder if morality can exist outside of the language that describes it. In a purely physical universe, if human beings don't cast morality in language, does morality actually exist somewhere out there in the world? Where? Why should matter and energy care about morality?

But if Tom is suggesting that we can distill at least a broad sense of morality from the common agreements across cultures down through the ages, I think we're still talking about propositions – statements that describe these behaviors and that recommend them to others as objective. I am sympathetic to this type of historical sweep, and would also want to note that this approach is compatible with theism. Tom might say that the simpler way to understand this broad morality is without God. God, in Tom's view (I am speculating), would be an unnecessary add-on to the whole consensus view. But my thought is that God functions, essentially, as an attentive parent in a healthy household, as my analogy above describes. God is an integral part of this household and not an unnecessary add-on. That is, we needn't confine our observations of ethics to the behavior of the kids. We'd also want to consider the *source* of their guidance – their parents (God, by analogy). Similarly, guidance and wisdom for a broad consensus of humanity could, quite reasonably, flow from the creator of humanity. If God exists, this makes sense.

I should mention that while a broad consensus of morality from multiple cultures throughout history may provide "a broad consensus of morality," I think it's fair to question whether consensus is a sufficient principle for deciding right from wrong. As much as we might be able to distill moral values such as kindness and respect from consensus, I think it would be hard to rule out values such as violence, vengeance, power, and greed. There seems to be no shortage of these negative elements in almost every cultural moment in history. A few exceptions here and there simply prove the rule.

Another concern I have about consensus is that it could be overturned by a new consensus in the future. Objective morality of the past would just be temporary. But then it's fair to ask: Was this past morality ever truly objective? If we think of the word "objective" as denoting universal truth that is not reducible to the subjective judgments and preferences of humans, a possible ever-changing consensus would fail to meet our criterion of objectivity.

Having said that, if I were an atheist I'd be looking at broad consensus as a high-potential source of ultimate morality. I can't think of any other place to look – certainly not to feelings, or to an elite think-tank at a major university, or to the preferences and rules of those currently in political power.

Further, we might ask an Euthyphro-type question of consensus: Is something right because consensus declares it? Or does consensus declare it because it is right? In other words, is there a standard of right and wrong outside of cultural consensus? But what would that be? If Tom's answer is "reality," then precisely which parts of reality is Tom referencing? But if Tom sticks with consensus (as I would), there is still the problem of the shifting sands of consensus, which places the objectivity of morality in doubt.

Sixth, I think Tom and I may be entering an impasse of sorts, as follows: On naturalistic (atheistic) premises, objective morality takes a certain form. On theistic premises, objective morality takes a different form.

So the nature of these first premises is a key question and a key difference between us. My starting point for a discussion of ethics is God. Tom's is the natural world. This situation is like two trains starting off on different tracks. How can the trains talk with each other in meaningful ways as they move forward and diverge? How can they problem-solve together? In philosophy, this is sometimes called "incommensurability," meaning: two neighboring worldviews not sharing enough assumptions and language in common for effective communication to take place between them.

Now Tom may insist that naturalism is not, in fact, his starting point for ethics, but rather, the "data" or "evidence" of morality that he finds in the real world. Data itself is his starting point, which then leads him to naturalistic conclusions.

I counter by saying that God is, in fact, my starting point for a discussion of ethics. But of course in the background of my thinking lie reasons outside this discussion for holding to theism. I don't see the relevance of these reasons, however. This isn't a book about God's existence. Rather, I show up to our discussion about ethics not as a blank slate but as a committed theist.

Similarly, Tom shows up as a committed atheist. So I guess I must question whether the data for morality that he observes in the real world, which leads him to naturalistic conclusions, is perceived by Tom in neutral terms, or whether his naturalistic commitments function as a filter to first determine, and then interpret the data. One reason I question this is because it is common for atheists and theists to disagree on what counts as evidence for any given worldview. (I've been in that discussion many times! Typically, the atheist makes an assertion about there being "absolutely no evidence" for God or the life of Jesus, etc. Then when a Christian offers evidence for these elements, the atheist counters by saying it doesn't count as evidence at all. Ergo: differing definitions of evidence tend to derail the discussion.)

Seventh, Tom seems to imply a kind of aggregation of sources and thus a "cumulative case" for objective morality. One consults self, community, law, cultures, wide consensus, etc., then draws a conclusion. I really like the direction of this argument, and it seems to hold promise for further discussion. I want to say that each source consulted (self, community, law, government, culture, etc.) can and should be informed by God. Tom will disagree. But perhaps at this "train station" of multiple sources consulted, two divergent trains (Tom's atheism and my theism) can meet for a meaningful dialogue. We'll see.

Creating God out of nothing?

Tom states:

> Obviously, I believe I have answers to what morality's basis is, and where to find objective morality. But even if I didn't, this would not be evidence of God. Even if I said, "I don't know," to

both of these questions that wouldn't make God a better answer by virtue of the fact someone imagined it. That would be akin to saying, "What caused the earthquake? Oh, you don't know? Then, Thor did it!" So, the real question is what evidence indicates the God answer. If there is none that indicates a God, then the God hypothesis is eliminated, even if no other explanations were provided.

I can understand that from the theist perspective, for someone who believes in a triple omni being, it can be difficult to think of something lesser than God as objective. However, the fundamental nature of reality, whatever it is, is objective. So, even if the fundamental nature of reality is just naturalism or materialism, it would be the objective standard. And so, if there is some undiscovered law of physics governing morality, then it is objective. You do not need a triple omni being for things to be objective.

None of these points provide any independent basis for knowledge about morality.

I agree with Tom that you can't answer tough questions about morality simply by creating a super-being out of nothing. That is, you can't wave your wand and say, "Thor did it." And if questioned who Thor is, just insisting that Thor is some kind of ultimate-ultimate who has say-so over all things, wouldn't be a real answer. And my replacing Thor with the word "God" is no improvement. This atheist objection to made-up divinities is well-taken, and I'm glad Tom brought it up.

I think (and hope) I'm saying something quite different. I'm saying that atheism and theism are roughly parallel traditions, with one having no automatic priority over the other. In this way of thinking, theism is not an add-on to naturalism, it's there at the starting line. The theist asks, Why not see the world as an enchanted creation rather than a purposeless accident? An enchanted perspective on the world seems to make a lot of sense. It gives us a starting point for creation as well as a basis for morality and an ultimate telos or purpose for life – to love God and neighbor. This is the whole project of theistic philosophy beginning in the 20th century from thinkers such as Nicholas Wolterstorff (Yale), William Wainwright (UW Milwaukee), William Alston (Syracuse), and Alvin Plantinga (Notre Dame). Their work has been met with great respect (though with considerable disagreement) by atheist philosophers such as William Rowe, Thomas Nagel, Quentin Smith, and others. I mention all these philosophers of religion and epistemology merely to say that the right to philosophize from one's perspective, whether theistic or naturalistic, is rarely questioned anymore (that I know of). The content is questioned, but not the starting point.

This equalizing of starting points enables me, I believe, to pull even with naturalism as we approach the question of evaluating evidence for morality. We all begin somewhere. Nothing is proven at the outset. If God is an arbitrary starting point, then so is not-God. Naturalism is as much an unproven assumption as theism. And if Tom thinks the broad consensus of morality over time and many cultures is a decent basis for objective morality, then why think the best explanation for this phenomenon is naturalistic? Theism is just as compatible with a broad consensus of morality as naturalism. In fact, I argue, more so. People's inner sense of moral obligation across time and cultures is more likely to have arisen from God than from atoms. I realize this is a judgment call. Nothing is ultimately provable. But it seems to me moral obligation is a personal concept and is more likely to have arisen from a source that is personal than impersonal.

Just to reiterate, I believe starting points are simply unprovable assumptions that lead to possible fruitful principles for philosophy and human flourishing. My starting point is God, Tom's is the natural world. The project of this book is to see which starting point best explains and accommodates objective morality. It may be that Tom wishes to deny these starting points and begin our quest with something like "Tom's and Rick's neutral observations of the world." But I don't think that's possible. I'm not neutral. *I come to the table already believing in a theistic world.* So the big question for me, the theist, is whether the idea of objective morality fits my worldview better than Tom's. Thus in the present project, I must promise to listen well to Tom and take his arguments seriously without dismissing them out of hand. After all, even my own theology informs me of the "noetic effects of sin" (a fallen mind) and therefore my own fallibility in understanding the world. Put more simply, I have something to learn from Tom because of the limits of my own knowledge and my respect for Tom.

A further response to Tom's objection that "you do not need a triple omni being for things to be objective," is that I agree in a certain sense. The fundamental nature of reality is, in fact, objective. I take that fundamental nature to be God (or God-given). You do not need a godless material world for things to be objective.

Zooming out to the best explanation

As I muse in general on the character of the world and the human condition, I can't think of a reason to exclude God from my worldview. Tom dismisses Thor as an invalid explanation for an earthquake. So do I. But that doesn't mean all theistic explanations are false. Theism – and in my case, Christian theism – is a broad worldview with a rich store of resources available for intellectual and spiritual life. I read Lewis and Tolkien, MLK and Luther, Aquinas and Augustine, the Sermon on the Mount and the oracles of Isaiah, to great personal enrichment. This tradition seems to offer more philosophical resources than the fictional stories of Thor (as enjoyable as they may be).

So when I hear atheists lump all non-material explanations together, I wonder at the logic. An example would be calling belief in God the same as belief in unicorns. If unicorns are imaginary, then so is God (so it is said). But why? It seems perfectly reasonable that some immaterial beings could be real and others not. The rule that states all immaterial beings are of the same type is simply dogma. A more thoughtful investigator would take non-material claims, such as religious claims, on a case-by-case basis. I know of no universal rule that says immaterial beings (spiritual beings) are all the same and necessarily cannot exist. Who could know that?

One of the points here is that when the atheist critic equates Christian theism with Thor, a supporting argument is needed. As stated earlier, I am using a definition of God in a much different way than what we know of the mythical Thor. For example, Thor seems to be part of the world whereas God is outside it. Thor is an internal cause, God is an external creator. And in Christian theism, science is a perfectly legitimate (though not ultimate) explanation for thunder and lightning. But when you plug in Thor as the explanation, he becomes the sole and efficient cause, science not needed.

Tom states: "So the real question is what evidence indicates the God answer, if there is none that indicates a God than the God hypothesis is eliminated even if no other explanations were provided."

Again, I agree, somewhat oddly, with Tom. If there is no evidence for morality that points to God, God would be eliminated as an explanation. I assume Tom would accept the reverse of this idea. If there is no evidence for morality that points to naturalism, then naturalism too should be eliminated.

It so happens that my starting point as the overall best explanation for reality is theism. So when the morality question comes along, I find no data in morality that is incompatible with theism or would somehow overturn my theistic beliefs. Any broad consensus of morality would, for me, count more toward theism than naturalism. That is, it's more likely that God, not some impersonal force risen from atoms, planted morality in the human heart.

The supposed priority of naturalism

An assumption I find among the many atheists I've worked with over the years is that we're all required to start with naturalism, and the idea of God is simply an add-on (an unnecessary add-on). In other words, all phenomena have a naturalistic explanation unless the theist can prove otherwise. But it seems to me theists can play a parallel game (what Wittgenstein called our own "language game"): We start with theism, and it's only when naturalism can explain phenomena better without God that theism should be dropped. This latter project is more difficult than it may seem. The naturalist will explain natural phenomena such as gravity by citing science and empirical methods, but this is not incompatible with theism. For myself and most theists, science is a gift from God, given to humanity for the purpose of studying and enjoying God's creation, enabling us to live lives of gratitude (note that belief in God is common among science faculty in the university world).

When we move from the physical to the subjective world, it seems to me theism is in a better position to explain phenomena such as human relations, art, beauty, consciousness, and, for our purposes – morality. I'm not saying there are no naturalistic explanations for things. I'm simply suggesting that a personal loving God is a more native source for the subjective parts of life than are cold material forces. By a native explanation I mean a conclusion flowing naturally from its source data or first premises. Water flowing down a mountain is most naturally explained by the presence of snow and ice at high elevations, not by the color green or the number 17. The idea of morality flowing from atoms seems to me an odd fit, a case of category confusion. To change the metaphor slightly, morality arising from atoms is like a stream rising higher than its source. Atoms can never flow uphill, so to speak, to become something more than they are. Atoms don't seem to contain the potential for ever making judgments about ethical questions. Should I rob old man Biggie to feed the orphans? Should I cheat on my girlfriend? Mindless, purposeless, inanimate atoms have no preference. And in naturalism, that's all we have.

Atheist philosopher Michael Ruse, if I understand him correctly, seems to be saying something like the following: Let's admit that the universe and our lives have no ultimate meaning. The universe is cold and purposeless and uncaring. We are part of the universe. We don't rise above it. The best we can do is "act as if" meaning exists. Then we can survive as a species and maybe even thrive.

I respect Professor Ruse for being so honest about the implications of naturalism. But for the theist, meaning and purpose, and therefore ethics, are built into the universe. We have a sense of "soulishness" because the soul is really there. We seem to thrive on beauty and art and intimacy because the capacity for appreciating such things is given by God. The end product makes sense as the deliverances of its source. Humans beget humans. Receivers in the game of football catch passes from quarterbacks. Houses are built by carpenters. Music emanates from a choir and reaches the appreciative ears of listeners. A personal God gives the gift of personal existence. But atoms delivering an end product such as ethics? I cannot see it. Daisies don't grow from stones. So when Tom asks us to look at the evidence for objective morality and reason to its source, I think it's more reasonable to say that a source gives birth to its own kind. A moral God begets morality. Meaningless atoms beget meaningless ends. If we wish to call those meaningless ends "morality," simply because that's the hand we've been dealt in a pointless universe, then I'd say we've sunk pretty far in our expectations and aspirations. We're close to a tautology: whatever is, is. X is x. That's not saying a lot, in my opinion.

Stepping back for a moment, I worry that discussions of this type slowly (or quickly) devolve into put-downs and caricatures of the other side. Even in using the words "meaningless" and "pointless" above, I'm concerned about insulting my dialogue partner – my friend Tom, in this case, but also our atheist readers. I don't wish to insult (or be insulted), and I'm sorry if anyone feels I've not shown them respect with this nihilistic type of characterization.

But atheists, I'm also saying that if I were in your camp I'd be wrestling mightily with the lack of meaning in the universe, of which I am a living member. I realize many atheists don't feel their lives are meaningless, and I'm glad about that. I'm not saying otherwise. But if I were a believer in naturalism, I'd be different. I'd labor under the task of creating meaning in an empty universe, and I'd wonder if the meaning I was supposedly creating was actually meaningful – and that, perhaps, my feelings of having meaning were simply lying to me. Or maybe I would just accept the fiction of meaning and try not to think about it too hard and thereby survive each day. One time I had an email exchange with a philosophy professor in Minnesota where I live. I asked him about a lecture we'd both attended regarding the connection between human identity and the environment. His opening line back to me was quite revealing: "On the days when I'm not a nihilist I might have an answer for you, Rick." Then he went on to address my question quite helpfully. I appreciated the professor's transparency and honesty (similar to Professor Ruse) about the implications of his naturalistic worldview.

To summarize this section

I believe in the philosopher's right to philosophize from his own worldview and not have to prove his worldview to anyone before starting a project. That puts naturalism and theism even up at the start. Neither has automatic priority. Then when we move down the path together and consider a topic such as ethics, theism provides, in my opinion, a more native (that is more natural, organic) explanation of moral obligation. Additionally, the charge against

Christian theism that it's simply another Thor-type explanation created by pre-scientific humanity doesn't hold up under scrutiny. There's no reason to think that just because one spiritual being doesn't exist, another also doesn't. I think it's quite possible to cancel out Thor without also canceling out the risen Christ. And it's quite possible for God to exist even if unicorns don't. The atheist might object that there's really no difference between made-up animals and a made-up god. But that objection is simply dogma. If theism is true, for example, it doesn't follow that unicorns (or Thor) also exist. Why are these entities bundled together by atheists in such an all-or-nothing fashion? I answer: because atheists typically think the proper starting point for constructing a worldview is naturalism. But that is also dogma. In starting with theism, as I do, it's not difficult to eliminate both Thor and unicorns. The determining factor is whether one's first premises are naturalistic or theistic.

Nor are these the only two options. We could bring into the discussion pantheism, Star Wars style dualism (the force), deism, other theisms (such as Islam or Mormonism), or an essentialist naturalism that says there is such thing as true "human nature." This last option seems to be what's held by atheist philosopher Evan Fales, for example. That is: meaning is found within, as part of the essential self.

Whatever the options, it still makes sense for me to begin with theism and see where it goes. Neighboring worldviews operate on their own respective premises, and if there is a degree of charity around the table, we'll all learn something from each other. The important thing is to be willing to embrace change if another viewpoint makes more sense of more data than your own, with fewer unanswered questions. In the present discussion, Tom's naturalism and my theism are the only options on offer. I mention the other views simply to acknowledge that there could be other starting points and that the main goal is to account for reality in the most comprehensive way possible, not to stay entrenched dogmatically in one's own camp.

Tom

Post Hoc Rationalization

"I start with God" – Rick

Rick's statements betray what I believe to be a weakness in theistic based morality. One of the biggest problems with theistic morality is starting with your conclusion. Imagine we see a gold brick on a table and we were wondering how it got there. Imagine I said, "I start with leprechauns," as my explanation, and then I look at the evidence and try to make it fit my conclusion of leprechauns. Does that sound like a compelling reason to believe leprechauns are the cause? Probably not.

In fact, it seems to be going about the question entirely backwards. We should start by analyzing the phenomenon—the gold brick in this case—and try to infer what caused the gold brick based on some properties it has; fingerprints, weight, chemical composition, etc. We need to look at the evidence, and follow the evidence wherever it leads, rather than starting with our preferred conclusion and trying to make the evidence fit.

Notice, if we compare the methodology Rick employs vs. the methodology I am employing. My method is starting with the phenomenon of morality and looking for patterns which we can use to infer some common principle to describe its nature. Whereas, Rick's method is starting with his God and trying to make the evidence fit his conclusion.

This I believe is a fundamental problem with theistic models of morality. I do not believe it is possible to look at the evidence of morality, and rationally use the patterns in morality to lead to the conclusion of a God. The only way it seems to get to that conclusion is if you started with it before considering the evidence.

This is a problem because for any unknown, you can always start with an imaginary cause and make all the evidence fit. This is known as "post hoc rationalization." "In rationalization those cited justifications are sought only after the conclusion is already in hand. Rationalization is post-hoc. The conclusion is accepted or at least favored in advance, and one's desire to show the predetermined conclusion to be rational then motivates the search for explicit justifying grounds."[4] Post hoc rationalization is a form of fallacious reasoning which we know does not provide a rational basis to believe anything, because any hypothesis can use post hoc rationalization to make any and all forms of evidence fit.

For example, many years ago it was unknown what caused lightning. Imagine my conclusion was "I start with Zeus as the cause," and as we discover more about clouds and friction of atoms producing electric charge, this would seem to indicate it is not caused by Zeus. However, because I am starting with my conclusion of Zeus, I can use post hoc rationalization to make the evidence fit by saying, "All of this friction between particles is actually designed by Zeus to work in this way, therefore it actually is Zeus!"

Because post hoc rationalization can work for any hypothesis, (including the one correct explanation, but also all the infinitely many purely imaginary ones), it does not provide a way to differentiate imagination and reality. Therefore, it is not a rational way to justify belief. This is just one example of thousands of fallacies, biases, illusions, delusions, misconceptions, etc., that

---

4   Eric Schwitzgebel, "Rationalization in Moral and Philosophical Thought." Department of Philosophy, University of California at Riverside.

have been discovered (and, named by science as forms of reasoning which our human brains find very compelling). But these probably fail as rational justification for a belief. These pitfalls of human reasoning have led many down the wrong path which is why science labeled them. So, we can know if this is the justification you are using, you are making a mistake, and need to use one of the other non-fallacious forms of reasoning which can differentiate imagination and reality.

For example, looking at the evidence without forming a conclusion and following the evidence wherever it leads. Notice that in my opening, I do not start with my conclusion but rather start by looking at patterns in the evidence of morality, and see where those patterns lead.

Post Hoc Rationalization Continued

A related issue is where Rick states, "Embedded in Tom's analogy is an appeal to natural causes, which automatically rules out theism."

This is a common belief among many theists, that atheists are simply ruling out God from the outset. But it is almost always false, especially concerning academic atheists. Ruling out a conclusion before looking at the evidence has the same problem as starting with your conclusion without looking at the evidence, and would be equally irrational. Because I recognize this is fallacious, I would never do such a thing. I never rule out any hypothesis before looking at the evidence; that would be completely contradictory to my epistemology, (my theory of knowledge).

My ship analogy applies to any cause of any kind, whether spiritual or physical–magical or natural. The analogy is simply of cause and effect. If objective morality is real, and has an effect on us, then we should be able to see a pattern in this effect. This is true regardless of what the source of morality is. If God is the cause of objective morality, and morality has an effect on our nature, then we would also see a pattern in this effect, presumably the pattern would be in line with the holy book which accurately describes the God who created it. Clearly this does not rule out God.

To bring this into the ship analogy: If there is a pattern in the currents of water affecting the boats, we should be able to see the pattern, even if that pattern is caused by Poseidon. Therefore, it is false to say my analogy rules out God. The analogy is simply illustrating we first need to look at the pattern of the phenomenon/the evidence, before we come to any conclusion whether it be God or Nature.

The Family Analogy

Rick uses an analogy of children looking to the example of their parents as the phenomenon of morality. However, I don't think this analogy provides us with any reason to think morality is objective. In fact, it seems to indicate the opposite. If the phenomenon of morality is simply how some people embody their lives, based on some set of verbal rules or idealist goals, how does any of that indicate morality is objective and not just a product of imagination or social construction?

If there is some pattern to these rules which transcends the subjective culture, or the family, or the society, and is independent of any of the family, (whether that be those who embody the ideal or those who are learning it), then we could say that fits exactly into my analogy of the currents. There is some pattern that exists across cultures, is independent of any person, and affects each of the groups in the same way. Indicating this is caused by some outside force which governs this pattern—like a current.

If we say that morality itself is based on one of the agents, why are you concluding that person is the ground of morality, and not affected by the external force, just like everyone else? Which is more objective, the model based on a subject or the model based on an objective force?

Mind-Independent

"God is, in fact, mind-independent because God creates all minds." – Rick

What?!? That is literally not what it means to be mind-independent. A potato is mind-independent. A potato is mind-independent because it exists regardless of what any mind may, or may not think of it. Even though, (and this may come as a surprise to many), the potato did not create all minds. Yet, it still manages to be mind-independent.

For something to be mind-independent, it simply means it exists independently of any thoughts, opinions, feelings, or dispositions of ANY mind. If something only exists because you, or ANY mind, are thinking about it, then it is mind dependent. For example, if you are imagining a unicorn, that unicorn is mind-dependent. If you stop thinking about it, then it will cease to exist. If you change it to bright purple, then it will become bright purple.

The moon, on the other hand, continues to exist even if no minds ever thought about it. And, no matter how you try to change it with your mind, it is unaffected. Therefore, the moon is mind-independent. And, keep in mind, the moon did not create all minds, but it's still mind-independent.

If morality only exists because God thought it into existence, is morality more like the unicorn or more like the moon? Is it mind-independent or mind-dependent? If morality is a law of nature like gravity, then is morality mind-independent or mind-dependent?

I fully grant that if God exists, then he would be mind-independent just as you or I exist mind-independently. Even though we are minds, we exist even if no minds are thinking of us. However, if morality was a product of God's mind, or his thoughts, or his opinions, or his dictates, or dispositions, then morality is mind-dependent and therefore subjective.

In order to tell if morality is mind-independent or mind-dependent, you can ask one simple question, "Is something moral because God, (or any mind), says it is, or did God say it is moral because it is moral independent of what God, (or any mind), says?" If something is moral simply because God, (or any mind), said it was, then it's subjective–because it is contingent on the opinion of a mind.

If something is moral independent of anything God, (or any mind), says—meaning morality is grounded in something else, (not any mind), then it's objective. It is objective because it is independent of the opinions of a mind.

Unchanging

Rick says that God is "unchanging in a sense" but we can say anything is "unchanging in a sense." Meaning, even if everything else about the thing changes all the time, we can still say "there is this one part of the thing which never changes."

This is an example of "ad hoc reasoning." Ad Hoc reasoning is when someone adds an explanatory factor, condition, or reason that is posited—without evidence—to counter a specific objection, or argument in order to protect one's original assertion, hypothesis, findings, or conclusion from falsification.

Imagine if I said, "The ocean is the unchanging ground of morality." You could reply, "But the ocean changes all the time!" This seems like a good counter argument if the ocean is always changing. It seems unreasonable to believe it is the unchanging ground of anything. However, by using ad hoc reasoning, I can save my position by saying, "Ah, but there is an unchanging part of the ocean you simply cannot see, which is the foundation of unchanging morality!" Clearly there is no evidence of such a thing. Therefore, it is *ad hoc*–posited to defeat the clear counter argument which has significant evidence.

The same applies to God. Take the Abrahamic God of the Bible, who changes his decisions and plans all the time. At one point morality was "an eye for an eye." Then it changed to become "turn the other cheek." Is it reasonable to think that God is an "unchanging ground"? No, just like it is not reasonable to think the ocean is an unchanging ground. We have an abundance of evidence of it changing and no evidence of it being unchanging. So, while you can assert it could be unchanging in some unforeseen way, that is an ad hoc assertion.

What are some things we do have evidence of that are unchanging? Laws of physics. Many of the laws of physics, (like the laws of thermodynamics, e.g., energy), cannot be created or destroyed. We seem to have very good reason to believe these laws are eternal and unchanging, which is the consensus in the academic field of physics. And so, if we are looking for a candidate of something which is unchanging to explain the unchanging nature of morality, a law of physics is a far better candidate than something which we have no evidential reason to believe is unchanging—like the ocean, or a God.

Says who?

"But I wonder if morality can exist outside of the language that describes it. In a purely physical universe, if human beings don't cast morality in language, does morality actually exist somewhere out there in the world? Where? Why should matter and energy care about morality?" – Rick

If morality does not exist outside of language, then it is by definition subjective. Language is a subjective construction of cultures. One way it could exist outside of language—if it is a law of nature, like gravity. Where? It's universal–everywhere in the universe. Why should matter and energy care? Why would they need to care? Again, that seems to be imposing an inherently subjective quality that undermines objective morality.

If something is moral only because someone "cares" that's a thought, feeling, opinion, or making morality contingent on thoughts, i.e. subjective. For morality to be objective it literally can't matter whether or not anything cares.

Purely Physical Universe

Rick mentions the phrase: "In a purely physical universe." However, I don't quite understand theists' fascination with this term as if it is some form of knockdown argument.

Anything that can be achieved in a supernatural world, can be achieved in a physical world; free will, an afterlife, a soul/floating consciousness, meaning, purpose, morality, etc. These can all equally exist in a physical world, as they can in a spiritual world.

Consider a chair. Does it matter if the chair is made of metal, wood, plastic, or magic potatoes? No, it's still a chair no matter what it's made of. The same applies to free will, morality, meaning, a soul etc. If these things can exist being made of some spiritual stuff, then they can equally exist and be made of some kind of physical stuff.

Now, I grant we have not made any discoveries in any scientific lab of any physical particles that could produce these things. However, we also have made zero discoveries of spiritual stuff that could produce such things. So, by asserting these can be grounded in a spiritual plain of existence you are going beyond the evidence to posit something we have not discovered. And, guess what, the physicalist can do the same. And, posit new kinds of physical particles that also have not been discovered and we have no idea how they work, (just like we do not for the spiritual stuff), to provide physical alternatives which are equal explanations to ground each and every thing you believe could exist in the spiritual realm. Or, to put it another way: Anything the supernatural can explain, the unknown natural can also explain.

Consensus

I agree consensus isn't the ground of objective morality, as you will see in my opening. I believe what grounds objective morality is an undiscovered law of nature. It affects people in the same way leading to consensus. So, consensus would be one line of evidence pointing in the direction of what objective morality may be. But consensus is not what grounds morality. The reason I don't think violence is the consensus will be explained in my opening, based on the pattern of moral progress.

Can the consensus change over time? Sure, it can. Any evidence you have can change over time. That's just how evidence works. Suppose we discovered the bones of Jesus, proving once and for all he didn't rise from the dead. Would you be unable to accept reality because you are so dogmatically obsessed with your beliefs? Would you never accept evidence to the contrary? Suppose we die and get to heaven and God is there with many other gods. And he says, "Yah, that whole Bible thing I wrote? That was a joke." Would you still refuse to accept you were wrong?

The evidence can always change. That isn't a bad thing. It's intellectual honesty to acknowledge that you will be willing to change your beliefs to fit what we discover about reality. Assuming the evidence cannot change is another example of post hoc rationalization—trying to make anything you discover fit your predetermined conclusion which is a type of delusion. A delusion is a false belief held despite significant evidence to the contrary.

God, Thor, Leprechauns, Fairies and Santa

There is an often-made criticism of theism that God is the same as Thor, fairies, leprechauns, Santa, etc. Many theists often rebuke this statement saying there are relevant differences between the Abrahamic God and Santa. I want to clarify the core of the argument atheists are making, because it will likely be a point I will use in this book.

> The "God is like Santa" argument is illustrating two classes of things:
>
> A: Things which are made only of properties which have been demonstrated to exist independent of our imagination. Class A includes all things in the material world that have been proven to exist using novel testable predictions, such as the experiments used in the scientific method.
>
> B: Things which have at least one property, which has not yet been demonstrated to exist independent of our imagination. Class B includes all miracles, magic, mythical creatures, paranormal, and supernatural.

In science and physics, only models using Class A objects are taken seriously. Models using Class B objects are not taken seriously. Many theists' first inclination is to label this a kind of naturalistic bias. But it is not. This is another example of using proven rational methods and excluding proven fallacious methods. Of the models which have posited miracles, magic, etc., none have ever been able to make successful novel testable predictions at a higher rate than chance, (i.e. predict news things about the world we didn't already expect). However, models using Class A objects are reliably able to do so.

Excluding methods which have never worked isn't a bias. It's rationality. It's the reason you don't trust a Magic 8 Ball to tell you the future. Do you consider yourself biased or just rational?

This does not mean you cannot use Class B objects in hypothesis. There are many times in physics and science where a scientist just made something up with no evidence, but then was able to make novel testable predictions based on that made up idea. These were proven correct, leading to that property which was Class B becoming Class A. Pauli and Dirac would be examples of this. The same can be applied to any other Class B object as well. Once it is able to make successful novel testable predictions, it will be reasonable to consider it a Class A object.

So, when atheists say "God is like Santa" they mean that both have at least one property which has not yet been demonstrated to exist independent of our imagination. Making that hypothesis less reasonable than any Class A hypothesis. And, this is an accurate assessment regardless of the differences there may be between God and Zeus. They are the same in this respect.

The Two Tracks

I agree with Rick that we do have two separate starting points. From my perspective Rick's starting point is post hoc rationalization. This is a demonstrably false track which has been proven unreliable by thousands of years of human brains being led astray by the same exact track, (which is why we labeled it fallacious reasoning to warn people not to use that track).

My track, which is starting with the phenomenon/evidence and looking for patterns—without assuming any conclusion—seems to be unquestionably a better logical starting point. Rick may have some background evidence which he believes indicates his God exists. And, while I believe no such evidence exists, that is a separate topic. In my opening I will make no background assumptions about naturalism or theism. I will simply start with the evidence of morality alone and follow the patterns in morality wherever they may lead.

Another of the biggest weaknesses of the theistic worldview is, if you exclude these background arguments and evidence Rick holds for his belief in God, I believe it will be impossible for him to follow the patterns in evidence of morality alone to come to the conclusion of a God. Meaning his argument for morality only works if other unrelated arguments also work. I believe the same is true for every argument used to indicate a God:

- The physics arguments are only evidence for God if the moral arguments succeed.
- The moral arguments are only evidence if the historical arguments succeed.
- The historical arguments are only evidence if the testimonial arguments succeed.
- The testimonial arguments are only evidence if the physics arguments succeed.

This is affectionately called, "the cumulative case" by theists. This leads to a carousel of one argument, (which is only evidence if the previous argument succeeds), and that argument is only evidence if another previous argument is. However, when we explore each argument individually by starting with the evidence in the relevant field, excluding the other arguments, they all fail.

Instead of asking you to accept my background arguments and evidence for naturalism, I will simply start with the evidence of morality alone and we can see where it leads. As a side note to attempt to explain this further—the carousel or "the cumulative case" argument is attempting to use those "other arguments" as Class A Objects, (something that has already been demonstrated). Already been demonstrated as providing some evidence for a God, thus justifiable to use in defense of a Class B object, (an argument we are denying has been demonstrated). However, all arguments for God are Class B objects. You cannot start with the evidence in the relevant field alone to lead to the conclusion of a God with any of them. This is why they incorporate the "cumulative case" which includes the other arguments, (which also cannot start with the evidence in the relevant field alone to lead to a God). So, whenever theists use one argument for God as supporting the other arguments, ("the cumulative case"), it is akin to using the existence of leprechauns as supporting evidence for the existence of unicorns. For an argument to be justifiably considered evidence, it must be able to start with the evidence in the relevant field without appeal to any other arguments for God. And, from that evidence alone, lead to the conclusion of a God.

Compatible with Belief in God

Near the end of Rick's previous section, he says repeatedly, "This is compatible with belief in God." This is another example of a statement which is common among many theists as a kind of knockdown argument. However, you can use post hoc rationalization to make anything "compatible" with any presupposed conclusion.

Being able to explain a phenomenon to make it fit your worldview is not evidence, and it is not special. Any worldview can do so for any phenomenon or fact. In science this is known as the problem of underdetermination.

The problem of underdetermination states there are infinitely many ways to explain all data/evidence. For example, I could say the universe was created by magic pixies five seconds ago, and they implanted false memories of everything prior. This would be compatible with all the evidence we have. The way we filter out these hypotheses, (even though they are compatible with all the evidence), is by only accepting models which make novel predictions about the future. It's very easy to use post hoc rationalization to make the evidence fit your preferred hypothesis. It's very hard to use your preferred hypothesis to accurately predict things about the future we don't know, and don't expect. So, if you can do that, then you have a genuine reason to believe your hypothesis is more than simply imaginary.

Discoverable

Rick says that God is discoverable. But what does it mean to be discoverable? If I am imagining riding a unicorn, did I discover unicorns? Obviously not. However, if i were to find fossils of a horse with a horn, then I could say I had discovered unicorns.

The difference between these two is, one is purely in my imagination, and the other is something which can be demonstrated to exist outside of my imagination. So, to be "discoverable" means to be able to differentiate something being true in reality as opposed to just an idea in your imagination. That's what happens when you "discover" something. You find out it's true in the world outside of your imagination via evidence.

What is the standard to know if something is discoverable? Because anyone can make any evidence fit their hypothesis by using post hoc reasoning and underdetermination, just being able to make something comparable with your belief does not do anything to differentiate imagination from reality. In fact, it counts for nothing.

However, there is one thing which not all hypotheses can do: make successful predictions about things in the world we don't know yet, and don't already expect. If you have an idea and say, "If this idea is true, then here is what we will find in future!" If you end up being correct, that is a truly impressive feat, giving us real evidence your idea is something in reality above and beyond your imagination.

As far as I know, no God hypothesis has ever been able to make successful novel, testable predictions. Novel means new. So, predicting something we don't already see or expect. Predicting the sun will rise tomorrow is a prediction, but not a novel one, because we already see/expect that.

The only claims of God seem to be testimony, revelation, personal experience, and intuition. All of these are conceptual–in your imagination. And, none of them can differentiate imagination from reality. We know this because science has been studying these methods for thousands of years. And, we know they do not work.

Now to be fair, these can be evidence of the Class A hypothesis I mentioned earlier. Like, if you were to have personal testimony you saw a dog. That would be reasonable to believe. However, if you were to claim you saw a unicorn, that would not be reasonable to believe. So, testimony can be evidence of things which have already been demonstrated to exist independent of our imagination. However, testimony is not evidence of things which have not been, such as miracles, magic, mythical creatures, the paranormal, supernatural, etc.

The reason for this is, we have an abundance of historical evidence of people making claims of paranormal/supernatural things based on personal testimony, (for tens of thousands of years). When tested, they have been proven false, or unverifiable, in every case. This is why in the academic field of history and in law/courtrooms, testimony is not accepted as admissible evidence for miracles, magic, mythical creatures, etc. First you would need to empirically demonstrate they exist to the court, before testimony of them occurring previously would be accepted.

Moral Obligation is More Likely to be from a Personal Source

"Moral obligation is a personal concept and is more likely to have arisen from a source that is personal than impersonal." ... "A source gives birth to its own kind" – Rick

This point Rick makes seems to be one of the core arguments in his position, and likely is for many theists. But I do not understand how. This argument seems to be based on Rick having a kind of "like comes from like" intuition about the matter. This "like comes from like" intuition is a composition/division fallacy. One of the thousands of false forms of reasoning which are compelling to human minds but are provably not rational.

A division fallacy is to assume that something which is true of the whole must be true of the parts. A composition fallacy is to assume something which is true of the parts, must be true of the whole. In the case of the "like comes from like" intuition, the fallacies are in the form: what is true of the product must be true of the origin. Or, to phrase another way: A property that is in the product must also be in the origin.

All such reasoning is proven false by something called "emergent properties." For example, let's look at water. Water is wet. Using the "like comes from like" intuition I could say, whatever makes up water must also be wet. However, this is clearly false. Water is made from H_2O, (one Hydrogen and two Oxygen molecules), and neither Hydrogen nor Oxygen is wet, as they are gases. Wetness is an emergent property of how Hydrogen and Oxygen bonds and interacts with each other when in the H_2O form, and is not a property of the parts at all.

This could be the case for ANY property. Because we know emergent properties exist, and any property could be emergent, you cannot ever use the "like comes from like" intuition as evidence for believing it is not. You would need some other form of actual evidence, (like novel testable predictions), to rationally conclude anything. Therefore, the intuition that "like comes from like" is not evidence of anything.

Right now, you may be thinking of examples where like does come from like. But this is not evidence that using it as a rationale is justified. It is of course possible to use fallacious reasoning and get to the correct conclusion. This is described by something called "the fallacy fallacy" which is the fact that many people will say because an argument is using fallacious reasoning, the conclusion is necessarily wrong. This is a fallacy, because using fallacious reasoning does not prove the conclusion wrong. It only proves the justification wrong.

So, we know it is possible that even when you are using fallacious reasoning, you could get to the correct conclusion. But the fallacious reasoning is provably not evidence to make the conclusion justified. Because we know emergent properties exist, and the "like comes from like" intuition can't differentiate emergent and non-emergent properties, then it is not ever evidence. Even though, sometimes it happens to be true. And just to be clear, the times it is true, is the vast, vast minority. Notice with most of the examples you may have been thinking of, where like does come from like, eventually those properties are actually emergent from something entirely not "like" it at all—matter, atoms, protons, neutrons, etc.

One example where like does come from like is, the property of existing. If an object has the property of existing, then it is reasonable to say its origin also has the property of existing. This is not because using "like comes from like" is evidence, or rational. But because we have good evidential reasons to conclude non-existing things can't cause things to exist. So, even though the "like comes from like" intuition happens to be correct in this case, it is not evidence nor a justification.

Furthermore, there is a huge epistemic problem to this "like comes from like" thinking. Let's say X was created by Y, and X has some property. So you think "like comes from like" and conclude: therefore Y also has that property. What about the origin of Y, does it also have the property?

If Y was made by Z, and "like comes from like," then Z also must have that property. And, if Z was made by something else, so must it. This continues ad infinitum. Meaning, whenever you claim "like comes from like," in essence, you are claiming the property is not emergent at all, ever, at any point in its history.

If you are claiming something is not emergent, what is it? The only other option is a fundamental property to all of reality. (Notice in my earlier example where "like does come from like"—existing, that was not by chance.)

Now, that is a big claim. Especially seeing as how we don't have any way to tell which properties are truly the fundamental ones in science as opposed to being emergent. Even Space and Time are considered emergent in science. Many physicists have valid models where causality is also emergent. Almost anything could be an emergent property.

99.99999% of all things we know of are emergent from more fundamental things. So, if you think a certain property is one of those 0.000001% of fundamental things, you are probably wrong. But more importantly, you would need a substantial amount of evidence to justify that whatever property you think is special, actually qualifies as fundamental. And, the "like comes from like" intuition is no evidence at all, because it cannot differentiate emergent from non-emergent, (fundamental), properties. So, to claim some property is a fundamental part of reality, you are going to need a significantly more substantial evidential basis than your intuition that "like comes from like."

Here are several more examples of this kind of fallacy often used in theistic arguments:

- Mind can't come from non-mind.
- Life can't come from non-life.
- Consciousness can't come from non-consciousness.

Each of these is using the same fallacious "like comes from like" intuition, leading to the consequence that each of these properties is being asserted as fundamental to all of reality. When in fact, it is far more plausible to think they are emergent from other more fundamental properties, like protons and neutrons. Not only is this a priori more rational, but also it's what all the evidence indicates. Which is why it is the consensus in every academic field specializing in these topics. Life does come from non-life, (abiogenesis), and mind does come from non-mind, (physical brains).

Now let's bring this back into the realm of morality. Have you ever been hungry? It's a relatively unpleasant sensation. But if we give you the right chemicals or shock you in the correct part of your brain, you will cease being hungry. So even though—in order for you to experience hunger you need to be conscious because hunger is a conscious sensation—that doesn't mean it's caused by consciousness. It is caused by unconscious neurons in your brain which affect your consciousness.

So, it would be an example of a composition fallacy to assume that because hunger is a conscious state, then whatever grounds or causes hunger, must also be/have a conscious state. Clearly your stomach is not conscious... probably. Why not think morality is the same? Something non-conscious affecting your consciousness? So, even if obligation is a personal concept, (just like hunger is a personal experience), that does not imply it cannot be caused by an impersonal source. In fact, this seems to be a much more likely situation, as pretty much all our subjective personal experiences are caused by non-conscious, impersonal brain states that are affected by physics. Why think morality is any different?

Rick

Tom's boat analogy

Tom says, "My ship analogy applies to any cause of any kind, whether spiritual or physical–magical or natural. The analogy is simply of cause and effect."

I accept this explanation, thanks.

Post-hoc rationalization

I know this fallacy but don't think it applies to my argument. I'm simply conducting a thought experiment, as follows: Does the idea of objective ethics seem to fit better with theism or naturalism? If theism, great. That is a credit to my worldview. If naturalism, equally great. That is a credit to naturalism.

Tom asks this question: Would you be unable to accept reality because you are so dogmatically obsessed with your beliefs? Would you never accept evidence to the contrary? Suppose we die and get to heaven and God is there with many other gods. And he says, "Yah, that whole Bible thing I wrote? That was a joke." Would you still refuse to accept you were wrong?

My answer in a word: no.

Compatibility with theism

Tom seems to think that "compatibility" is a weak form of argumentation, and that once you admit your starting point you can make any evidence fit that starting point. My starting point is God, and Tom accuses me of making any and all evidence fit with God – that is, seem compatible with God.

Tom has a different starting point: the data of morality. He then examines the data and concludes that it is better supported by naturalism than theism.

Notice the difference in the two starting points: God (me) vs. data (Tom).

Tom says, "Notice, if we compare the methodology Rick employs vs. the methodology I am employing. My method is starting with the phenomenon of morality and looking for patterns which we can use to infer some common principle to describe its nature. Whereas, Rick's method is starting with his God and trying to make the evidence fit his conclusion."

Tom adds further, "I will make no background assumptions about naturalism or theism. I will simply start with the evidence of morality alone and follow the patterns in morality wherever they may lead."

I commend Tom for beginning with the "phenomenon of morality" of examining the data to see where it leads. However, he mistakenly states that I am attempting to make the evidence fit my conclusion.

To summarize what Tom seems to be saying, and perhaps overstate the case slightly:

a) Tom has conducted his examination of the data – and his subsequent argument – impartially. One might even say, *scientifically*.

b) I, on the other hand, am prejudiced by my starting point and can only see the data of morality through the lens of theism. Therefore, all data will be interpreted by me *theistically*, in a manner of what's often called "confirmation bias." That is, you only accept data that confirms your prior-held belief.

Starting points

But starting points are tricky things. The rule that says "begin with the data" as your starting point sounds like an arbitrary rule to me. In the practice of science, for example, you often begin with a hypothesis, and then go to the data to confirm or deny the hypothesis. And that's simply what I'm doing. I begin with the God hypothesis, and despite the temptation of confirmation bias, I seek to confirm or deny the God hypothesis, via argumentation, as the best explanation for objective morality. The verdict could go either way, to theism or naturalism.

Is theism vulnerable?

I'd like to name the kinds of things that would count against theism: If the "data" of morality showed that religious people always and everywhere act immorally, it would be a strong critique of theism. In fact, these people sometimes do act immorally, which *does* count against theism to some extent. Or let's say the Bible is shown to be full of lies. Ethically, that would count massively against the theism which I hold.

Aside from the topic of ethics, other items could be marshaled against theism in various degrees: prayers never answered, religious experience absent, the bones of Jesus discovered, a historical man or woman of the 3rd century revealed as the sole author of the Bible, philosophical incoherence exposed. We could add parallel examples from other theistic religions, such as Islam. The point is, lots of things could falsify theism. When that happens, I will be there to listen, which is one reason I engage in this dialog with Tom in the first place.

To repeat, I'm arguing that not any and all data can be made to fit with theism. Theism is falsifiable, in varying degrees, by the sorts of "data" (and argumentation) just mentioned.

Thus far, however, nothing I've heard from Tom or anyone else in the area of ethics is "incompatible" with theism. But of course *that doesn't prove theism.* I'm making a much smaller claim than proving anything. My claim is simply, *on the whole, given all the factors, ethics fits more natively, more "compatibly,"* *with theism than with naturalism.* That's likely because theism is true. But of course, the compatibility between ethics and theism could be accidental, in which case theism may not be true. I am fine with that. I agree with Tom that you shouldn't force the data into your worldview. Contrary to what Tom says, I'm not "attempting to make the evidence fit my conclusion." I just haven't seen any evidence in the area of ethics that conflicts with my starting point (aside from the sometimes unethical behavior of the religious, mentioned above. In my experience, however, belief in God tends to curb wrongful behavior due to believers' love of God and their sense of being accountable to God.)

I should also comment on the fact that Tom calls my belief in God a "conclusion." That's not quite right. It's actually an assumption, not a conclusion. Again, I "assume" God in our discussion of ethics, and I have background reasons for making that assumption. The real "conclusion," then, is whether objective ethics (if they exist) are best explained by theism (me) or naturalism (Tom). That conclusion is up for grabs in this book.

Neutrality?

As much as I admire Tom's attempt to evaluate the data of ethics with no prior assumptions such as naturalism, I must ask: Is that possible? Is there such a thing as neutrality and impartiality? An objective evaluation of the facts? Enlightenment thinkers said yes. These days, that belief is questionable. Philosopher Thomas Kuhn, for example, famously said that all observations of the world are theory-laden and locked within various paradigms. Thus, said Kuhn, there is no neutral perspective from which to view the data. In any case, the question of objectivity is a complex philosophical problem and I'm not claiming to answer it here. But I think it's appropriate to at least question anyone's objectivity in evaluating data. Put simply, different people see the same car accident or ball game or sunset differently. Certainly, the assessment of something as complex as the "data" of ethics, say, by a hundred people, would yield vastly diverse opinions. Not to say that one or more of the people couldn't get it "right," but who could tell? How would that be decided? A long argument would ensue. The point is that the argument against human objectivity says we all wear tinted glasses of various shades through which we see the world and evaluate the data of perception. This is simply the phenomenon of "perspective," and is shaped by one's background, desires, culture, relationships, economic status, etc. Setting aside these factors in order to rise above oneself to see the world precisely "as it is" seems a tall order. Immanuel Kant agreed with this. He said that we don't have direct access to the external world itself but only to our own internal perceptions of the world.

Myself, I've abandoned the notion of perfect human objectivity. Only God could have that. And if God has revealed his wisdom to us, it makes sense to listen to him. Jesus said, "Everyone who hears these words of mine and does not put them into practice is like a foolish man who built his house on sand." Hence, I read the accounts of Jesus with great interest. As for science, as it advances, our understanding of the world becomes more accurate. Will that understanding be perfect? No. Science keeps changing. But greater accuracy is a worthy goal. Thus, insofar as the theist is equipped with the tools of science and the wisdom of God, a coherent picture of the world emerges, including that of ethics.

The mind of God: objective or subjective?

Tom seems to think that God's thoughts are subjective. He says: "My main criticism of God-based morality wasn't that it is arbitrary, but that it is subjective, i.e. contingent on the opinions of a mind."

Here, Tom has reduced God's thoughts to mere opinion. That may be true of Thor or Poseidon, whose status in mythology places them within the universe. But the theism to which I hold positions God outside the universe as the creator of everything, including ethics. That's what I mean by "objective" ethics. If I am the author of a book and I give the book's universe a certain moral code, that code is objectively true for that universe. We can, perhaps, disagree on the definition of "objective," but that is the common-sense definition with which I'm working.

Like begets like

Tom makes a good point in saying that not everything in a product or endpoint must be present in its source. He states that it's false to believe that "What is true of the product must be true of the origin." And he gives the example of the wetness of water: water is not composed of elements that are, in and of themselves, "wet."

Agreed. But I'm saying something slightly different: certain elements in a product or endpoint must be present in the creative powers and capacity of its source. For example, let's say we examine the "data" of a 90-mph fastball but don't know its source. We don't know how it got moving so fast. In this example, the two options available to us are a major league pitcher or Rick Mattson. We'd naturally choose the major league pitcher. And because we didn't see the actual source of the fastball, we don't know for sure who threw it. There's no proof because we didn't witness the source. But it's "most likely" (plausible) that a pitcher threw the fastball, not me. Philosophically, that's a pretty small but reasonable claim.

Thus, the smallish claim (philosophically speaking) I am making about ethics is that the rules for human behavior are more likely to have arisen from a personal rule-maker (God) than from impersonal forces such as atoms. Tom is looking for an undiscovered natural source of morality, a pattern built into the universe similar to a law of gravity. But a universe comprised solely of atoms is, in my view, an unlikely source of moral wisdom. Atoms don't seem to possess the creative powers or capacity to produce moral wisdom. They can't throw a moral fastball. In short, in regard to ethics, atoms are impotent.

Somehow, Tom thinks this judgment commits a formal fallacy of division or composition. But I'm not actually saying that the property in the product (a swiftly moving baseball in the example above) must be actually in the source. I'm simply saying that the source must have the ability or capacity to produce the product. God does. Atoms don't. That's a fairly common-sense judgment. It's not proof. I wish my argument could rise to that level. Rather, it's a "most likely" statement of belief or judgment and is sometimes called an inference to the best explanation.

Another analogy

Let's say I walk into a theater and see a play. Afterward, two people present me with opposing explanations of the play. Person A says, "Producing plays is what theaters do. Plays are a natural element of the theater, just like chairs, lights, costumes, and the stage. Plays are built into what it means to be a theater. Anything people can do, theaters themselves can also do."

Person B says, "No, plays don't just happen. They're not built into the nature of a theater per se. Plays require directors and producers who recruit actors and conduct the play."

Do I believe the explanation of person A or B?

I can look objectively at theaters and try to discern a pattern of meaning in their operations. But it's only when I admit to the personal nature of a theater production that I see its most likely source. Theaters (source) don't naturally give rise to drama (product). That capacity is simply not there. Nor do impersonal universes, comprised of impersonal forces, give rise to the human drama of ethics.

Again, I wish this portion of my argument could rise to the level of proof or empirical verifiability – that would be a gigantic philosophical achievement. Rather, it's a modest, "most likely" claim in my overall case for theism as the source of ethics.

God as a mind-independent reality?

Tom states, "If something only exists because you, or ANY mind, are thinking about it, then it is mind dependent."

In other words, it doesn't have its own existence. It's simply a product of the mind. Agreed. And I like the reference to a potato as being mind-independent because it exists whether minds think about it or not. Awesome, I'm still on board. A bit later, Tom states my position well: "If God exists, then he would be mind-independent just as you or I exist mind-independently." And since I believe that God *does* exist and is the creator of all reality, this God is mind-independent. Of course, if God doesn't exist, my argument fails. But again, God's existence is not the topic of our discussion.

Note the oddity of this logic: A unicorn is a product of our imagination. Therefore, so is God.

But just because unicorns don't exist doesn't mean God doesn't. Christian theists like myself believe God has revealed himself to us on his terms. He is "discoverable" because he has taken the initiative to self-disclose. And he's done so in his own ways. Though not outside of science per se, God's revelation comes in many additional ways. But again, I'm not here to demonstrate God's existence. That's another book. The question before us is whether the God of (roughly, Christian) theism – or naturalism – is the best explanation of objective ethics. So when Tom continues to poke at the existence of God, I think he is wandering off-topic.

Besides, even if God is merely a product of human imagination (which I'm not granting), Tom seems to appreciate and employ imagination in his own position. As we'll see, he imagines an ideal ethical world – the Best Possible World – that doesn't currently exist. He imagines an undiscovered law of nature that unifies all ethical judgments. He imagines a technologically advanced future that would create maximal human autonomy and harmony. Tom, I applaud your use of imagination. It's fun to think of the possibilities. Let's agree that imagination is a useful tool. But that doesn't mean that God is necessarily a product of human imagination.

Testimony

Tom also dismisses testimony as a basis for judgments about entities such as God. But this sounds like dogma to me. Why be prejudiced against testimony? Tom uses the example of a court of law, where testimony is not accepted for miracles, magic, and the like. He says, "First you would need to demonstrate they exist . . . before testimony of them . . . would be accepted." But how is this relevant? A court of law that assumes naturalism is not inclined to accept the testimony of supernatural events. That fact says nothing about the existence of supernatural events but says much about the naturalistic assumptions embedded in the court of law. Furthermore, testimony is an indispensable tool for everyday living and basic beliefs. I take it on the testimony of scientists and doctors that medications are safe and effective. But I wasn't there in the lab when the testing was done. Testimony also informs my geographical understanding of the planet. I've never been to China but I believe the "testimony" of Chinese residents, maps, charts, history books, and the like that China is a real country.

It's a difficult task to isolate the testimony about religious experience or the life of Jesus as automatically unreliable without also canceling testimony about other historical people and experiences. Assuming an "anti-supernatural filter" is one way to do it. But of course, that is question-begging. If Jesus really did perform miracles and rise from the dead, as testimony would have it, the anti-supernatural filter would miss the truth. In other words, if I filter for natural phenomena only, a supernatural event would be overlooked.

So it seems wise to take testimony on a case-by-case basis. Some testimonies are more reliable than others. Multiple witnesses help but don't guarantee the case for something. It's a judgment call on whether to believe any given testimony. But testimony shouldn't be ruled out automatically. And the billions who testify to the power of God in their lives over the centuries should at least receive a hearing and not be dismissed by philosophical prejudice. Nor should the early church's presentation of Christ to the world be automatically dismissed because it is given in the form of testimony. The early church was absolutely convinced it had encountered God in the flesh in the person of Jesus. Many were martyred and were otherwise persecuted for this belief, which they held undeterred.

The 18th c. philosopher, David Hume, is famous for dismissing accounts of miracles because in any given case, he said, which was more likely – that witnesses were mistaken and/or dishonest, or that the regular laws of nature were overturned? Odds were always against the witnesses. But of course, if a real miracle ever took place and was reported by witnesses, Hume's way of thinking would miss the truth. So again, it seems wise to take testimonial accounts on an individual basis, neither rejecting them out of hand nor accepting them without question.

Predictive power

One of Tom's arguments against theism is that it lacks predictive power. This is simply not true. As a theist, I believe in science, which has plenty of predictive power. It's one reason so many scientists in academia are theists. They think an orderly universe is more likely to have arisen from an orderly Maker than by chance. Many times I've said to my atheist friends: "Which would I rather have, science alone, or *both* science and God?" That's an easy choice for me. For theists like myself, science is a wonderful gift from God, used properly to discover the order and beauty of his universe (and make predictions).

Aside from the gift of science, why should I expect belief in God to have predictive power in the first place? Many things in life, such as love and purpose, are valuable and important but are not measured by their predictive power.

Conclusion to this section

I haven't responded to all of Tom's objections, but hopefully the selection above covers the basic ground. Starting points seem to be a central issue. Tom starts with the data of ethics and sees where it goes. I start with God and see if theism holds the data. Starting with God may seem an arbitrary choice, but there is ample precedent. There's an entire discipline called the "philosophy of religion" that includes both theist and atheist philosophers. Beginning with God as a starting point in that discipline is common. No one starts from nowhere. Everyone begins with something. Why not begin with God? And if someone comes along and says, "Let's start with potatoes," there's no rule against it. Have at it. If it can be shown that potatoes provide massive explanatory power for big-ticket items such as the origin of the universe, ethics, and the meaning of life, and can do so in a coherent manner, all the better for potatoes. Most atheists start with naturalism and build out from there. But naturalism has no inherent, automatic advantage over theism. Any advantage can be shown only in subsequent argumentation – in the competitive race, not at the starting line. Hence the question: Do ethics fit better with naturalism or theism? We don't know until the race is run. And now, halfway through the competition, I believe theism commends itself well to the thoughtful reader who is open to possibilities.

Tom's Case for Naturalistic Morality

I MAGINE YOU FOUND a magic lamp with a djinn who will grant you a wish. What would you wish for? Money? Power? Fame? Fortune? Immortality? Cure all disease? End world hunger? World peace? What would be the most moral wish you could make?

What is Morality?

When you see someone being hurt, or stolen from, or insulted do you get a gut reaction—a feeling that there is something wrong about whatever is happening? If you do, then you are experiencing the phenomenon of morality.

Ultimately when we speak of morality, we are referring to these specific feelings we get when we see or think about certain kinds of actions. Some actions make us feel a positive feeling, which we label as moral actions. Some give us a negative feeling, which we label immoral actions. When trying to discover what morality is, we are trying to find out what causes these feelings and what, if anything, do the feelings refer to.

It is possible that these feelings are just an illusory byproduct of evolution and refer to nothing in reality independent of our imagination—like a mirage off in the distance—in which case, there is no objective morality. It is simply a subjective evolutionary inclination. But maybe, just maybe, our feelings about morality are more like our eyes. Perceiving something that is actually there—existing in reality outside of our imagination. If that is the case, then morality refers to something which is objective.

If there is such a thing, what might it be? A God's nature? An undiscovered law of nature? A moral particle? An abstract or platonic object? A new law of logic? There are many possibilities it could be, as with any currently unknown phenomenon. In order to come to an answer, we must follow the evidence to try to discover the truth.

Subjective Morality

If morality is subjective, that means what makes something moral is simply the fact that some mind thinks it is, e.g. opinion, thoughts, feelings etc. All of the best evidence we currently have supports the subjective morality hypothesis—that morality is just a byproduct of evolution. However, I am a moral realist. Meaning, I believe in objective morality. The reason I am a moral realist is because there are indications morality may be more than just a subjective byproduct of evolution.

For example, if we were to discover other kinds of life, such as aliens from different galaxies, or discover true artificial intelligence—will they also have some view on morality? If they do, will all the different forms of life seem to be converging on a single model of morality? If this was the case it would be good evidence morality is something more than a subjective inclination.

If we were to create artificial intelligence or discovered similar such beings on other planets that did not evolve, and these developed without having been preprogrammed with morality, and if they happened to discover morality on their own, this would be conclusive evidence morality is not contingent on evolution. I believe it is highly likely that if/when such beings do occur, they will eventually develop a morality of their own. More importantly, I believe the morality they develop, (as well as the morality developed by all or the majority of conscious beings in the universe), will converge on a single model—just as scientific discoveries made by all of these different species will also converge on a single model. Indicating there is some deeper truth outside of just our subjective imaginations for morality—just as there is for science.

I believe both of these conditions are highly likely. That other forms of life will develop morality independently and they will all converge on a single model. Which is the reason I am a moral realist. So, even though we don't have any conclusive evidence of objective morality today, it is worthwhile to try and figure out what this ultimate model of objective morality, (upon which all consciousness beings will converge), might be and what might ground it.

Objective Morality

If morality is objective that means what makes something moral is independent of what any mind thinks or feels, e.g. a law of nature, a fact of reality, etc.

Morality is a term that is often confusing because we are very anthropocentric beings. We humans like to think of ourselves as the center of the universe. Because of this, when we ask questions like, "What is the moral thing to do?" we have a tendency to contextualize this question by comparing it to our personal limitations. This is often seen in the form of the phrase "ought implies can." Meaning, that if something is the moral thing to do, and you are morally obligated to do it, this assumes you must be physically able to do it. I agree, it would not make much sense to call someone immoral for not doing something it is physically impossible for them to do.

For example, using a classic moral dilemma—if you see a baby drowning a few feet away and there would be no cost to you to save it, would you be obligated to do so? We would never say a paraplegic was immoral for not saving the baby, because they are literally incapable of doing so.

That is perfectly reasonable. However, when talking about objective morality, this is a fundamental mistake we must overcome. If there is an objective morality, it would be self-contradictory to base that objective morality on subjective human limitations. Therefore, this "ought implies can" mentality is a flawed way of thinking when talking about something being objective. We need to filter out our subjective limitations, rather than use those subjective limitations as the basis to evaluate what the objective standard would be.

The objectively moral thing is the standard that would apply to all beings of any subjective kind—including the most capable being in any given moral situation. This is what we mean by objective morality. The moral fact of the matter is independent of any subjective context. So, if you imagine the most capable being, i.e. a being that is infinitely powerful in any given moral situation—the objectively moral thing to do is the standard that being is measured against. Meaning, if the all-powerful being would be immoral if it did or did not do X, that action X is the objectively moral action.

Once we know the objectively moral actions, we can then apply the subjective limitations of any individual to know what is the best action they can do subjectively. This would obviously not be the objective moral action; it would only be the best subjective moral action that individual can take.

So, when asking the question of whether or not something is moral, we need to clarify if we are asking if something is objectively moral, i.e. moral independent of subjective limitations, or if we are asking if the action is subjectively moral, i.e. the best action an individual can do given their limitations to get as close to the objective standard as possible.

Most people usually mean the latter. However, in order to answer the question about subjective morality, you first need some objective standard that you can compare to, in order to know if the action in question is getting as close to that standard as possible, or not.

So, to answer any question of whether or not something is moral you need to start with the objective standard and answer what the objectively moral action is in that situation. And only then, (once you have that objective answer), can you apply the subjective limitation of an individual to know which action they can take. This would maximize the moral outcome by getting as close to the objective standard as possible.

We can use this same analogy to understand why a God-based morality does not work. If we imagine an all-powerful being in any given moral situation and want to know what the moral action is, we could not simply say, "Whatever the being happens to do is the objectively moral thing." Even if the being is perfectly moral and/or the grounds of morality, this answer fails because it is simply telling us the location of morality. But it tells us nothing about the principles that describe why the action is moral. Is something moral simply because the God would do it, or would the God do it because the action is moral?

If whatever God does is the moral thing, for no other reason than the fact he does it, then morality is arbitrary. However, if a God does an action because the action itself is moral, (based on some set of criteria that defines morality), then in order to know what morality is we need to know that criteria. Knowing what the God would do might give us the answer to which action is moral. But it doesn't tell us anything about morality itself. For that you would still need to provide the principles describing what makes that action the moral one.

Because of this, referencing God doesn't tell us anything about morality. It is simply asserting where morality is located. It does not provide any definition of the moral principles that would tell us what the moral actions are.

This leads to a rather perplexing problem. If you can't tell us what the moral principles are, then you must not have started with the moral principle as your basis to conclude a God was the source. So, how did the theists conclude God was the source at all?

A serious model of morality would start with the phenomenon we observe, create principles to describe the patterns in that phenomenon, and only then try to infer based on those patterns what the ground of morality is. It seems theists are going about this entirely backwards. Starting with their conclusion and trying to make the evidence fit.

This is the key to why secular models of morality are so much better, and preferred by the consensus of experts in the academic field of ethics, (over theistic models). Theistic models of morality usually start with their conclusion. A God or holy book which says God is the grounds of morality. Then work backwards, making up principles to fit the God.

Secular models do the opposite. They start with the observed phenomenon of morality, then try to come up with principles that accurately describe morality. Only then, they try to infer what the ground of these principles may be. The secular method is the same method science uses.

So, as any serious model does, we will start by looking at the phenomenon—the feelings we get of morality, and try to discern a pattern in these feelings which we can describe with some moral principle.

Moral Intuition

Would the world be better without rape? If you think it would, you are experiencing moral intuition. Our moral intuitions tell us certain actions are right and others are wrong, i.e. moral and immoral. For example, we tend to see killing for fun as immoral. But why? What is it about certain actions that makes them immoral?

The best approach to answering this question is to analyze the various kinds of moral and immoral actions to try and find some common factors that outline what the essence of morality is. We can imagine different ways the world can be, and use our moral intuitions to assess which ones are more moral than the others. And, continue comparing possible worlds, filtering out the less moral ones to try and get to the best of all possible worlds.

You might worry the worlds we imagine might have some unforeseen consequences. But we can evaluate those worlds as well. Which would be more moral: the world we imagine with these consequences, or a world we imagine with the consequences being optional? Meaning, people can opt out of the consequences and reject them from existing in their world. Clearly, having the consequences be optional rather than forced, would be more moral. So, we can evaluate those cases as well.

Moral actions: saving, assisting, helping, healing, freeing, giving, self-sacrifice, protecting, etc.

Immoral actions: killing, rape, torture, slavery, theft, lying, cheating, bullying, etc.

Of this list, we can see some actions are contingently moral/immoral—like killing. For example, killing in self-defense, or killing to save the lives of others, is not at all the same as killing for fun. It seems like certain immoral actions can be made less immoral, or even moral, depending on their context.

However, there are some immoral actions that cannot be contextualized—like rape. There is no context in which rape is moral. Even if there were some case where rape could save the lives of many people, it would still be immoral. So, while some actions, like killing, are contingently immoral, other actions, like rape, are necessarily immoral.

What is the difference between contingent and necessary immoral actions? Let us look again at the action of killing. If you were to kill someone who wanted their life to end, then it may be moral to kill them in order to end their suffering, (such as in euthanasia/assisted suicide). Therefore, consensual killing is not immoral at all.

When we try to apply the same criteria to rape, there is a problem. Rape is by definition non-consensual. If it were to be consensual, then it would no longer be rape. The term "consensual rape" would be like the equation "1 + 1 = 5." It is a self-contradiction. So, just as we can say is it objectively the case that 1 + 1 = 2, we can also say it is objectively the case that rape is non-consensual.

This consensual factor seems to be the difference between rape and killing. It is why one cannot ever be moral but the other can. It seems that consent is a determining factor in whether an action is contingently immoral or necessarily immoral. It seems that all necessarily immoral actions entail being, by definition, non-consensual.

Therefore, it seems we can tell the difference between contingent and necessary immoral actions by what happens when we make the action consensual. If the action is made consensual, and it becomes moral or amoral, then it is only a contingently immoral action. Whereas, if making the action consensual the action becomes self-contradictory, then such an action is necessarily immoral. When talking about objective morality, it is these necessarily immoral things we are concerned with. The contingently immoral things are only subjectively immoral to the context. So, they are not relevant to objective morality. It would be incorrect to say killing is objectively immoral.

Because we can use consent as a means to separate immoral actions into kinds, this implies consent is something that is pivotal in determining what the essence of immorality is. In fact, it seems that many, if not most immoral actions, stop being immoral if we make them consensual. We can thus conclude immorality is a non-consensual…"something."[5]

Another important aspect of morality is discovered if we look at examples of non-consensual actions. For example, if I pick up a rock. You did not consent to my doing so, making it a non-consensual action. However, picking up a rock is clearly not immoral. Therefore, it seems consent only applies to yourself and your property. You cannot consent on behalf of someone else or something you have no say over, such as a rock. So, for something to be immoral, it has to be a non-consensual "something" that affects a person or their property, i.e. an imposition. So, immorality is an imposition on someone without their consent.

Another consideration is that is it obviously not immoral to harm a rock. The reason for this seems to be that rocks don't have the ability to feel. Even lacking the ability to feel, it can still be immoral to harm something, such as in the case of an unconscious person. So, it seems the fact that it is unable to feel, (because it does not have consciousness, nor the potential of being conscious), is what makes it not immoral to harm a rock. Therefore, morality seems to be in some way related to things with consciousness, or the potential to have consciousness in some respect.

By looking at the evidence of our moral intuitions and connecting all the dots, the picture it portrays I believe can be expressed by the principle: involuntary imposition of will is immoral. We can mirror the same methodology for morality to come to the conclusion: voluntary assistance of will is moral.

If this view of morality is correct, that any involuntary imposition is immoral, this has counterintuitive consequences that go against a great many of our moral intuitions. For example, if this model is correct, then killing one person to save another, or five others, would be immoral. Disciplining children without their consent would be immoral. Putting criminals in jail would be immoral. Giving a drug addict all the drugs they want would be moral. And, helping someone to commit a crime would be moral.

---

5   I define 'consent' as: If person X could know every possible action that could occur to them in every possible context, and could place each on a list of "allowed" and "not allowed," those on the allowed list would be consensual.

For a model of morality primarily based on moral intuitions, having consequences that contradict many of our moral intuitions is quite a big problem. If this were all the evidence we had for morality, we would be in a bit of a bind. However, there is still another line of evidence to look at—moral progress. Let us see if adding in the other data points from moral progress can help resolve these issues. But before we jump to moral progress, let us explore some more features of morality by looking at our moral intuitions.

Another common feature of the feelings of morality is the sense of "oughtness" we get when we see an immoral action. We feel as if the person *ought* not have done that. Or, if we see someone who could have done a moral action, but did not, we feel they *ought* to have done it. This feeling of "oughtness" is a key topic in moral discourse. Many believe this sense of "oughtness" is fundamental to morality. Therefore, if an objective morality exists, it must have some "oughtness" quality to it in order to accurately reflect these feelings about morality.

However, I think that is incorrect. I believe our feelings of "oughtness" are not fundamental to the essence of what morality is, but rather an anthropocentric addition. In other words, it is not the "oughtness" that makes something moral. What makes something moral is something else entirely.

We can demonstrate this is the case. Is something moral because we ought do it, or ought we do it because it's moral based on some independent criteria? It seems to be the case that something is moral because it fits some set of criteria. Only after something has met those criteria, do we add the prescription that we ought, or ought not, do it. Therefore, oughtness is not intrinsic to morality but is rather a corollary addendum.

However, "oughtness" represents one of the most common features of our moral feelings. We only apply moral language to agents, e.g. that person who killed someone for no reason is immoral, but that rock which fell on someone and killed them is not immoral. The world would have been better had both actions not occurred, but we only call one of them immoral. The reason I believe this is the case, is because we only have perceived control over one of the actions. Meaning, we believe we can influence the person to not kill by creating laws, providing deterrents, teaching people social norms that guide their actions. We can do none of this to affect the actions of the rock.

Therefore, this sense of "oughtness" only seems to apply to individuals who are aware of these social norms, and are intellectually capable of recognizing their action goes against them. So, an action which would be immoral for an adult human of some reasonable level of mental acuity, would not be immoral if done by a child. Or, someone who is mentally handicapped, or a lion, or a rock, because they lack the intellectual ability to understand their action goes against the social norms.

However, this seems to go against another of our intuitions about morality—that it is supremely important. There is nothing higher than being a morally perfect being. A pacifist Buddhist monk who owns nothing but the clothes on his back is a superior person than Caesar, or Genghis Khan, or Attila the Hun, (powerful warlords who conquered half the world and could have anything they wanted).

If morality is what is supremely important, isn't the consequence of the person losing their life more important than who or what caused it? If that is the case, would it not make more sense for the consequence to have more moral weight than who or what caused it? It seems to me, the supremely important fact in that scenario is the death of the individual. If that's the case, why do we call someone who died by a falling rock simply "bad"? Whereas, if a person is doing the killing, it is given the more significant label "immoral"?

The fact that a person is the one doing the killing seems almost trivial in importance in comparison to the significance of the lost life. To call someone's death simply "bad" seems to be entirely insufficient to convey severity of the event.

Morally Perfect World

I want you to imagine a Morally Perfect World. What does it look like? Is there no death, no murder, no torture, no aging, no hunger, no strife, no poverty, no disease? Is the morally perfect world the same as a perfect world? Or, is there a difference?

If you define morality as only having to do with the actions of agents, then even if all agents were perfectly moral, the world would still have death, suffering, disease, and all manner of terrible things. By this definition, a morally perfect world is nowhere near a perfect world. In fact, most of the bad things that happen are caused not by agents, but by nature. Nature kills more people every year than all human wars combined. So, defining morality to only pertain to actions of agents seems strange to me.

When I talk about objective morality, I am using that term to refer to the essence of goodness itself—the ground of all goodness. The idea that a morally perfect world would still have so much bad seems to miss the core of what morality is—as it is oblivious to many, maybe even most, of the goods and evils in the world.

For this reason, when I imagine a morally perfect world, for me, it is the same as the perfect world. Therefore, instead of defining morality as how agents should act, I define morality as the principles that describe the nature of the perfect world. Not just for actions of agents, but any actions. If you think a morally perfect world could still have billions of people suffering from disease and dying painful, natural deaths—and yet, the world could still be perfectly moral—then, I think you have an inane understanding of morality.

Criticism of Philosophy

Unfortunately, this is how most philosophers understand morality. This is one of the primary reasons I think moral philosophy is unproductive and unrelatable for most people. Also, if you think morality only pertains to actions of agents, then there must be some other kind of "goodness" to describe all the "goods" which don't have to do with human action. In fact, there seems to be far more of this other kind of "goodness." So, if they are separate, this other kind of "goodness" supersedes morality by a significant margin. However, when I use the term "goodness" I don't tend to think of it as having greater significance than morality. On the contrary, I think morality has greater significance than "goodness."

If our intuition about morality—that it is supremely important—is correct, then I believe it is more accurate to apply moral language to the more significant event: the death of the individual, independent of who or what caused it. Of course, this leads to the question, "Why do we only use moral language to apply to agents?" As I mentioned earlier, this seems to be due to the fact that we have some perceived control over agents—in that we can influence their actions with social norms.

If my interpretation is correct, then if we are able to gain a similar level of influence over rocks falling on people, we would begin to see that as morally significant as well. Do we see moral intuitions shifting under certain circumstances to give us a reason to expect they may shift in this way? I believe we do. In the example of the moral progress we see across time.

Moral Progress

Societies tend to have shifts in their moral intuitions and beliefs over time. Some of the best examples of moral progress are; women's rights, gender equality, LGBT rights, decreases in racism, abolition of slavery, increases in freedom of expression, decreases in capital punishment, helping the elderly, helping the mental and physically handicapped, increases in charity, human rights movement, reduction of child labor, workers' rights, civil rights, veganism/vegetarianism, animal rights, universal healthcare, etc. Are these changes random, or is there a pattern in them across cultures—something that connects them?

There are examples of things which were culturally seen as moral becoming culturally seen as immoral. Such as certain kinds of disciplining children, like spanking—causing a child physical pain to deter them from doing certain actions. This was once seen as the moral duty of parents to make sure their children are prepared for living in the world. But as society has progressed, and a greater understanding of the psychological harm this can do to some children has been determined, and the fact there are non-violent ways to achieve the same outcome—society at large has begun to see such a method as cruel and immoral.

There are also examples of things considered amoral becoming seen as moral. Such as, caring for the environment, (as we gain the resources to be able to live without damaging ecosystems). For example, it begins to be seen as immoral to damage the environment with pollution, or over hunting/fishing a species to extinction. Another common example is veganism/vegetarianism. In many developed nations it is becoming seen as immoral to kill animals.

We also see the opposite—things once being seen as immoral becoming moral. Such as killing the enemy in war. Or, rationing resources while prioritizing certain groups. These can begin to be seen as moral if there is a loss or limitation of the availability of resources and such actions become necessary for survival.

Each of these advances only seem to take place in extremely specific circumstances. Namely, as the society involved makes technological advancements or gains access to an abundance of resources. Societies implemented many required actions and prohibitions which were believed to be beneficial to the society in some respect. As the technological limitations of societies are removed, the old prohibitions and requirements are no longer perceived as necessary or beneficial. These begin to be questioned, causing the perception of them as being moral/immoral to begin to shift. As society gains enough excess resources to allow for more individual freedoms, without causing a detriment to the society, it appears as if we begin to allow for those freedoms to be seen as morally neutral. Whereas, if the action would be a detriment to the society by requiring resources and not producing enough in exchange to be beneficial, we would see the action as immoral.

For example, gay marriage. Because gay couples cannot produce biological children it is not as evolutionarily beneficial to a society as they still require food and other resources. So, it makes sense societies with very limited resources did not provide resources to gay couples, and would instead give the resources to heterosexual couples. This would allow for the society to survive longer giving societies who happened to demonize gay relationships an evolutionarily advantage. However, once agriculture provides an abundance of food and other resources, resulting in no detriment to the society for providing them to gay couples, societies begin to shift to being more accepting of gay relationships.

Of course, this process is slowed if there is a prominent ideology in the society which inherently demonizes such relationships. Such ideologies become prevalent because of the evolutionary advantages their doctrines provide. Their more explicit doctrines will only begin to be questioned once the less stringent required actions and restrictions lose relevance, in a similar fashion due to technological progress in other domains.

All of the examples I have provided so far involve culpable agents. But there also examples of moral progress that seem to be applying moral language to non-agents. Such as in the modern social justice community which uses morally charged terms like: racist, sexist, misogynistic, transphobic, etc., applying such terms to non-culpable individuals and non-conscious entities. For example, a system or argument can be racist without a culpable person being involved. Also, arguing that someone can be subconsciously racist without having any ill-intention. That pattern hidden in these examples is—as technology or access to resources increases, the scope of morality also increases. Starting from those of the highest social status, then eventually trickling down to those of lower social status. For example, from men in positions of authority, to men of a lower social status, to women, to animals we like, to the elderly and handicapped, to other cultures and races, to criminals, to animals of higher intelligence, to animals of lower intelligence, etc. Each of these stages being a result of the technological advance of the society. Allowing it to have excess resources, which can then be used to support the lives of those with lower social status. Doing so previously would take resources away from those of higher social standing, whom the society is perceived to depend on for its survival. Thereby, putting the society at risk. The pattern also goes in the opposite direction. Once we lose access to resources or means to sustain ourselves, the pattern reverses. Harsh environments create harsh people.

If we follow this pattern to its extreme, and imagine we had infinite resources, the scope of moral progress will continue to grow until it encompasses every conscious entity. One by one, humans would begin to feel morally compelled to provide all conscious entities with the resources they require to live, and then, additionally to live well—free from involuntary impositions.

As mentioned in the section on moral intuition, some immoral actions are only contingently immoral, and others are necessarily immoral. Moral progress tells us there are also contingent moral intuitions that were adopted for the purpose of survival, but really have nothing to do with morality. Just as contingent immoral actions are irrelevant to objective morality because they are only subjectively immoral to certain contexts, the same applies to our intuitions. If our intuitions are only subjective to specific social contexts, then they do not tell us about objective morality, and we must filter the contingent intuitions out of our consideration of determining what objective morality is.

This might just be able to solve the problems presented earlier in the proposed definition of objective morality/immorality, (involuntary imposition of will). If our intuitions in the counterintuitive examples are all contingent intuitions, then we need to filter them out of our consideration of objective morality. They are only relevant in the subjective context of our social situations and will change in accordance with new social situations. Therefore, having no bearing on objective morality.

Let us look again at the counterintuitive examples. Are these actions contingently immoral? To find out we must take moral progress to its extreme and imagine we have infinite resources, and then see if the proposed solution is moral or if there is a more moral alternative.

Criticisms/Objections Killing One to Save Many is Immoral

If we imagine we have infinite resources, killing one to save many is never the moral option because there will always be a more moral option available to us. Such as, teleporting the victims to safety. It's only justified to kill the one because you don't have infinite resources. So, it's the lesser evil option. Being the lesser evil doesn't make it moral. It's still evil.

Punishing Children is Immoral

If we imagine we have infinite resources, punishing children is never the moral option. There will always be a more moral option available to us. Such as, giving them the intellectual capabilities to recognize the implication of any action, (essentially making them adults, at which point they have the right to make choices for themselves). It is only justified to punish children, because if you don't, they will suffer far worse consequences imposed on them by reality—if they do not learn to avoid certain actions. But again, that does not mean it is moral to punish children. Only the lesser evil done to prevent the greater harm if you do not.

Putting Criminals in Jail is Immoral

If we imagine we have infinite resources, forcing a person to be in jail against their will is never the moral option. There will always be a more moral option available to us. Such as, teleporting the victims to safety or giving each person their own personal force field to protect them from criminals. It's only justified to imprison the criminal because we don't have infinite resources. So, it's the lesser evil option. Being the lesser evil doesn't make it moral. It's still immoral.

Giving a Drug Addict Drugs is Moral

If we imagine we have infinite resources, we could create a cure to any of the negative side effects of any drug. The reason it is considered immoral to give an addict the drugs they desire is because of the harsh negative consequences on their body/life. Therefore, if we can remove any such consequences, there is no reason not to give the addict the drugs he desires, (as there are no consequences). In such a case, it would actually be moral to give the drug addict the drugs. If we have infinite resources.

Helping Someone to Commit a Crime is Moral

If we imagine we have infinite resources, we could create a virtual world where the person can commit as many crimes as he/she likes with no consequence to others, allowing them to fulfill their will with no consequences. Thus, it would be moral to help them commit their desired crime. If we had infinite resources. If they specifically willed to impose involuntary restrictions on someone else's will, then it would necessarily be immoral to help them. As it would entail imposing on someone else without their consent.

Rocks Falling on People is Immoral

One obvious example of this being accepted is religious and it is called "natural evils." In Christianity, these include tornadoes, hurricanes, earthquakes, etc. One of our biggest intuitions is of blameworthiness. How can something be immoral if it can't be considered blameworthy, (as rocks obviously cannot)? I believe this contradicts with our intuition that morality is supremely important.

Which is more important, the blameworthiness of the perpetrator or the consequence to the victim? I would say the impact on the victim is far more important by comparison. So, if our intuitions that morality is supremely important are correct, then the impact on the victims would be far more relevant to moral language. In which case, if we compare a rock falling on someone vs. a perpetrator deliberately killing someone, the vast majority of the moral significance is in the death of the victim, not the intentionality of the perpetrator. Therefore, we should not discount the rock falling and killing someone from having moral considerations. I believe this is the primary reason the social justice community so readily apply moral language to non-culpable entities, such as systems, arguments, and subconscious tendencies.

One of the biggest indications that we will begin to see inanimate objects as morally culpable is advances in the field of neurology. Neurology indicates we are all subject to our brain chemistry. So, no one is ultimately to blame for their actions, as there is no such thing as libertarian free will. We are all victims of our physical brain chemistry. So, there is no such thing as blame-worthiness. Therefore, morality ultimately does describe non-culpable objects. Namely, chemistry and matter in motion. We know many actions we would often label immoral are not caused by the choice of an individual, but by the physical processes in their brain, such as brain tumors:

"The sudden and uncontrollable paedophilia exhibited by a 40-year-old man was caused by an egg-sized brain tumour, his doctors have told a scientific conference. And once the tumour had been removed, his sex-obsession disappeared." [6]

Such facts discovered in neurology are causing a change in how we view criminality. Making it more of a medical condition in need of treatment rather than a punishable offence. I believe morality will have the same shift. We will begin to see immoral actions as actions that should be prevented, not actions done by agents who are blameworthy.

---

6   Charles Choi, 21 October 2002, Brain tumour causes uncontrollable paedophilia, newscientists.com, Retrieved from: https://www.newscientist.com/article/dn2943-brai n-tumour-causes-uncontrollable-paedophilia/

To use an example, I first heard from Sam Harris—psychopathy. We tend to see the actions of psychopaths as immoral. They do actions which actively harm others for their own benefit or pleasure and feel no remorse. Because of this we see them as bad people deserving of punishment. But imagine with future advancements in neurology, we discovered a cure for psychopathy. Where you could just take a pill and open the pathways in the brain which were impaired, allowing the individual to feel the empathy and compassion they were unable to feel before. Now, they feel the guilt and remorse for their actions. Once we get to this point, we will no longer see psychopaths as morally culpable for their actions. Rather, victims of their biology—exactly like the brain tumor.

This is not just true of brain tumors or psychopathy but all mental conditions. Once we find out any action that we perceive as immoral was caused by some curable brain state, we will no longer see it as a morally culpable action done by an evil person. Rather we will see both the perpetrator and the victim as victims of a disease. If we intend to be honest in our search for morality, we must incorporate these facts discovered in neurology and other modern scientific fields and follow the evidence wherever it leads.

Many people do this by adopting the compatibilist approach. Compatibilism being the position that free will is compatible with determinism. Meaning, even though we are determined, we can still have free will in the sense that, insofar as our brains act without outside influence, even though our brains are wholly determined by physical and biological forces, then we are free. Others do away with morality all together as a fictitious concept relating to the myth of free will. There is a third approach. That adopted by the social justice community I mentioned earlier, which is broadening the concept of morality to apply to things with no culpability. Such as, system, arguments, and subconscious biases.

But I take a different approach. I believe the concept of morality will evolve, much like the criminal justice system is doing now, into a more realistic understanding that incorporates advances in our knowledge of reality. For example, recognizing morality does not refer to some persons culpable choice to do good or bad, but rather their brain chemistry and whether or not it predisposes them to help or harm others. Thus, changing the concept of morality to mean something like, "Does the physical structure of that brain assist people or harm people?" This shift from seeing morality as actions done by agents, to actions done by physical brain states. is moving us a step closer to seeing inanimate objects as having moral significance.

We can then ask, if physical brain states in agents can be moral/immoral, then why not see physical states outside of agents as being able to do moral/ immoral actions? Like, rocks falling on people? We can potentially make a moral comparison between physical states just as we do for brain states. This physical system is predisposed to harm wills, more than that physical system, and is thus, more immoral.

I believe this is likely to occur. So, I argue in the future, people will intuitively see morality/immorality not as actions done by agents, but any action done to agents—regardless of who or what does the action.

It seems as if these counterintuitive consequences are not so counter intuitive after all. They are simple contingent intuitions based on our current subjective circumstances. We can see the evidence of such intuitions changing, even today. In the future when our technological means progress sufficiently, these criticisms will themselves become examples of moral progress. Where a past society did not see the moral significance, the future society will.

Now that we have analyzed the evidence of morality from moral intuition, and moral progress, and have derived principles based on the patterns in each, let us build a more comprehensive model of what an objective morality will look like if we project these principles to their extreme.

Contradictory Wills Objection

If one person wills to not be alone, or for a particular person to be with them, yet the other wishes to not be with that person, in my model this will result in the person who wishes the other to be with them, to be rejected their desires and end up being alone. This seems like an involuntary imposition on the will of the person who is alone, thus being immoral or providing a contradiction in my model.

This is incorrect. The principle "no involuntary imposition of will" is not limited to "your will" but "all wills involved." Your will only applies to yourself and your property. If you will something involving another person, for there to be no involuntary imposition of will, ALL parties involved must consent. So, if you will for another to be in your universe, and they do not consent, that is not an involuntary imposition of your will. Because your will only applies to yourself and your property and does not apply to other conscious beings. Their will applies to themselves and their property. So, if they stay in their own universe, neither yourself, they, your property, nor their property has been involuntarily imposed upon. Therefore, no involuntary imposition of will has occurred.

The Moral Standard

Based on moral intuition we can conclude that morality can be described with the principle "involuntary imposition of will is immoral." Based on moral progress, we can conclude this principle extends to all conscious agents. And, the imposition we currently see as justified are all contingent on subjective limitations. Following these lines of evidence, we can conclude the objective moral standard is a world where there is no involuntary imposition of will of any conscious agents. What would such a world look like?

If we imagine having the infinite resources to accomplish this. Every conscious agent would get a universe of their own which they can design however they wish and decide all the actions that are allowed to occur in their universe. Any other such actions would be physically impossible in their universe. You may invite others to your universe, or be invited to theirs. And, they may consent to joining you if they are fully aware of all the rules you have in place and agree to them. It will also be possible to make new worlds jointly with other people. The only limitation being—you cannot create or force other conscious beings in your universe or program them with desires set by you. Once created, they would immediately get their own universe and the freedom to design it however they see fit.

In such a morally perfect world, all interactions will necessarily be consensual. If someone tries to harm you without your consent, it will be physically impossible. For example, if someone throws a cup at you it will simply pass through you like you are a ghost, unless you consent to it hitting you. In such a world, immoral actions such as rape and murder are impossible.

I call this world "The Best of all Possible Worlds" (BPW for short). This is the morally perfect world we can use as a basis to measure all actions to see if they meet the standard of this world. If an action would not be allowed in this world, then it is objectively immoral. To know the objectively moral action for any given situation, we would imagine the same situation occurring in the BPW. Whatever would be expected of us in that case would be the objectively moral action.

If anyone can design their universe as they choose, will moral actions even be possible as anyone can simply snap their fingers to achieve anything they desire in their universe? Yes, though they will be more about relationships. For example, if someone desires companionship or company, spending time with them in their universe or inviting them to yours, will be moral actions. As you are voluntarily assisting them to achieve their wills—the definition of a moral action.

Let us see how this model addresses the classical moral dilemma of the trolley problem. If there is a trolley heading down a track toward five people, and you are at a switch which can change the direction of the trolley to a second track; however, there is one person standing on the second track, and you will hit them instead, should you flip the switch?

Assuming none of the persons involved consented to being hit by a train, this entire situation would be impossible in the BPW. Any of the individuals being hit by the train, without their consent, would be immoral. Therefore, we know, no matter what we choose in our realistic world, an immoral action will occur either way. To resolve this, we must consider what action we can take to bring us as close as possible to the BPW, given our limitations. If we do nothing, five immoral actions will occur as the five individuals are hit by the train. If you flip the switch, only one immoral action will occur. In this case it is reasonable to flip the switch to save the five, even if you kill the one, as you have prevented a net four immoral actions—getting as close the BPW as possible given your limitations. However, there is another consideration to remember: culpability. In the case you flipped the switch and saved four lives, you have done four moral actions which you take credit for. However, you have also done one immoral action which is also *partially* your fault and you should be obligated to try to accommodate the victim or their family. If you had done nothing, five immoral actions would have occurred. However, none of which you are responsible for as the physical environment itself and the moving trolley is to blame. This is why you are only partially to blame for the one immoral action caused by flipping the switch. The vast majority of the culpability lies in the physical environment of the trolley, (which is not your fault).

However, consider a similar example. If instead of there being a switch to change the direction of the trolley, there was a very fat man standing in front of the track. And, if you pushed him onto the track, it would cause him to be hit by the trolley, stopping it and saving the five. In this case, you would almost entirely be responsible for the death of the fat man. The culpability being mostly on you, rather than the trolley. Therefore, in this case it would be wrong of you to push the fat man. Whereas, it is not, for you to flip the switch. This illustrates that justification for doing an action, which will lead to an immoral outcome, is based on culpability. If the majority of the culpability is not on you, and you are simply mitigating already immoral circumstance, then such an action is a justified immoral action. This can also be called a subjectively moral action. As it is the best you can do given your limitations. However, if the majority of the culpability is on you, then it is an unjustified immoral action. In other words, both objectively and subjectively immoral.

At the beginning of my opening, I asked a question: Imagine you found a magic lamp with a djinni who will grant you a wish, what would be the most moral wish you could make? My answer to this question would be to wish for the djinni to create The Best of all Possible Worlds as I have described it. Where every conscious being gets their own universe, they can design however they like. And, it is physically impossible to force any conscious being to do anything they do not consent to doing.

If you feel this answer is more moral than the answer you came up with when you began reading, or you feel this answer is a good contender for what the most moral wish would be, then I have done my job.

This provides us a fairly comprehensive model to contrast actions with, in order to determine if they are moral or immoral. But it does not answer the last question about morality—what grounds morality? What is the ontology of morality/what is it made of?

Moral Ontology

Ontology of morality: we have intuitions that are separate from moral intuitions. Like the intuition that is A = B, and B = C, therefore A = C. Nothing can be completely green and completely blue at the same time. These are also intuitions like moral intuitions.

Logic and math are languages to describe our intuitions about these fields. We also have similar intuitions about morality. So, the field of morality is analogous to the field of math and logic. Math and logic are languages humans invented to describe patterns of how reality operates. In other words, logic and math describe some feature of reality akin to a law of nature. I believe morality also describes some feature of reality—a moral law of nature.

If we understand morality in the way which I have proposed, what could possibly ground such a thing? Obviously, the BPW does not exist as anything more than an abstract ideal, (as there are clearly many involuntary impositions of will all around us every day). But it does not need to exist to act as a ground. A perfect triangle is an object with three perfectly straight lines, each with an adjoining angle of 60 degrees. In our world, it is impossible to draw a perfect triangle. As an example, when we use an electron microscope to zoom in on the lines, we will see they are never perfectly straight as the electrons move in rounded bubble shapes. However, we can still use the non-existent abstract idea of a perfect triangle to get as close as possible given our limitations. We can do the same with the BPW, even though it also does not exist.

However, there is something that does exist which is leading us to this abstract ideal. As I mentioned before, I believe that all conscious agents will develop morality independently from one another, including non-evolutionary consciousnesses. In addition, they will all converge on a singular model of morality. If this is true, then there is something inherent to all minds causing this phenomenon.

Such properties commonly resulting among diverse groups are referred to as higher order emergent properties. Some other example of higher order emergent properties are health and fitness. Fitness is the ability for an organism to survive in an environment. Some organisms are more fit than others, as they can survive/thrive in more and harsher environments. Is fitness objective? Yes, it is an objective higher order emergent phenomenon describing a relation between an organism and environment in which it can live— which is true independent of minds or opinion.

Is there a highest level of fitness, like an objective standard to compare the fitness of other creatures? Yes, it is possible for an organism to be capable of surviving in any environment. Thus, making it the objective standard of fitness. We know of no such organism, but we can use the abstract ideal as a guide in determining the level of fitness of any given organism.

Morality is a higher order emergent property like fitness. But instead of measuring the relation between an organism and its ability to survive in an environment, morality measures some relation between an environment and consciousness and the entities interactions within these. Or, in the case of my model, the ability for conscious entities to act without involuntary imposition of will in any given environment.

Why call this higher order phenomenon morality when we could just call it something different? Remember, ultimately morality is whatever is causing those feelings we have when we see certain actions, we call moral or immoral. Whatever is causing those feelings and what those feeling refer to is morality. If such a higher order emergent property exists, it would explain why we have the moral intuitions and progress we observe and why such things are also present in all conscious agents. Therefore, this definition seems to exactly map onto what we are referring to when we are talking about morality.

We can go one step further. This higher order emergent property view of morality can be seen as an undiscovered law of nature, i.e. the moral law. This law can be ultimately grounded in Naturalistic Pantheism—the position that the fundamental nature of reality is unguided natural processes, i.e. not a mind or non-physical consciousness. Value, meaning, purpose, etc., can also be naturalistically grounded in similar way.

In order try and make Naturalistic Pantheism into something those who believe in a God can relate to and/or understand, we can describe it in terms of God's properties. A theistic God is usually described as having the properties: eternal (or outside of spacetime/the first mover), all-powerful (or necessary), all-good, all knowing, personal, conscious being. If you remove "personal" you get a deistic God which is eternal, all-powerful, all-good, all knowing, and conscious being. You can think of Naturalistic Pantheism as removing all the conscious aspects leaving only eternal, (or outside of spacetime/the first mover), all-powerful (or necessary) nature. Or put simply—Naturalistic Pantheism is eternal, all-powerful nature.

This can act as a ground for objective morality in a similar way theists believe God does. Objective morality, the undiscovered law of nature, is a part of the nature of Naturalistic Pantheism. So, just as a God can be said to ground objective morality, Atheistic models of reality can also ground objective morality and are far better by comparison.

Rick's Response to Tom's Case for Naturalistic Morality

TOM LAYS OUT his opening argument in a thoughtful way. He asks us to use our imagination in conceiving a Best Possible World (BPW), which would serve as a standard for measuring morality in the present real world.

A tempting response is to dismiss the BPW as being so other-worldly as to have no practical value. But I love lofty, creative ideas, and the BPW certainly qualifies. And while I'm familiar with "possible worlds" theory in philosophy, and even the most famous "best of all possible worlds" concept of G.W. Leibniz, I have to admit I've never read anything like Tom's BPW idea before.

Thus, to me, Tom's essay seems an exercise in constructive philosophy, and therefore quite daring. You put something out there and let the scholarly and popular critics have at it. (Tom, as your partner in this book, I admire your courage.)

There are three main topics in Tom's essay on which I'd like to comment: objective morality, materialism, and the BPW.

Objective morality

Feelings. Tom sees a close connection between objective morality and our feelings. Morality is what causes our feelings of moral "oughtness." We see someone harmed by another person and we feel angry toward the perpetrator and sad for the victim. We have intuitions that an immoral act has been done, and I think Tom is telling us that something out there beyond ourselves, something called "objective morality," is what causes these feelings or moral intuitions.

So, morality causes feelings. We may not know precisely what this morality is, but when we discern patterns in our feelings, we can begin to describe the moral principles to which they point. Or put another way, we can describe the moral principles which gave rise to the feelings.

If I may therefore suggest: in Tom's system the logical priority is morality, then feelings. Otherwise, the feelings would have little significance. But sequentially, it's the reverse. We observe the feelings first, then infer a moral principle that caused them. He writes, "We will start by looking at the phenomenon—the feelings we get of morality, and try to discern a pattern in these feelings which we can describe with some moral principle."

I wonder, however, if feelings are an adequate basis for judging morality, even if those feelings are shared widely. Regarding certain generic fundamentals, feelings are nearly unanimous. We feel that helping is better than hurting and flourishing is better than torture. Most of us agree on that. However according to atheist philosopher J.L. Mackie, "To say that there are objective values would not be to say merely that there are some things which are valued by everyone." That is, wide agreement on values doesn't make them objective.

And as soon as we get into more specific issues in the real world, feelings seem to diverge widely and irreconcilably. My feelings may not be your feelings. 9/11 was condemned by the West but cheered in parts of the Middle East and elsewhere. Slave owners in America felt it was right to enslave what they considered to be sub-humans who didn't deserve full human rights. Pro-slavery feelings were so strong, in fact, that Southerners were willing to die for their version of economic morality, even dividing families and neighbors in the Civil War.

In present-day America, progressives and conservatives are locked in persistent, severe (and perhaps endless) gridlock over what constitutes the common good for society. This is a war of feelings, values, morals, laws, freedoms and restrictions, capitalism versus socialism, family norms and parental authority, gender and sexuality, and most intractable of all – race relations. In my six-plus decades on this earth, I've never seen such extreme political entrenchment, strife, and uncivil public behavior. So I'm having a hard time trusting the reliability (and stability) of feelings and the moral intuitions they engender to serve as the required phenomena or data of morality. Feelings are running wild these days and are wildly divergent and conflicting. I can't see how they will come into eventual alignment.

Convergence. If I understand Tom accurately, he's saying that moral intuitions observed broadly will tend to converge into moral principles that most people can accept. And even if they don't accept them now, eventually they will, given the principle of moral progress that Tom holds. Moral progress is aided by advances in technology that enable more people to enjoy resources once possessed only by the elite of society. Thus, I see a parallel in Tom's thinking between technological advance and moral advance, between scientific convergence in describing how the physical world works and moral convergence in how morality works. I'd like to hear from Tom whether I'm describing this accurately. The Best Possible World (BPW), then, will be one in which massive technological achievement will enable individuals to enjoy maximal freedom of choice without interference or imposition from anyone else.

How do we arrive at objective moral principles? We use our "moral intuition" to determine which actions are more moral than others. And we continue to compare possible worlds, filtering out those with greater immorality, to narrow the field down to the BPW. The BPW then becomes the gold standard by which to measure all actions in the present actual world.

Further, it should be noted that for Tom moral intuition is akin to the intuitions we have in other disciplines, such as math and logic. We have an intuition that 2+3=5, and that if something is square it can't, by the same measure, also be triangular. We know these truths to be self-evident, even if we can't verify them empirically in every instance.

In summary, I take Tom to mean by "convergence" a kind of consensus of feelings and even beneficial actions of human beings across time and cultures. We observe these phenomena and reason our way to the principles behind them. These principles represent objective morality.

Tom claims to be a moral realist (meaning, he believes in objective morality). He and I have this in common. I guess I'm not convinced, however, that feelings or convergence provide a solid basis for objective morality. 99% of people could feel something or agree on something and still be wrong.

Consent. One of the hallmarks of morality for Tom is the idea of consent. Persons must give consent for any action performed on them or their property. Lacking such consent, the action is immoral. "Immorality is an imposition on someone, without their consent." At first blush, one can think of many counterexamples of this broad principle, and Tom anticipates these. Must we expect a child to *consent* to be disciplined by a parent? A criminal to consent to incarceration or punishment? Yes to both, Tom answers, counter-intuitively so (he admits).

In a maximally advanced society, technologically speaking, we could give children the "intellectual capabilities" to essentially become adults, and thus make their own decisions and avoid the imposition of parental discipline. Criminals could also avoid the imposition of imprisonment against their will by implementing technological safeguards for victims (such as teleporting them away). Of course, in the present world, lacking such technology, we must settle for disciplining children and locking up criminals. These actions are immoral because they violate the principle of consent, but they're necessary in the form: *If all choices in a situation at present are immoral, the least of all "evils" should be carried out. We're stuck with these immoral actions for now.*

I'm very much on board with the value of consent as a crucial factor in human relations. Tom rightly criticizes acts of imposition on unwilling persons. An obvious example is rape, one of the most egregious forms of nonconsensual behavior. But I'd like to reign consent in, just a bit. Tom's version of consent seems to rest on radical individual autonomy and assumes, I think, that we always know what's best for ourselves. I recently heard a similar concept preached on a nonreligious podcast: *Only you can decide what's best for your own mental health.* By the principle of radical autonomy, then, athletes know better than their coaches, mentees know better than their mentors, pupils know better than their teachers, and the mentally ill know better than their therapists. The autonomous self always knows what's best for itself.

I'm troubled by this paradigm. I guess I'm not convinced that I always know what's best for myself. If I were given the privilege of living in my own world, making my own autonomous choices, and only interacting with others as I see fit, I'm afraid I'd lose something of myself. I'd lose the benefit of what Tom calls an imposition on my autonomy. I agree with Tom that imposition can be harmful at times, but the benefits of living in community and submitting oneself to its authority is what it means to be fully human, from a Christian perspective. Yes, such communal life can be abused in religious circles, as in jihad or cultic authoritarianism, but that's no reason to reject it as an essential good. A good system is not nullified by misusing it.

It seems to me that cultures and other groups (such as business teams, educators, etc.) which are set up for the growth and development of their members actually recognize the benefits of "imposing" order, discipline, and healthy practices on their people, even if it involves, at times, unwanted hardship. In my own Scandinavian heritage of the 20th century, for example, we were taught that our individual autonomous preferences and choices had *communal* consequences. Thus, we learned to work hard, save our money, stay off drugs, tell the truth, share our resources, etc., not as isolated individuals in possession of indisputable self-understanding, but in the concrete give-and-take of communal relations and economic systems. That is, if I went on drugs or stole money, I was damaging the common good. I realize Tom envisions a BPW that eliminates many or all of these corporate consequences through a maximally advanced technological state, but even in that world, the assumption seems to be that each self knows what's best for the self, that it's better to be isolated in the realm of one's preferences, untouched by unwanted conflict or challenge, than to be enmeshed in the involuntary crucible of community.

A theology of Christian community begins with the Triune God who exists as one being in three persons – rather than as a singularity, as in Islam. While this isn't the place to explain the doctrine of the Trinity (as much as that is possible), its historic, philosophical influence has been vast. Of many applications, it forms the basis for human community. Yes, we are individuals, each responsible to God for our own actions. But this individual existence takes place inside the community of faith whereby, "I" am a member of "us." That's biblical anthropology.

As for personal development, we "disciple" each other into maturity (again, at our best; sometimes we fail in this). Part of this development is the admission that none of us as individuals know what's best for ourselves, and that it takes the wisdom and time-tested practices of the church community to organize, motivate, and discipline its members. Yes, the authority of communal organization can be abused, as mentioned above. But overall, a healthy community brings prudence, correction, accountability, and "orthopraxy" to its members. I've served in this system for many decades and appreciate it greatly.

The above paragraph assumes the reality of the Trinity and its attendant implications for anthropology. If naturalism rather than theism is true, of course, any such reference to God is instantly canceled. Yet, I believe it's within the purposes of the present discussion to at least briefly summarize a Christian way of "doing life."

So that is my attempt to affirm a portion of what Tom says about consent while moderating it a bit away from radical individual autonomy and more toward robust community. I'll say more about these communal relations below, in the section on interdependence.

Undiscovered law of nature. Tom writes, "This higher order emergent property view of morality can be seen as an undiscovered law of nature, i.e. the moral law."

I take this to mean that the abstract principle of morality (objective moral law) is based on a level of conjecture, and is thus technically "undiscovered." Tom even hints it may be a physical law of nature.

This was among the least clear ideas, for me, of Tom's overall position. I do respect a humble "it's the best we can do with what we've got" attempt at describing moral laws that most likely give rise to our moral intuitions. If I were an atheist, I'd do something similar. I'd admit that there's nothing outside of human feeling and models of apparent human flourishing – in contrast to human misery and suffering – to ground morality. Then I'd construct moral principles based on those feelings and examples of flourishing. I'm pretty sure I wouldn't call these moral principles "objective." But I think Tom would and does. I think he's saying we don't *construct* moral principles, we use language to describe what's already there. The principles that guide human feeling and action already exist out there somewhere. That's what makes them objective. They're part of the natural world, what Tom calls the world of Naturalistic Pantheism. I hope I've understood this properly.

Starting point revisited. Tom asks, "If you can't tell us what the moral principles are, then you must not have started with the moral principle as your basis to conclude a God was the source. So, how did the theists conclude God was the source at all?"

To repeat an earlier statement, my starting point in this book is God. I'm asking the question of whether the data of morality fits my starting point or not. Tom has accused me of jumping to God as my *conclusion*. But that's not quite right. My conclusion is still an open question: *Does the data of morality fit best with theism or secularism?* If Tom convinces me through argumentation that moral data is best explained by secular sources, my conclusion would then be settled and Tom would win the argument of this book. But my starting point of theism, technically speaking, would remain untouched. The existence of God is not the question of this book. However, I would need to subtract ethical arguments from any case I might wish to make for God's existence in a different book or conversation, or even in my belief system.

Furthermore, I can ask Tom a parallel question: *If you can't tell us what gives rise to the moral feelings we have, how can you conclude that natural law was the source?* A speculative assertion that natural law could *possibly* be the source provides little reason for holding this view.

Following the evidence? Tom admits: "All of the best evidence we currently have supports the subjective morality hypothesis—that morality is just a byproduct of evolution."

Despite this best evidence, Tom identifies himself as a moral realist. We've been led to believe that Tom is following the data of morality (the "evidence") as closely as possible before drawing any conclusions. But the best evidence leads elsewhere – toward subjectivism (given by evolution), away from Tom's position. Tom seems to be calling for an honest analysis of the data while adopting a position that, by his own admission, is contrary to the data.

Additionally, I'm struggling to identify the locus of this supposed objective morality in a purely naturalistic world. Physical reality doesn't tell us how to behave. It has no morals, no preferences. Atheist philosopher Michael Ruse says the world is just "matter in motion. It has no meaning. It has no values." Thus, how can the natural world, for example, tell Smith whether or not to cheat on his taxes? In Smith's own version of the BPW, he cheats whenever he wishes and gets away with it. In Tom's BWP, probably not. Whose BPW is better? Who decides? To adjudicate between Smith and Tom, Tom seems to appeal to "reality" – a built-in natural law that exists objectively on its own, independent of human thought.

But this is speculation and, in my view, lacks the most important attribute of all (the same as stated by atheists against God): *existence*. Tom asks us to consider "what if?" this law of morality exists. It would explain our feelings of oughtness. But so could many other sources, such as cultural norms, evolutionary advantage, God, or aliens who may have planted humanity on Earth. Any of these sources, if posited as a "most likely basis for morality," would require supporting argumentation. Tom's "what if?" and "maybe, just maybe," sound like speculation to me, not theoretical or evidence-based argumentation. This is what I'm hearing from Tom: "What if there's an objective moral law of nature? If there is, I believe it will eventually guide us to a BPW that we can envision even now. And the BPW will be ushered in by a convergence of worldwide morality that parallels massive scientific advancement." This sounds like one man's vision of a possible future (and quite intriguing!), not an argument for a secular basis of morality.

I've contended throughout our discussion that ethics flows quite naturally from a personal God, while from the material source of nature only, ethics is absent. Atoms don't yield morality. "You can't squeeze blood from a turnip." Richard Dawkins insists the universe is comprised of "blind physical forces." One need not be a theist to think the world lacks inherent meaning all on its own.

Mind. A reading of atheist philosopher Thomas Nagel's *Mind and Cosmos: Why the Materialist Neo-Darwinian Conception of Nature is Almost Certainly False* is instructive here. If I may summarize Nagel's position, the reductionist program of scientific materialism is insufficient to account for mind and meaning. He writes, "If evolutionary biology is a physical theory—as it is generally taken to be—then it cannot account for the appearance of consciousness and of other phenomena that are not physically reducible."[7] Quoting an authority like Nagel doesn't make my position true, but it does show that even in the atheist camp there is discomfort with materialism (sometimes called "physicalism") as a comprehensive explanation for the world.

In the same way Tom critiques theism on this line of thought, I believe the tables can be reversed. Tom tells us that God's morality is arbitrary, that in theism we learn nothing of true morality, only the *location* of such morality (in God). So here I'd like to ask Tom, does this undiscovered law of nature tell us anything about true morality, or is it merely a location for it to be housed? Isn't it as arbitrary as God? Is it right because it meets another moral standard, or is it right in itself? But isn't "itself" just a secular, arbitrary form of God to which we must submit?

Tom's reply to this question might be that the objective law of morality is embedded in "reality." That would make it an absolute standard, not subject to any other standards. How this is an improvement on God, the creator of all reality and all standards, is unclear to me – unless, of course, God doesn't exist. In that case, the battleground for morality would take place between moral realists like Tom and "subjectivists" (my term) who deny inherent meaning in the world and rely on ethics shaped by evolution and/or created by humans.

This is a good time to pause and express my admiration for Tom's willingness as a moral realist to stand out from the crowd. To my thinking, there's a vast chasm between those who create morals and those who (supposedly) discover them. Tom discovers morality and thereby stands in the minority of non-theists. As mentioned earlier, I agree with Tom that morality is objective and is discovered, not constructed. We stand together against subjectivism but stand apart and oppose each other on the source or basis of true morality.

Back to natural law. I see a possible overlap between Tom's position of believing in a law of nature for morality and the "natural law" theory of, say, Thomas Aquinas or the "*Tao*" considered by C.S. Lewis. Aquinas says that natural law is a reflection of the nature and character of God and is built into the universe, including in humanity. Humans flourish when they obey this

---

7   Thomas Nagel, *Mind and Cosmos* (Oxford University Press, Kindle Edition, 2012), p.14.

law, which they know innately to be true. For our purposes: if God exists and has embedded his character into human nature, perhaps Tom's awareness of objective morality stems from God. I doubt Tom would agree to this but on the God-premise it's not illogical. Let's say I secretly install a morality chip, reflecting my morals, into an android. At a future date, the android somehow learns about me (however that might happen) and concludes that I was the source of its morality. This inference is not indiscriminate and seems to draw on the idea of an intelligence (me) passing along a sense of moral obligation felt by the android. On this analogy, we've all received a "morality chip" (conscience) from God which enables us to tell right from wrong.

A related way that nature contributes to the present discussion is Lewis's notion of the *Tao*,[8] which represents common ground for a variety of traditions such as Norse, Egyptian, Chinese, Roman, Christian, and Jewish. Each tradition reflects something of the ethical laws of nature and seems to converge toward moral categories such as "duties to parents, elders, and ancestors"; "the law of justice"; the "law of good faith and veracity"; and other obligations. This understanding of *Tao* could almost be marshaled in support of Tom's model where worldwide morality converges (eventually) into a BPW. Ethical systems around the globe, each reflecting objective morality in varying degrees, could be woven together into a single tapestry or *Tao* of morality. I like the direction of this scheme in Tom's favor.

The question thus becomes whether the *Tao* is a composite of the other views or a stand-alone view to which the others point. For Lewis, it's the latter. He argues that the other views point indirectly and, in their own respective ways, to the one true God as revealed in Christ, the ultimate source of morality. In other words, the *Tao* in all its diverse expressions reflects the law of God embedded in the collective conscience of humanity.

The preceding section is another way of saying that whenever "convergence" or "consensus" is brought into the service of objective morality, it's not obvious that secularism is the correct framework. Natural Law (Aquinas) and the *Tao* (Lewis) both point back to God. That is, when you discover that nature produces obligations of conscience, it's likely those obligations were created and planted by an intelligent Mind. Indeed, I'm struggling to see how a moral law

---

8   See Lewis's discussion in *The Abolition of Man* (MacMillan paperback ed., 1965).

of nature could exist *without* Mind. That is, without God – not "a god" like Thor who's inside the world, but an external, uncreated Creator of the world.

The mirror. Further, is Tom's objective law that exists somewhere in reality anything more than a mirror? It seems to me this law simply represents the supposed best of how humans already behave. That is, we look within ourselves, find the best of what we do, and project it into a law that supposedly exists independently of ourselves. This reminds me of the projection technique 19th c. philosopher Ludwig Feuerbach accused theists of using. For Feuerbach, God was nothing more than human nature writ large, a projection of the ideal self. In Tom's case, it seems the undiscovered law of nature, which is an objective morality, is simply human goodness writ large – a projection of us at our supposed best, and thus a kind of "descriptivism" – that is, a factual description of human behavior. But arguing from these facts to an underlying objective morality seems difficult to me. Again, Mackie's point is relevant: things valued by everyone do not constitute objective morality.

Additionally, I'm wondering how an "undiscovered" law of nature can be known to ground morality. If the law is undiscovered, how do we know about it? We can speculate that it may be out there, a diamond hidden somewhere in the cosmos. To give the benefit of the doubt, Tom may be saying that even if this diamond's exact nature is unknown to us, it's still the best explanation for what gives rise to our feelings and moral intuitions. The undiscovered law is thus a kind of law-of-the gaps explanation for morality: we believe in it until a better explanation comes along. It's not provable because it's undiscovered. We don't even know if it's discoverable. What we know, on naturalistic premises, is that God cannot be the source of morality. So it must be an undiscovered law.

Similarly, Nagel, in trying to explain human consciousness, confines himself to naturalistic explanations (which he finds wanting). But the alternative explanation of God cannot be true. Nagel admits he doesn't *want* theism to be true and that he has a vested interest in atheism. So he seeks solutions to the problem of consciousness that exclude theism as a contender. He exercises faith in the future of science, which in his view needs a radical upgrade to explain how, in essence, matter could come to "think." The God solution to this problem is unthinkable.

Perhaps this automatic exclusion of God is what Tom is thinking regarding morality, I don't know. Nor do I wish to speculate on his motives. In any case, he states that secular versions of morality are "far superior" to those of theism. But I'm having a hard time seeing how an undiscovered law of nature is superior to a revelation of God. That's like saying an undiscovered diamond is superior to a diamond in hand. Actually, that's not quite right. The atheistic diamond isn't simply undiscovered, it's *unknown*. It's speculative. The speculative diamond that might possibly exist in an ideal world – at least as we imagine it – is "far superior" to a fully given diamond already on display for the world to see.

God revealed himself in Christ to a whole community: first-century Palestinian Jews and Gentiles. This disclosure is not hidden or undiscovered but is plain in the historical record. So, for example, the Sermon on the Mount, recorded in Matthew chapters 5-7 in the New Testament, purports to be the wisdom of God spoken by Jesus, the Son of God. The early church described the Son as the "heir of all things, through whom also he made the universe. The Son is the radiance of God's glory and the exact representation of his being, sustaining all things by his powerful word." Lofty words that generated thousands of Christian martyrs at the hands of Roman soldiers (and the teeth of lions). In any case, such was the early Christians' view of Jesus which caused them to value his teachings at the cost of their own lives.

I understand that a declaration of moral authority and wisdom, such as the Sermon on the Mount, doesn't make it true. Yet, I find the Sermon, one of the greatest wisdom passages in the Bible, to be a much more compelling basis for morality than an undiscovered law of nature, which appears in any case to be a projection of human aspirations. That is, a mirror of our supposed best selves. When the Sermon calls me to contrarian behavior such as loving my enemies, blessing those who curse me, and being generous with the one who robs me, I think quickly of typical secular (cultural) alternatives: vengeance, retribution, and getting even. To my thinking, the commands of the Sermon are much more sublime.

Lastly in this section, I'd like to ask the question of who it is among mortals that is entitled to observe the phenomena of feelings, interpret the patterns therein, and generate a description of the undiscovered law of nature.

The late Yale Law professor Arthur Leff wonders who has "the power to declare careful, consistent, coherent, ethical pronouncements 'better' than the sloppier, more impulsive kind. Who has that power and how did he get it?"

In reply, we might suggest that a group of university professors be given this power. But would they agree on true morality? Having worked in the university world for four decades, I doubt it. How about a cadre of world leaders represented in the United Nations? Given the amount of global conflict, competing interests, and disparate cultures in the world, the U.N. seems an unlikely candidate for the consensus or convergence Tom envisions.

Regarding the Best Possible World, for example, could professors or U.N. leaders agree on what it would be? Tom's version of the BPW values radical individual autonomy where everyone is free from the impositions of everyone else. But that sounds to me like a hyper-Enlightenment, Western, white, individualistic ideal, not something people of color around the globe, who tend to be more communal in their anthropology and sociology, would wish to embrace. In the black churches where I sometimes hang out, for example, the vibe is not freedom from the imposition of others, where each person knows what's best for themselves. Rather, the *community* knows what's best for the individuals. Individuals are expected to submit their wills to the authority of community. This is true in many Hispanic, Asian, and Native American communities as well. *We comes before I.* But in Tom's BPW, the autonomous "I," which consists of me alone in my own universe, reigns supreme. I think Tom is overly optimistic in believing that moral convergence is in the future of humanity in a manner that resembles scientific convergence. At least in science, we can all look under the microscope or into the telescope and generally agree about what's there – at least in the essentials (scientists, of course, disagree on many things).

Professors and U.N. officials: two unlikely candidates to provide consensus on morality. Perhaps we should look elsewhere – to professional ethicists or lawyers or Democrats or to the overall atheist population who claim to be the most rational of all and would thereby judge these complex matters most impartially.

Some might wish to exclude theists and other religious believers, all of whom make up perhaps 90% of the world's population, from serving in the

Tom Jump and Rick Mattson

elite group of decision-makers who seek consensus on objective morality. They are, after all, blinded by their religious beliefs to objective truth. Please forgive a note of sarcasm there.

I've been reading of late about white-collar crime in America, with many examples given from the state of Mississippi. The overall picture is not encouraging regarding the future of ethics, and I'm having trouble envisioning a qualified representational committee that sorts it all out on behalf of humanity.

In Christian anthropology, *humanity is created good but fallen into bad, though a vestige of the original good remains.* Left to themselves without accountability, moral agents usually default to selfishness, even at the expense of others. That's what's happening in a massive 70-million dollar government scandal in Mississippi, with a hundred other smaller cases pending in the state auditor's office.

Conclusion: When no one is looking, even supposedly good people are prone to doing bad for personal gain. The biblical anthropology just mentioned of "good-turned-bad with some good left over" seems exceedingly realistic and accurate to me in our world. So I don't really share Tom's optimism for humanity's future convergence/consensus around a secular, objective moral standard. Indeed, despite certain headway made in the treatment of minority communities in America, I'm still quite pessimistic about the human heart and its ability to define the good and embrace it, tomorrow and beyond.

Examples of right and wrong. Tom helpfully gives us some specific actions and attitudes that can be classified as right or wrong: "The good ones are 'Saving, assisting, helping, healing, freeing, giving, self-sacrifice, protecting.' The bad ones are 'Killing, rape, torture, slavery, theft, lying, cheating, bullying, etc.'"

He also provides further treatment of rape (necessarily immoral under any circumstances), and murder (immoral aside from rare exceptions).

I do not argue with these lists and categories. I do wonder about their basis, however. In a famous debate between atheist Sam Harris and theist William Lane Craig at the University of Notre Dame a few years ago, Harris offers a list of moral and immoral actions that parallel Tom's. When asked for their foundational support by Craig, Harris replies, in essence, that such moral values are self-evident. Whatever promotes human well-being is good; whatever

102

hurts it is bad. Thriving is good, suffering is bad. Who could disagree with such obvious common sense? Not Craig. He agrees with the observations, but he continues to press the point of their origin and authority, and why anyone would be obligated to obey these admittedly commonsense moral principles.

Honestly, watching the debate now for the second time gives me a new appreciation for Sam Harris. Obviously, he cares for those who suffer in the world, such as women among the Taliban who are forbidden literacy and other basic human rights. And he seems in the video to be exasperated by anyone who needs a divine being to teach them right from wrong, especially in such clear cases (as he provides) of moral goods and ills.

I have the same appreciation for Tom. I love that he cares for the well-being of others and that he's not afraid to publish a scorecard of obvious wins and losses regarding human behavior, perhaps daring a theist like myself to demand a philosophical argument, say, for the value of "helping" or "healing." Or to say that opposing rape is merely an arbitrary subjective judgment. Who could be heartless enough to criticize a list of these "apple pie and baseball" items, or fail to condemn pointless suffering in all possible worlds? Perhaps Rick Mattson?

Well, I hope I'm not that heartless! But in a book like this, you can't simply assume a solution to the question at hand without showing why your worldview best supports it. This is a form of question-begging: assuming the conclusion in your premises. Meaning, that assuming the "no one could disagree with this list of rights and wrongs" solution is, without argument, a true solution.

Of course, I do agree with Tom's lists. And they are perfectly compatible with theism. Helping and healing are basic practices of the Christian faith, not only commanded by God but modeled by Jesus. But in Tom's naturalistic world, these positive practices seem to arise merely as observations of human behavior. They simply "are." And my question is whether it's more likely such practices arose from an impersonal, purposeless universe or one that is personal and purposive. To state again the illustration of a household, if I observe the polite and helpful behavior of a couple of teenagers in a home, it seems more likely they were tutored and nurtured by their parents or other mature adults, even if those adults are not in view, than that the kids were inherently polite and helpful. But in Tom's universe, we ignore the adults (God) and focus only on the kids. We observe their good behavior and call it objective morality. To my thinking, it's more reasonable to infer the presence and teaching of adults in the home, even if not presently visible.

An even deeper philosophical question on this point is why, in a naturalistic universe of unguided evolution, we should trust our moral intuitions at all. Evolutionary advantage is given to the most powerful, not necessarily the most moral or truthful. To paraphrase, Darwin himself wondered whether he could trust his monkey mind to apprehend the truth about the world, including the truth about evolution. These are deep waters and I'm not sure I am competent to press the matter further, but I don't think it's a stretch to question the plausibility of truth-producing minds evolved from apes in a mechanistic universe even if that universe is called Naturalistic Pantheism.

In a famous quote, former atheist Lee Strobel writes, "Looking at the doctrine of Darwinism, which undergirded my atheism for so many years, it didn't take me long to conclude that it was simply too far-fetched to be credible. I realized that if I were to embrace Darwinism and its underlying premise of naturalism, I would have to believe that: Nothing produces everything. Non-life produces life . . . Unconsciousness produces consciousness. Non-reason produces reason. Based on this, I was forced to conclude that Darwinism would require a blind leap of faith that I was not willing to make."

If I may add to Strobel's list: I'm not convinced that non-morality produces morality.

Tom may argue that morality already resides in the natural world, and this "morality" gives rise to our moral intuitions. He writes, "Maybe, just maybe, our feelings about morality are more like our eyes. Perceiving something that is actually there—existing in reality outside of our imagination. If that is the case, then morality refers to something which is objective."

That's a very big maybe. Even if true, it most likely points to God, the true morality-giver.

Materialism

I'm glad Tom brings up the idea of materialism because it plays a crucial role in ethics. Put simply, if we are material beings and nothing more, then our behavior is physically determined. Human free will is an illusion. And without free will it's hard to assign blame to wrongful actions. Tom writes, "Neurology indicates we are all subject to our brain chemistry. So, no one is ultimately to blame for their actions, as there is no such thing as libertarian free will. We are all victims of our physical brain chemistry. So, there is no such thing as blameworthiness."

There's a partial truth in this statement with which I agree: chemistry imbalances can lead to neurotic behavior. Courts of law recognize such conditions as excusing various crimes by pleas of insanity.

But the notion of a completely materialistic universe, including the total of what a human being is, seems counter-intuitive to me and perhaps philosophically untenable. Intuitively, it seems in my self-awareness that I possess a mind that exists beyond my physical self and that I'm aware of other such minds around me. I don't *seem* to be locked into predetermined choices. So when a certain segment of atheist thinkers such as Tom informs me that I don't transcend my physical self and that the exercise of my supposed free will is just an illusion, it comes as quite a surprise.

Here I sit in my living room. The refrigerator is right around the corner. I have a strong notion that I have a free choice about whether to grab a snack from the fridge. I could do it or not. It's up to me. At the moment, I choose to refrain. Too many calories in those snacks. But in Tom's physical world, which includes my comprehensive physical self, I don't have any choice. Brain chemistry already chose for me. In these exact conditions of my brain state in any possible world, I would make the same choice to refrain from the fridge. That is, *it's not possible under the exact same physical conditions of time and place and the state of my body and brain to have chosen otherwise.* Hence the imprisonment of materialism. I'm locked up in the physical world.

To Tom's credit, he makes lemonade in this prison. He offers the example of a pedophile suffering from a brain tumor that warped his desires. When the tumor was removed, his sex obsession was cured. In theory, then, one could take a pill for almost any moral malady and be transformed into a good person. Morality is thus rerouted through medicine and therapy. This is the logical conclusion of a material universe and I commend Tom for his consistency. No one is ultimately responsible for their moral failures because they are a product of, or a victim of, their physical states.

One way Christian philosophers have responded to materialism is to suggest a different underlying reality. Instead of just one substance in the universe, there are two: material and immaterial. This is called "substance dualism." For human anthropology, it means a person possesses a material nature and an immaterial nature. A human being is defined as an embodied mind or soul. Returning to Thomas Nagel, the renowned atheist philosopher seems to allow for this possibility, dismissing as irrational the power of physical reality to produce minds: "Materialism requires reductionism; therefore the failure of reductionism requires an alternative to materialism." Foregrounding mind over matter, he continues: "The possibility opens up of a pervasive conception of the natural order very different from materialism—one that makes mind central, rather than a side effect of physical law."[9] It's apparent from Nagel's assertions that one need not be a theist to doubt the power of material reality to produce mind and meaning – and therefore morality. For Nagel, physical nature simply can't perform that kind of work.

Dualism frees the mind to make choices that are influenced by material factors but not completely determined by them. That is, consciousness and such functions as choice and intention rise above the material housing of the brain. Thus, it's not merely my brain loving my wife, it's "me" – an objective entity not reducible to my body – who loves Sharon Mattson. This is made possible by a creator God who made human beings in his likeness, endowed in miniature with the creator's attributes of consciousness, intention, and the like.

In a world of substance dualism, human beings are, in fact, responsible for their choices. Hence the criminal justice system. To my thinking, this makes more philosophical and intuitive sense than the surprise revelation that we are locked into physical determinism, do not possess free will, and are not responsible for our choices.

Let me zoom out for a moment and share what kind of argument I'm attempting here. It's a "seems to make more sense" (plausibility) argument rather than a philosophical proof (whatever that might be). I'm trying to say that given all the factors in the complex problem of human ethics, the best solution is to assume substance dualism and accept free will and human responsibility.

9   Nagel, pp. 14-15.

The denial of these three items leads to the absurdity of determinism, where a man could rape a woman and *not be held responsible.* Imagine that. The rapist is simply sick. He needs an anti-rape pill. He doesn't pay for his crime, he merely checks in for health care.

Substance dualism could be false. I haven't given a metaphysical argument for it. I'm simply saying that its denial leads to absurdity. Perhaps you know of someone who's suffered the horrors of rape. I do. There's a moral urgency that rises in us that demands justice. The perpetrator is *guilty and must be held responsible.* This same demand fuels the social justice movement in this country. Racism and oppression are wrong, the violators must pay, the innocent must be protected. But if materialism is true, no one is culpable, which I find unacceptable – morally, intuitively, and philosophically.

Judgment calls. In the myriad interactions with atheists that I've enjoyed (mostly!) over the years, one of the constant themes I hear is that we must get past our fantasies and face the hard truths of reality. One of those is materialism – that matter and energy are all that exist. There is no soul, no heaven, no angels or demons. There is no afterlife, just bodily decay. The deceased live only in the memories of the living. In a strange sense, I admire the consistency of this whole position. There is no possible emotional rescue from a divine source, no spirits of the dead visiting their living relatives with assurances of eternal peace. And for many atheist philosophers, the blunt reality of materialism has led them to deny ultimate meaning and objective ethics. Two examples are J.L. Mackie and Jean-Paul Sartre. This is a logical conclusion, in my view.

But Tom is different. Tom is trying to construct objective ethics (and therefore objective meaning) in a material world, even though he admits, perhaps embraces, the denial of human responsibility. And he thinks my God a fantasy, on the level of the mythical Thor.

Maybe so. Maybe the God of the Bible is wishful thinking. Maybe the Trinity is plugged in just to solve problems, such as those in ethics, despite lacking the most important attribute of all: existence. I've thought of this countless times in my four-plus decades of Christian faith (beginning at age 19). But as much as atheists find the fantasy of God untenable, I find the dehumanizing robotic existence of materialism even more so. The more

I interact with consistent-minded atheists, the more I must conclude that from their perspective a human being is nothing more than a complex machine operating inside a giant machine called a universe. It is only fantasy to embrace the higher truths of art, loyalty, nobility, poetry, familial love, intimacy, compassion, and the like. These are elements of the subjective life. The "hard truth of reality" is that these qualities are not native to machines. We grasp at them desperately and fool ourselves into thinking we experience them. But such experience is an illusion, akin to the surprise given to me by atheists that free will is an illusion. Better to find subjectivity in a subjective (personal) Creator who grants it all as a gift, something that flows from his very character and nature. The idea of a God who is personal is not so strange when we find ourselves in a universe full of wonder and meaning. I guess my atheist friends and I see differently when we look to the heavens. They see physical stars and planets. I see a divine hand at work and hear a clarion voice:

> The heavens declare the glory of God;
>> the skies proclaim the work of his hands.
> Day after day they pour forth speech;
>> night after night they reveal knowledge. – Psalm 19:1-2

Thus, one of the challenges of ideological debate is that there are judgment calls to be made. I judge that materialism is robotic and inhuman and doesn't adequately explain the human experience. I hear God speaking in the heavens. But Tom accepts the material explanation of human nature and *doesn't* hear God in the heavens. Imagine two friends, Tom and Rick, standing together in an art gallery, viewing a painting. Tom interprets the work in one way, Rick in another. Yes, we can share reasons for why we see things as we do, and perhaps these reasons will influence the other. But at some point, disagreement is simply person-centered. Philosopher C. Stephen Evans notes, "The testing of theories is a complicated affair, requiring an element of good judgment as well as honesty and concern for truth. Some theories fit the facts better than others. But the process of testing is not one for which formal rules can be given. Common ground may be hard to find, and rational discussion may sooner or later reach an impasse where both sides say, 'This is how it appears to me.'"[10]

This is how it appears to me: belief in a personal Creator for personal subjective experience is more sensible than believing in an impersonal universe that generates mechanistic beings with no moral responsibility. To me, moral responsibility is a self-evident truth of human nature. Its best explanation is God. That's me looking at the painting. My friend Tom, standing next to me in the gallery, disagrees. So be it.

I would also add that the theistic version of the universe just offered also provides the hope of deliverance from slavery to self, extending to eternal life, where every believer achieves their ultimate destiny, becoming their truest and most fulfilled self. I'm attracted to this biblical vision of eternity, in contrast to the popular but mythical notion of spending the afterlife in a state of boredom, perhaps seated on a cloud playing the harp. Christian theism is a place of human authenticity and progress. We *develop* into our ultimate selves as envisioned by a loving Creator. This is eternal life: to know and love God and to grow ever more into his image, which is the ultimate *telos* (endpoint). Unbelievers should read Augustine about this. Better yet, they should read the Bible cover to cover rather than criticize it from afar. They should join a church for six months instead of criticizing *that* from afar, and observe there the vast proportion of Christians performing their ordinary task of service to humanity and worship of God faithfully and quietly, behind the scenes, away from the media, in the power of the Spirit. This is the lived reality of a fine ethical life.

I realize some have left the church due to bad experiences and "church hurt." To the victims: I am truly sorry. The church is a collection of sinners who are "on their way" toward sanctification. Along the way, it's very possible to run into a small percentage of church-goers (and church officials) who say the wrong thing or do the wrong thing, to the harm of others. Having been active in the church all these decades, I've seen it. But the *vast* majority are comprised of kindly, quiet servants, hidden from view, who extend themselves to the world in the name of Christ (check out the origins of hospitals in the

---

10   C. Stephen Evans and R. Zachary Manis, *Philosophy of Religion: Thinking About Faith* (InterVarsity Press, Kindle Ed., 2009), p.32.

West, for example, and you'll find Christians at the center). I don't know how to put this any plainer.

The Best Possible World (BPW)

I've already made a few comments about Tom's BPW – mainly, that autonomous selves know what's best for themselves, which I doubt.

Additionally, it seems to me the deeper we get into the discussion, the more other-worldly and impractical Tom's model becomes. I'd like to suggest that in Tom's model, moral guidance doesn't come from natural law or from an ideal, futuristic world (which of course is also naturalistic and composed only of atoms). Rather, such guidance comes from Tom's own imagination, which I greatly appreciate. As stated earlier, I enjoy novel ideas and blue-sky thinking, and Tom's version of the BPW is one way to frame morality. I wonder, however, whether his perfect world would be considered perfect by many people. I, for one, would reject it as too nebulous, too other-worldly, devoid of concrete reality. The BPW sounds to me like a video game or a Star Trek hollow deck where you live in your private virtual world that is. . . not real.

Guests could enter your virtual space but the space is still virtual. Every crime you commit in your world has no victim; thus, you've gained nothing from your illegal action. Who would "consent" to be victimized by your crime? Every game of chess you play could be derailed by an opponent who consented to play the game but, in the end, doesn't consent to lose. In the BPW, what's at stake? How would I *develop* as a person, as a moral being? What would constitute real-life, tough moral choices that, over time, enlarge my character? Where is the wisdom born of experience and hardship? Technologically-endowed intelligence is one thing, wisdom is another. Even if one doesn't adopt the virtue ethics, say, of Aristotle, character surely counts for something. In my thinking, character comes with challenge – a real-world challenge where outcomes are uncertain. To have knowledge (and perhaps even wisdom) downloaded into my brain, as into a robot . . . is that real life? Humanity's ideal future? I'm not signing up.

There's an episode of the TV show *The Twilight Zone* from 1960 in which a criminal dies in a shootout with police and finds himself in the next life, a paradise where all his wishes are granted. An angel played by Sebastian Cabot serves as his guide. In this wonderful afterlife the criminal wins every card game, gets all the girls, grows rich at the casino, and lives in luxury. Pretty soon he hates it. There's no challenge, no barriers, no setbacks, no victories over formidable opponents. He complains to the angel that heaven is boring. He can't bear to live this way for eternity. The angel responds, and I paraphrase: "Sir, what makes you think this is heaven?"

To my thinking, moral fiber is developed at least partly through *involuntary* challenges – situations I would never choose. One of my friends witnessed the I-35W bridge collapse in Minneapolis in 2007 in which 13 people were killed. Instinctively, he exited his car and made his way down to the river to rescue people trapped in their vehicles. This incident made him a better person, certainly better than if he'd stayed home in his world playing out the scene virtually, which he'd probably never choose anyway.

Without constraints and accountability, people default to their pleasures and preferences. In Tom's BPW, I could see myself, for example, sinking into unceasing hedonism and losing my soul in the process. In Christianity, human beings are created for work. Tending the garden and the like are built into what it means to be human. Yes, in the BPW, you could work if you prefer. But to what end? What is there to accomplish? Tom's answer might be, "Anything you want." But why want it? What non-consensual barriers stand between me and success? What handicap must I overcome? What limitations must I learn to navigate? How will I *grow* without non-chosen adversity? Is personal well-being related mainly to the satisfaction of personal preferences? I cannot agree with this. Put me on the battlefield with an unchosen, non-consensual opponent, and see what comes of it. Don't put me in charge of choosing my opponents, if there be any to choose. That's no challenge. I don't want to slouch into eternity, a slave to my preferences and desires.

In a well-known essay, philosopher Robert Nozick introduces a thought experiment where people plug themselves into an "experience machine" where everything goes well for them. But Nozick contends that most people would rather live in reality and face involuntary challenges than simply engage in the virtual experiences of pleasure – even if, while on the machine, they are unaware of their virtual living. That is, people would choose reality rather than plugging into the machine in the first place. Some studies show this preference in the population.

I suppose Tom could respond to my argument for involuntary adversity by saying that in the BPW you can have anything you please – even "non-chosen" challenges. The menu of choices is infinite or nearly so. Choose whatever you want. That's the nature of the BPW. But this response doesn't solve the problem. "I choose to face unchosen situations" is still a choice of the self. It represents an unfettered egoism and individualism that seems to me misguided for society as a whole – a Flawed Possible World. Contrast this state of affairs with the biblical vision of human flourishing, which perhaps can be summed up in the word "interdependence." Interdependence is neither raw independence as in Tom's BPW nor a sickly dependence where people fail to carry their own weight. Rather, it's a fully functioning body of people who work as a team to grow the character of its members and influence the world for good. This is the church at its best and is often referred to in the New Testament as the *body of Christ,* a place of mutual love and service. Occasionally, the church fails its members and the surrounding world. These failures make headlines and exaggerate the impression of dysfunction. The quiet provision of food, clothing, shelter, healing, and spiritual hope to a needy world, which is the bread-and-butter of most churches, makes for boring media content and is rarely featured.

In any case, while Tom's BPW seems to exist as a thought experiment in the distant future, we need an ethic that applies today, an ethic that tells Smith whether or not he should cheat on his taxes (or his wife). Going through the arduous process of determining the ethics of the BPW for any situation – even getting people to agree on a BPW – is hopelessly clumsy and ineffective, in my view. The cacophony of "oughts" in contemporary life, many conflicting with each other, cries out for a standard of morality that steers clear of Tom's BPW and focuses on the loving and just will of the creator of the universe, the author of all values. This seems obvious to me. But not to Tom. Hence, this book.

Would "infinite resources" help? Tom writes, "If we imagine we have infinite resources, forcing a person to be in jail against their will is never the moral option. There will always be a more moral option available to us. Such as, teleporting the victims to safety or giving each person their own personal force field to protect them from criminals. It's only justified to imprison the criminal because we don't have infinite resources. So, it's the lesser evil option. Being the lesser evil doesn't make it moral. It's still immoral."

The perfect world of infinite resources that Tom envisions seems quite fanciful to me. It may even be a tautology in the form of, *In a perfect world, everything would be perfect* (including morality). And in the present imperfect world in which we find ourselves, the morality of the perfect is used to judge the imperfect. In other words, the morality of a fanciful sci-fi world of moral perfection, where context and conditions are radically different from our own, and in which I doubt we could agree on the "perfect" morality anyway – that utopian standard is imported back into our reality and is used to judge right and wrong. To give just one famous example, in Tom's model the imprisonment of Derek Chauvin for the murder of George Floyd a few miles from my house in St. Paul, Minnesota, was actually *immoral.* The value of consent outweighs the value of punishing a crime. Chauvin was incarcerated without his consent, so regardless of the severity of his crime, locking him up would necessarily be unethical. Yes, it would be the "lesser evil" in this imperfect world, yet, nevertheless: immoral.

Let's push things to the extreme. Let's say a Soviet dictator starves out four million Ukrainians or a fascist dictator kills six million Jewish people. Only as a concession to the contemporary world (which lacks infinite resources) would we carry out the "lesser evil" and punish the guilty. Behind the scenes, in the ivory tower of moral philosophy, we would know better. We would declare immoral any non-consensual punishment of genocidal dictators.

I must pause for a moment to let all this sink in. Let's say an ethicist came along who, through new insight and the rearrangement of certain definitions, began calling wrong, "right," and right, "wrong." By elevating the value of personal consent to the #1 ethical value, everything else is subordinated. Every action against a person without their consent creates a victim. Victimhood, whether at the hands of another person or the force of a falling rock, is the ultimate violation to be avoided at all costs. *All* costs. What used to be right – punishing a criminal – is now wrong, though we may punish criminals in the short run as the lesser of evils. What used to be wrong – raping a woman – is now *not* wrong, or at least not blameworthy, due to the physical programming of the rapist's brain.

Leave it to the philosophers (the ethicist just mentioned), we say to ourselves, to render common sense unintelligible.

Tom writes, "I argue in the future, people will intuitively see morality/ immorality not as actions done by agents, but any action done to agents— regardless of who or what does the action."

Again, avoiding victimhood is the standard by which the world in all its complexity is measured. If you are injured on a ski hill, you're an agent *to whom something immoral was done*. Nature caused it – the same nature, incidentally, that contains an objective law of morality. Any event with a victim is a moral event.

I'm wondering if we're even talking about ethics anymore. The topic under discussion sounds more like cosmology or metaphysics. It's about the whole world – a theory of everything. A perfect world isn't just a morally perfect world, it's perfect in all respects. Even assuming we could define and agree on a definition of "perfect," my head is spinning right now. Ethics should measure the actions of human agents.

I fear that when Tom expands the topic of ethics to include nonhuman forces, we're losing touch with reality. I want to say to Tom, "You talk about the kind of lofty, abstract ideals that I absolutely love. And you do so in a matter-of-fact way that indicates this material is commonplace and no big deal. For this, you have my utmost respect! I consider myself a fellow dreamer right along with you. But why not write a book with me about *first things* or *being* or *ultimacy* rather than ethics? I feel as though you are using ethics as a springboard to a much bigger topic, such as cosmology or metaphysics or Platonic ideals."

For readers of this book who are practical thinkers, you must be wondering when this project will be grounded. Sorry. I live in the clouds. I think Tom is there as well, or at least he visits often. To my thinking, abstract theory is an absolute *must* before practical action in one direction or another can be justified. Should Smith cheat on his taxes? Should I rob a corrupt billionaire who would never miss the money to help an orphanage? The answer to these questions necessarily involves ethical theory. If grounded in God we may get one solution, and if grounded in a future BPW as defined by Tom, another solution. Theory matters.

Due to the mechanistic world Tom is positing, where brain states are physical and are locked into physical determinism, the line between human and nonhuman is breaking down. "I" as a subjective being has disappeared. I am my brain. I am not my mind, which implies substance dualism, but my brain. I am a robot of sorts, and when the physical world acts against me – when the wind blows me over or I stumble on the gravel – I am a victim. A wrong has been done to me which is hardly any different than a stranger punching me in the mouth. Everything in this world is material, so a material cause such as a tornado is nearly identical, in kind, with the material cause of a fellow human (a sophisticated robot like me) punching me in the mouth. It's all meant to happen. It all *must* happen. And it's all *physical*.

Zooming out for a moment: naturalism is like a room full of marbles. The blue marbles are human beings; the red, animals; the green, nature. The colors may vary, but the substance is all the same. Marbles have no inherent value. The only value they possess is the value they assign themselves. "We are valuable," the blue marbles insist. But the red (animals) and green (nature) marbles have no opinion on the matter. To read into the green marbles a law of morality that should govern the world sounds to me like the same wishful thinking atheists accuse theists of exercising when they believe in God. On naturalistic premises, perhaps we all invent our unicorns.

Candide. To close this section on the BPW, I turn to Voltaire's *Candide* (written in 1759) which I've been reading with great interest. The castle where the youthful Candide first appears in the story employs a tutor, Pangloss, who glibly interprets every situation as the best of all possible worlds since everything of the past – all that led to the present moment – was determined. As the story unfolds, however, the tutor's words ring hollow in the face of human conflict, malice, violence, and suffering. This can't be the best of all worlds. Surely, things could be better than the torture and rape found in Candide's actual world. It seems for Voltaire human nature is *not* aimed at the good, despite the humanistic optimism (and Pangloss's naïve determinism) of 18th-century Enlightenment Europe. Voltaire himself is more pessimistic about human nature.

Similarly, American optimism about the future of humanity, even bolstered exponentially by technological advances, seems dubious to me. I agree with Voltaire: unrestrained power and autonomy bring out the worst in the human heart. Or to quote Russian dissident Aleksandre Solzhenitsyn: "The line between good and evil runs not through states, nor between classes, nor between political parties either — but right through every human heart." This statement seems eminently true, to my thinking. If the Gulag survivor is correct, a future moral convergence into an agreed-upon BPW seems unlikely.

Tom

RICK HAS DONE a good job understanding and outlining my model. The only area I think he may have misunderstood is what exactly I mean by a "law of nature" when I refer to the source of morality. Laws of nature/laws of physics, are not abstract concepts or figments of language, they are physically existing objects who have effects on the world. We describe the patterns of these effects as laws, but they refer to an actually existing physical thing which is causing that pattern. The law of gravity is the physical curvature of spacetime. The laws of thermodynamics are the physical nature of energy. The same would be true for my proposed "law of morality." It is a physically existing field in the universe like spacetime, or gravity, or EM fields.

Imagine for example, the belief helping people is good takes less energy. Or, is easier to form in brains because of some law of physics which causes those beliefs to be entropically more efficient than believing "helping people is bad." If all correct moral beliefs are entropically simpler than incorrect moral beliefs, and this is caused by some field fundamental to the universe, then this would be one example of an actually existing law of physics—outside and beyond any human—that has always been there, and existed before any

117

language, grounding objective morality. This is just a hypothetical example and is far simpler than I expect the true ground of morality to be.

Let us use this example to answer Rick's questions. Rick asks, "Does the undiscovered law of nature you're proposing tell us anything about true morality, or is it merely a location for it to be housed?" Let's take the entropic moral beliefs example. If correct moral beliefs are more entropically efficient because of some supervening force or field in the universe, then, yes, it would tell us everything about morality. Morality is a fact of reality that certain beliefs have a certain physical property making them identifiable and prevalent in conscious beings, more so than other beliefs. And the grounds of morality is the force or law of nature that causes this phenomenon.

Rick asks, "Isn't it as arbitrary as God?" No, arbitrary means to be based on random chance or personal whim, rather than a reason/system. In this case the system is the laws of physics. So, it would not be arbitrary. You could say it was a necessary part of every universe or a determined feature of reality, but not a result of random chance. My main criticism of God-based morality wasn't that it is arbitrary, but that it is subjective, i.e. contingent on the opinions of a mind. A model based on a law of physics is not contingent on a mind. So, it's not subjective.

Rick asks, "Is it right because it meets another moral standard, or is it right in itself?" If moral beliefs are correct because they correspond to those which are entropically more efficient, that would be morality in itself. There wouldn't be another standard. The standard is "correct moral beliefs are those which are more entropically efficient."

Rick asks, "But isn't "itself" just a secular, arbitrary form of God to which we must submit?" Unlike God, laws of physics don't require submission. They establish the truth. So, the moral law would tell us what is objectively moral, but whether or not you choose to be moral is wholly on you. Again, I'm not advocating that this entropic system of morality is true. It's simply an example of how physical laws could produce objective morality. As you can see, it does provide very clear answers to these questions—unlike a God.

Rick asks, "Is the objective law that exists somewhere in reality anything more than a mirror? It seems to me Tom's moral law of nature simply represents the supposed best of how humans already behave. That is, we look within ourselves, find the best of what we do, and project it into a law that supposedly exists independently of ourselves." If this law existed as a fundamental aspect of reality, our beliefs would be a result of it, not the other way around. If you are asking, "Why believe it exists and is not simply a hypothetical reflection of human imagination onto reality?" The answer is the same for every hypothesis, including Rick's God, as well as any hypothesis in science, i.e. novel prediction.

All hypotheses start as figments of human imagination UNTIL they can make reliable novel predictions about the future. At which point we would be justified in believing they correspond to something in reality outside of our imagination. This is how you know when a hypothesis is more than just humans writing their imagination of human nature onto reality as Feuerbach's put it.

Rick asks, "If the law is undiscovered, how do we know about it?" This is a similar question to the previous. The answer is—the same way we do for any and every law. We look at phenomena, find a pattern, infer the cause, then make novel predictions about what we would expect to see if the proposed cause is correct. All laws begin this way long before they are discovered, we discover them by confirming the predictions.

Naturalism of the Gaps

This is another example of an argument theists often use, but seem to not understand what a "gaps" argument actually is. Gaps arguments are when something which has never worked as an explanation is proposed in a gap, and the person is claiming that because there is a gap that hasn't been explained yet, which their hypothesis can explain—their hypothesis is reasonable to believe.

If we see: White goose, white goose, white goose, _____? And, we wanted to know what was in the blank/gap. And, someone proclaimed, "It's a black goose!" Then, we discovered it was another white goose and saw another _____? And, the person was to again say, "It's a black goose!" This would be an example of a black goose of the gaps. Something with no previous examples being posited to fill the gap. If we were to see white goose, white goose, _____? And, I was to say, "It's a white goose!" That's not a white goose of the gaps. It's just induction because we have past evidence of white geese.

Using an explanation which has consistently worked, like laws of physics explaining fundamental things, isn't a "gaps" argument. It's induction. Laws of physics have consistently made novel predictions about reality. So, they are the "white goose."

Using a God to explain anything would be a "gaps argument" because God models have never successfully made novel predictions. So, it's the "black goose" of the gaps.

Feelings

Rick is correct when he says feelings differ widely, but the pattern in the change in feelings related to morality does not differ much at all. All societies everywhere around the world, (and I argue anywhere in the universe), follow the same pattern of moral progress, i.e. the way those feelings change over time. As technology and intellectual growth occur, society begins to see impositions that were justified in the past as no longer justified, and consequently immoral in the present.

More importantly, when talking about morality we are talking about feelings. Morality refers to the feelings we get when we are exposed to certain kinds of actions. Like, harming an innocent person. We don't get moral feelings when someone picks up a rock. That is the only phenomenon of morality that exists for us to investigate.

So, when Rick criticizes feelings as being changing, implying they are a less reliable form of evidence than say empirical science, I would agree wholeheartedly. That is why the current consensus in most scientific fields is that morality is simply a by-product of evolution.

But what else is there? What else does Rick propose we use to investigate morality outside of our feelings of morality? We can't gain any knowledge of morality from reading the Bible. The Bible is a hypothesis just like any other. To get evidence of a hypothesis, you need to show it corresponds to something in the world independent of our imagination, e.g. novel predictions specifically related to the topic. So, what in the world can we look at which gives us some insight into morality other than our feelings?

I argue the patterns in these moral feelings over time and across cultures and analyzing how these feelings respond to moral dilemmas, can give us a pattern into whatever morality fundamentally is.

If Rick disagrees, I would need to know what Rick is using as evidence of morality. Because moral feelings, as far as I know, are the only candidate for moral phenomenon to investigate in the first place.

We Always Know What's Best for Ourselves?

Rick says, "Tom's version of consent seems to rest on radical individual autonomy, and assumes, I think, that we always know what's best for ourselves." This is not the case. My model is impartial to whether or not you know what's "best" for you.

One initial problem with this argument is that it assumes there is something which is "best" for you. Rick would need to provide some kind of proof there is such a thing, rather than simply asserting it. I grant pragmatically that in the world we currently live, there are things which help you survive or gain happiness more than others, but this would not be the case in the BPW. In the BPW you would be able to set the amount of happiness you receive from any action and set the actions which will benefit your future life in that world. In such a world there is no "best." There is no preordained outcome you are trying to achieve. You could live a million different lives, good, bad, malicious, virtuous, and erase your memory each time to start anew. The idea there is such a thing as a "best" seems shallow, ignoring the value in the diversity of ways you can live and experience life. Having the option of that diversity seems far "better" than being stuck in some preordained "best" path. Even if we suppose there is a "best" you, in the BPW you can simply snap your fingers and become the "best" you. If you so desire. If you do not desire to be that version of yourself, why would society have any right to force you to become such a person without your consent?

I want to try to steelman Rick's argument. I think the argument Rick is making is: suppose there is someone ELSE looking at your life and they are thinking about forcing you to act a certain way, the first thing they would likely consider is whether or not the thing they would be forcing you to do is "good/best" for you. Aside from the issue of whether or not there is such a thing as "best" outside of our pragmatic world, this is a valid moral dilemma which is important to consider when trying to define a moral principle, so I appreciate Rick presenting it.

In other words, if you don't know what is "best" for you, but someone else does, is it moral for them to force you to do that thing? *Again, in the BPW, if you didn't know what was "best" and wanted to, you could simply snap your fingers and you would know what's "best." So, there would be no justification for society forcing you to do or learn anything. Clearly this only applies to pragmatically limited situations. Meaning, it is not representative of true morality, only what is pragmatic/the lesser evil.*

For example, if you are a child, and you don't eat your vegetables you will get diabetes. So, your parents force you to eat your vegetables. Is this moral? No, It's the lesser evil. The moral thing to do would be to put the vitamins required into cake so children no longer need to eat vegetables. Or, to cure diabetes all together. More importantly, you are not a child and you are not mentally impaired. So as an adult, someone else forcing you to eat vegetables would be a form of physical assault, (and they would go to prison). The reason there are laws against this, is because it is immoral. Not all laws are designed to reflect morality, but this one definitely is.

What about personal development regarding character traits, (e.g. work hard, save our money, stay off drugs, tell the truth, share our resources, etc.)? Is it moral to force people to do things that build their character? No, for the exact same reasons above. Even if building a character trait could be beneficial, forcing an adult human who is not mentally impaired to go through some kind of ordeal to build their character without their consent is enslavement, (and they would go to prison). The reason there are laws against this is because it is immoral.

The moral alternative to forcing people to act in a way that is "best" for them, is to explain the consequences, for example, of not eating vegetables and let them decide for themselves. That would be perfectly fine. However, forcing you to eat vegetables against your will would clearly be immoral. Even if it was good for you.

Even Rick's own examples betray this:

- Athletes obeying coaches–athletes are not being forced to obey coaches, they are consenting adults and can leave the sport anytime they wish. So, this is perfectly moral and consistent with my BPW model as it is not an example of a community forcing people to act in a certain way against their will.

- Mentees obeying mentors–mentees are either children, e.g. not consenting adults/mentally impaired, or they are consenting adults who can leave the program anytime they wish. So, the same applies as athletes.

- Pupils obeying teachers–pupils are either children, e.g. not consenting adults, or they are consenting adults who can leave the program anytime they wish. So, the same applies as athletes.

- Mentally ill obeying therapists–people with a mental impairment are not considered adults with the ability to consent, like children. The moral thing to do in this case, both for children and the mentally ill, is to cure them of their mental impairment elevating them to the status of consenting adults. (An omnipotent being could do this with a snap of his fingers.) At this point the moral action would never be to force them to act in a certain way but to explain to them the benefits/consequences of the act in question and allow them to decide for themselves.

The same applies to Rick's further example of "cultures and other groups, (such as business teams, educators, etc.)".

- Disciplining abusive spouses–the moral thing to do is to prevent the harm in the first place by, for example, giving everyone a personal force field which would automatically activate when any harm to you would occur. Then, there would be no abusive spouses to punish. Punishment is not moral it is the lesser evil to deter future immoral acts.

- Substance-abusing teenagers–the moral thing to do is to prevent the harm in the first place by, for example, removing any harm drugs cause. If the drugs cause no harm, there is no reason to prevent anyone from taking them. The reason we try to stop substance "abuse" is because it is the lesser evil to prevent the harm caused by the drug.

If there was no harm, then taking drugs would be no different from any hobby such as knitting.

- Power-hungry church leaders—there isn't anything morally wrong with being power hungry, unless you abuse that power. If we can prevent the abuse of power by using personal force fields, then people can be as power hungry as they want.

- Reckless spenders/Excessive gamblers—the moral thing to do is to fulfill all of their and their families' financial needs, food, housing, luxuries, etc. Then, they can spend money on whatever they like. We pragmatically cannot do this (yet). So, we do the lesser evil and try to reform them to prevent the harm their actions can cause. If we eliminated the harm, there would be no justifiable reason to force them to change any more than someone who has any alternate hobby such as painting.

Many theists, especially Christians, see adult humans as nothing more than children with the responsibility to obey God because they are too incompetent to make responsible decisions for themselves. This comes in the form of the belief that it's ok for a supreme being to physically assault or enslave you, because it knows best. This is called special pleading.

Special pleading is an informal fallacy wherein one cites something as an exception to a general or universal principle. This is clearly demeaning and a result of religious indoctrination, but is a point that needs to be addressed. If being an adult human does not qualify someone as a rational or responsible actor, then God would be morally obligated to snap his fingers to bring any conscious agents to whatever level does meet that standard. Then he could take the moral action of explaining to the individuals the benefits/consequences of the actions and allow them to decide for themselves what to do.

God would be immoral for forcing anyone to eat vegetables, or to fulfill some trial to build character. Just as you would be immoral for forcing someone to do those things. What makes it immoral has nothing to do with the level of power or knowledge. Even if we know with absolute perfect omniscient knowledge, that forcing someone to eat vegetables will prevent diabetes and save their life, or even if we know with absolute certainty that forcing them to do some tasks to build character will drastically benefit their future life, it is still entirely immoral to force them to do those things. And, it is very easy to prove this. Simply ask, "Would it have been more moral to show them the effects of the actions so they could also know with certainty the consequences, and then let them decide for themselves what to do?" Obviously, that would be more moral. This means the desire to force people to do what is good for them is a pragmatic result of what works best to benefit our society, but is in fact the lesser evil, not a moral good. Which is why it is a principle common in conservative and authoritarian ideologies.

What is good for you doesn't matter to morality. Morally speaking, you should be allowed to make your own mistakes and learn from them at your own pace. If we had the power to abolish all severe consequences, like aging, death, and permanent diseases, (like an omnipotent being would), then, the moral thing to do is to eliminate those severe consequences and allow people to take their time learning at their own pace. Not forcing them to learn at your preferred pace.

Rick says, "If I were given the privilege of living in my own world, making my own autonomous choices, and only interacting with others as I saw fit, I'm afraid I'd lose ... the benefits of living in community and submitting oneself to its authority are what it means to be fully human, from a Christian perspective." That's fine—for Rick. In my Best of all Possible Worlds, he can choose to live in a Christian-centric world, where he is subject to God or the community's dictates. But it is not fine to force every living being into that world, without their consent. Rick can even explain to people the benefits of living in such a world, and allow them to choose for themselves if they would also like to live in such a world, with a community or God imposing on them. This would be perfectly moral and it is an option in my BPW. However, forcing people into such a world without their consent, (as the Christian God did in the Bible), is clearly a form of slavery. It is without a doubt immoral in every sense of the word and would not be allowed in my BPW.

In further discussion, Rick and I had some miscommunications on what I meant when I said God is "forcing people to be there" or is "forcing people into such a world." So, I wanted to add a section to further explain.

The Christian world is made up of three parts: Earth, Heaven and Hell. This is opposed to something like the Hindu world, which has: Earth, Reincarnation, and Enlightenment. Or, Norse beliefs which has the Nine Realms. Each worldview has its own "world" which refers to all the places your soul/consciousness could end up going, (voluntarily or not).

Suppose you were forced into the Norse religious "world" where you lived in the Nine Realms. So, you could travel between those realms, but you couldn't get to the Christian heaven or hell. In this example, you have been forced into the "Norse world" and you cannot escape. You are forced to live under the Norse paradigm, whether you like it or not. This would make you effectively a slave to the Norse paradigm. Where your life is spent working toward fulfilling the ethos of the Norse paradigm.

The same is true for people forced to live in the "Christian world" with earth, heaven and hell. So, if God created your soul/consciousness and placed it into the Christian world, and you could not voluntarily go to a different world, (like the Hindu or Norse worlds), then you have been forced to live in the "Christian world" without your consent. That is what I am referring to as slavery. You would be a slave to the Christian's paradigm and forced to live your life in a way which accommodates the Christian ethos.

This is what I am referring to whenever I say God "forces us to be here" or "forced the people at the Sermon on the Mount to be in that world." I'm not saying God forces people to stand at that location, nor that he forces people to obey/believe. I'm saying he forces those souls/consciousness to be in that world of earth, heaven, and hell, where they are only allowed those options and cannot choose to leave and go to a different world.

Rick says that my morality assumes that, "It's better to be isolated in the realm of one's own preferences, untouched by unwanted conflict or challenge, than to be enmeshed in the involuntary crucible of a messy community." No, in my model it's better for each individual to be given the knowledge of the benefits/consequences and have the freedom to decide for themselves if they would like to consensually be a part of such a community or not.

On Rick's theistic model the community and/or God are allowed to forcibly "gradually mold" you, without your consent, into "saints." Even if you may reject it, and even if it will not work, they still have a right to impose this "molding process" onto you. I will leave it up to the reader to decide which option they think is a more accurate representation of true morality.

Community vs. Individual Morality

Consider this, is it "immoral" for someone to make a harmful decision for themselves? No, that doesn't seem to fit. Is it "immoral" if society makes a harmful decision and imposes it on someone? Yes, clearly. Morality is not about making the best decisions nor personal growth. For example, it may be the best decision to go to college. You may be able to develop a lot of personal growth at college. Does that mean someone who didn't go to college and pursued their passions, but didn't succeed, is less moral because they did not make the best decision? Are they less moral if they have had less personal growth due to being around others less? Would it have been moral for society to force that person to go to college instead of pursuing their dreams? No, in fact that seems clearly immoral.

There is the argument their lives may be better if they were forced to go to college. While pragmatically that may be correct, it is still immoral to force that life upon them. The moral outcome is one where they can pursue their passions and not need worry about money, or housing, or food. If these pragmatic limitations on our lives were no longer a concern and were provided to us, then the conservative justification for forcing society's values on the individual is gone, and doing so can be clearly seen as immoral.

The moral world would look like this: any adult individual without cognitive impairment would all get their own world and would not need to worry about food, nor housing, nor money, nor aging and can pursue their passions, and grow at their own pace. Society gets no say or impact on the person whatsoever. Just like in the Best Possible World I describe. So long as the individual cannot harm anyone without their consent, there is no justification for the immoral act of forcing societal values on anyone, ever.

Why would Rick's proposed alternative of having a community/society with the ability to force such individuals to change faster, or force them to make "better" decisions be an improvement? It's not.

Each person should be free to pursue their passions—free to make their own mistakes and learn from them at their own pace. Now, if they choose to accept input from society, or ask for help, at that point it would be perfectly moral for society to have an impact in their lives. Never should a society have a *de facto* right to interfere with anyone without their consent.

Forcing people to abide by societal values is an immoral thing we must do to prevent greater immoral things in our pragmatic world where we are limited. That does not make it good, nor right, nor moral. It's simply the lesser evil. The lesser evil is still an evil. It definitely is not representative of objective morality.

Revelation

Rick seems to be using revelation as the evidence he is using to conclude God is the basis of objective morality. Revelation is a separate line of evidence unrelated to morality. So, what is Rick thinking? Rick's reasoning seems to be an argument by extension.

Rick, and many other Christians, have had revelation of an all-powerful being existing. *(Revelation cannot differentiate imagination from reality, but let us leave that aside for now and suppose it is as good as empirical verification.)* Therefore, they are justified in believing such an all-powerful being exists. By EXTENSION because it is all powerful, they are also justified to believe it's the basis of objective morality, even though it has provided no evidence, nor explanation to verify anything related to morality or moral phenomenon.

This is false. Rick seems to be unknowingly falling back on the carousel of the "cumulative case" argument. God is the basis of morality only if the Revelation arguments work. These arguments do not work. More importantly, they are not evidence of anything related to morality.

What properties of morality are you looking at to come to the conclusion of a God? You are not, you are looking at other unrelated arguments of Revelation and concluding that because those work, it's justified to believe God caused morality also. Even though you have said nothing about morality.

Let's suppose Revelation was a form of evidence, (it is not), and could differentiate imagination from reality, (it cannot). Let's also suppose it is equivalently as good as empirical verification, (it is not). With all these assumptions, this would justify the Christian in believing an all-powerful being existed. However, this would not by extension justify belief the all-powerful being is the basis of morality.

Suppose there was a super-powerful being named Bob. Suppose I can verify the existence of Bob. He lives down the street. I can introduce you to him. I can empirically verify his existence, address, height, weight, etc. He will even perform miracles for you! Creating things from nothing right in front of your eyes and for peer-reviewed scientific journals as well—giving you magical objects, etc.

Bob then tells you he caused Dark Matter, (extra gravity in galaxies), and Dark Energy, (energy density of empty space). Is this reason to believe Bob is the cause of Dark Matter/Energy? No. Even though Bob is very powerful and can be confirmed to exist, physicists would not begin writing papers about Bob being the cause of these unknown phenomena in physics.

To justify his claim Bob would need to provide examples of specific properties, and novel facts about Dark Matter/Energy, which we could perform experiments to confirm. Only then would we be justified in believing Bob created them. Likewise, even if God was proven to exist, we would need him to provide verifiable, novel information related to moral phenomena, which we could confirm to justify he is the cause.

Revelation Continued

Now let us address why revelation is not evidence. Let's say you walk up to two people talking named James and John. James says, "I had a revelation X is right." John says, "I had a revelation that X is wrong." How do you tell who is right and who is wrong? Maybe one had a true revelation and the other had a delusion. Maybe they both experienced delusions. Maybe they both had true revelation, but one or both of them misinterpreted the revelation? How do you tell who is right?

Clearly revelation itself doesn't work as they both claim to have had one. You would need a way to differentiate true revelation from delusion, i.e. differentiate imagination from reality. Without a methodology you can use to differentiate which revelation corresponds to reality, and which is imaginary, then revelation can't differentiate imagination from reality and is evidence of nothing.

Therefore, revelation is literally people imagining they experienced something. Like any hypothesis, you would need novel prediction, or some other way to differentiate imagination from reality, before revelation was reasonable to believe.

This applies even when you yourself had the revelation. You are unjustified to trust your own revelations until you have a method that can differentiate imagination from reality. As far as I know, the consensus in science is that revelation has never been able to make any successful novel predictions at a higher rate than random chance or guessing, and has not provided any way to differentiate imagination from reality.

We also have an abundance of scientific research on revelation. When people are having revelatory experiences, the part of their brain that shows activity is the same part that shows activity when they are speaking to themselves, (which would explain perfectly why it has never produced any results).

Revelation is not a "diamond in hand." It's a unicorn in your imagination. God is an imaginary hypothesis which has no empirical evidence of any of its properties existing independent of our imagination, and has made no novel prediction.

An undiscovered law is a kind of thing, (ex. laws of physics), which have been demonstrated to exist and make novel predictions consistently. Even though the particular law has not been discovered, an undiscovered, non-imaginary kind of thing is better than an undiscovered, imaginary kind of thing. An undiscovered horse is better than an imaginary unicorn.

Willingness to Die for Your Belief is Evidence?

Another common Christian trope is appealing to the willingness of the disciples to sacrifice their lives for their Revelation. Christians seem to be under the impression the willingness to sacrifice your life is somehow evidence of the truth of your beliefs. It is not. This is known as an appeal to consequence fallacy. An appeal to consequences is an argument that concludes a belief is true or false based on the consequences the belief had.

Let us ask the inverse. Is someone's unwillingness to die for a belief, evidence their belief is false? Clearly not. I believe that 1+1=2. If someone pointed a gun at me and told me to admit that 1+1=5, I would gladly admit it. Would that mean that my belief that 1+1=2 is less likely to be true? Clearly not. Whether or not someone is willing to die for their beliefs is wholly irrelevant to the truth of the belief, and Christians especially need to recognize this.

In 2022, Wynn Bruce set himself on fire on the plaza of the Supreme Court building. If you believe "willingness to die for your beliefs" is evidence of their truth, then in order to be consistent you must admit, his willingness to die for his belief is evidence his belief is true.

He was a climate change activist. Do you now accept climate change is real, man-made and something you should take seriously? If not, then you should realize the impotence of the willingness of the apostles to die for their revelation.

Do a simple Wikipedia search for "self-immolation" which is only one of many ways to die for your belief. There are hundreds of examples from all over the globe, spanning a multitude of religious beliefs. Is this evidence they are all true?

Being willing to die for one's beliefs is irrelevant to truth. Though it does show they have conviction in their beliefs, it does not say anything about the truth of the beliefs. And again, Christians, I'm speaking primarily to you when I say this.

Sermon on the Mount a Basis for Morality?

Rick says, "I find the Sermon on the Mount, one of the greatest wisdom passages in the Bible, to be a much more compelling basis for morality than an undiscovered law of nature, which appears in any case to be a projection of human aspirations. That is, a mirror of our supposed best stuff."

Ironically, the Sermon on the Mount seems to be very much "a projection of human aspirations. That is a mirror of our supposed best stuff," and while it holds emotional importance to Christians, it is nothing more than a collection of Platitudes and Deepities which are neither original nor profound, and mostly taken from previous religions including secular religions like Jainism.

Let us see if we can improve it. "Don't own other humans as property." Well, that was easy. I have now made the Sermon on the Mount many orders of magnitude more moral.

But, let's continue for posterity's sake. "Blessed is everyone. Every conscious being without exception." As an all-powerful being, I now give unto you the Best Possible World, therefore, "The mourning don't need comforting." How about:

"Everyone gets their own world/kingdom."

"No one ever needs to be thirsty or hungry."

"Everyone gets mercy, including unbelievers."

"Blessed are those who are persecuted for any reason at all."

"Rejoice and be exceedingly glad for great is your reward right here and now! You get your own world immediately! Because, instead of standing up here giving you a lecture, or healing several people occasionally—how about i just let you all into the BPW now, since that would be the moral thing to do? Peace out beeches."

Honestly, an all-powerful being standing on a hill offering platitudes to the masses of suffering individuals, (that he forced to be there in a world with suffering, hunger, thirst, etc., by placing their soul/consciousness in this world), seems vicious and malevolent. The only moral choice in that situation is to allow everyone instantly into heaven, or preferably my BPW.

Secular Alternatives?

Rick states, "When the Sermon calls me to contrarian behavior such as loving my enemies, blessing those who curse me, and being generous with the one who robs me, I think quickly of typical secular (cultural) alternatives: vengeance, retribution, and getting even. In my opinion, the commands of the Sermon are much more sublime." I think this quote shows Rick has a cultural bias against secularism. Secular morality is any model of morality which is independent of a religion and/or God.

One of the best examples is Jainism. Jainism has no God. It predates the Sermon on the Mount by 500 years. All of the things Rick states as moral doctrines: loving my enemies, blessing those who curse me, and being generous with the one who robs me, these come from Jainism and are embodied to a much greater extent than anything proposed in Christianity. Jainism advocates for absolute non-violence, even when being attacked. It advocates for never harming a living being—even flies or spiders. Jainism is the most moral religion by far and it is a secular religion, as it has no God.

When Rick says "I think quickly of typical secular (cultural) alternatives: vengeance, retribution, and getting even" I believe this to be nothing more than Rick's bias showing. Religious beliefs far more often embody vengeance, retribution, and getting even. In fact, I know of no secular moralities that advocate for any of those. Yet, I can name dozens of religious ideologies that do.

Vengeance/Retribution (they are synonyms) – "You shall acknowledge no God but me. . . . You are destroyed, Israel. . . . The people of Samaria must bear their guilt, because they have rebelled against their God. They will fall by the sword; their little ones will be dashed to the ground, their pregnant women ripped open." Hosea 13:4, 9, 16

Getting Even — "And if a man cause a blemish in his neighbour; as he hath done, so shall it be done to him; breach for breach, eye for eye, tooth for tooth: as he hath caused a blemish in a man, so shall it be done to him again." Leviticus 24:19-2

I could fill dozens of pages with examples like this. You will find no such examples in Jainism, Secular Humanism, Moral Naturalism, Situation Ethics, Virtue Ethics, nor any other secular morality I know of at any point in history. And no, Hitler, Stalin, Mao, nor Pol Pot, provided a model of secular ethics any more than David Koresh, Matthew Hale, Marshall Herff Applewhite, Jr., Charlemagne, or any of the other awful Christians provided a model of Christian ethics. An atheist being immoral is not a model of secular ethics, any more than a Christian being immoral is a model of Christian ethics.

Who is Entitled to Make Hypotheses?

Rick asks, "Lastly in this section, I'd like to ask the question of who it is among mortals that is entitled to observe the phenomena of feelings, interpret the patterns therein, and generate a description of the undiscovered law of nature." Everyone. Everyone, is the answer.

Anyone and Everyone is allowed to seek patterns in reality, try to describe those patterns with principles, infer what is causing those patterns, and make predictions about what they would expect if they are correct. That is the beauty of science. There are no authorities. Anyone can make a discovery about reality. Your biases don't matter. Your flaws don't matter. It doesn't matter if you are a good person or a bad person, a sinner or saint. You don't need to be perfect. You don't need to be immortal or all-knowing, or all-powerful. You only need a way to differentiate imagination from reality. To quote Richard Feynman, "It doesn't make any difference how beautiful your guess is, it doesn't matter how smart you are, or who made the guess, or what his name is … If it disagrees with experiment, it's wrong. That's all there is to it."

For example, if Rick or any theist, could look at the patterns in moral intuition and moral progress and find a pattern which coincided with a religious holy book, and could make predictions based on that model which were confirmed to be correct, poof! You now have evidence God grounds morality.

Academic consensus isn't just an opinion shared by a bunch of people. Academic consensus is a body of evidence which has demonstrated one hypothesis to be significantly more reliable than any other in the field. Anyone is allowed to create a hypothesis. If the evidence supports it, then the consensus will follow. Scientific consensus works by pitting everyone's biases against one another. Everyone has their own preferred model and they want their model to be correct. The only way to achieve consensus is to demonstrate your model has better evidence than all the other models. This is how you effectively filter out biases when discovering truth.

Isn't that better than giving up because we are imperfect, and resigning ourselves to being given a subjective revelation, which can't differentiate imagination from reality, and is no more accurate or reliable than a Magic 8 Ball or random guessing?

Purposeless vs. Purposeful

Rick asks, "My question is whether it's more likely such practices arose from an impersonal, purposeless universe or one that is personal and purposive." Why think morality would be a result of a purposeful creator? It seems Rick is again falling back on the "like comes from like" composition/division fallacy. "We are purposeful, therefore it's more likely whatever created us must also be purposeful."

"Looking at the doctrine of Darwinism, which undergirded my atheism for so many years, it didn't take me long to conclude that it was simply too far-fetched to be credible. I realized that if I were to embrace Darwinism and its underlying premise of naturalism, I would have to believe that: Nothing produces everything. Non-life produces life . . . Unconsciousness produces consciousness. Non-reason produces reason. Based on this, I was forced to conclude that Darwinism would require a blind leap of faith that I was not willing to make." – Lee Strobel. As we can see this fallacious "like comes from like" argument is a mainstay for theists.

These are all examples of compositions/division fallacies which intuitively seem compelling to people. However, when you actually dig into the logical justification of the argument, you find there is none, as I explained earlier in my section on composition/division fallacies. These kinds of arguments do not provide any reason to think any property is or is not fundamental.

More importantly, this was a legitimate question being asked in biology many years ago. We wanted to know if reciprocity and kindness, (like that described in Rick's analogy of the teenagers), is a result of social conditioning or biology and evolution.

The Purposeless Hypothesis was that if reciprocity was/is a natural result of biology/evolution, we can make the novel prediction that we would see these traits in animals, (whose family did not teach them anything resembling these kinds of moral acts of kindness). The research was done, and work by Frans Der Wahl, and many others, showed reciprocity and kindness among animals without any social conditioning to do so. It is biological. From the moment of birth these animals prefer kindness and reciprocity.

Evolution makes novel predictions explaining this. The consensus in all related academic fields is that it arose from purposeless natural processes, because that's what all the evidence indicates. The purposeful design hypothesis has made no novel predictions, ever, in any academic field.

Now, I am going one step further to say the purposeless cause is more fundamental than evolution and that hypothesis has not been confirmed yet.

But the Class A hypothesis is "purposeless natural processes" and the Class B hypothesis is "purposeful design."

This is an example of one of the foundation arguments theists often use. The argument from design— which is compelling to people because of an evolutionary bug in the brain called Hyperactive Agency Detection. Simply do a Google Search for "intelligent design." Under every academic source, it will be listed as a pseudoscience. For this very reason humans have a bias to see design, purposefulness, intentionally, etc., in everything. Especially unknowns.

But there is no valid argument there, no evidence, no justification. I implore you to fill out the argument in more detail so you can see for yourself. Why think a purposeful something is more likely to have been created by a purposeful source?

Do you have any evidence that purposefulness is irreducible and can't be an emergent property? Or, is it simply less counterintuitive to you? Do you have any novel predictions? What justification is there for this inference? How do you differentiate imagination from reality? Science, evolution, and non-purposeful natural processes have all made numerous successful novel predictions which is why they are the consensus in every related scientific field.

Moral Agents Usually Default to Selfishness

This is false. All the evidence in the field says otherwise. I agree this view is the Christian view. The Christian view is simply wrong, as it does not correspond to reality.

Christians have an anti-human bias, seeing humans as fallen and unable to help themselves without God's help. Therefore, they think the world must be getting worse due to human nature. But again, this is just false. All the evidence we have is the world, and people in general, are getting better in every respect. I would suggest reading Steven Pinker's book, "The Better Angels of our Nature," as well as look into the work of Frans Der Wahl on the morality of animals. Also, Game Theory, which demonstrates that societies who act cooperatively/morally do better than those that act selfishly, explaining why moral behavior is actually default rather than selfish behavior. There are also a number of studies that show animals, (such as humans), express more generosity and kindness to those whom are more closely related, decreasing as the level of relatedness does. Which explains things such as racism and in-group/out-group biases. Another great example of moral progress is, as technology and resources increase, the scope of the "in-group" increases to those who were once seen as an out-group. All of the evidence indicates humanity is improving.

I know this comes as a shock to many Christians who think the opposite—that we are moving toward the end times. But that is a socially constructed belief reinforced by religious newscasters. The news has a penchant for negativity. Religious newscasters exacerbate that penchant exponentially. To quote Richard Feynman, "It doesn't make any difference how beautiful your guess is, it doesn't matter how smart you are, or who made the guess [including God], or what his name is [Yahweh or Jesus] … If it disagrees with experiment, it's wrong. That's all there is to it."

Should We Trust Moral Intuitions Which Result from Unguided Evolution

Rick asks, "Why, in a naturalistic universe of unguided evolution, we should trust our moral intuitions at all. Evolutionary advantage is given to the most powerful and strong, not necessarily to the most moral or truthful." No, we should not. Intuitions are fine for building a hypothesis, but you don't trust hypotheses to be right. You test them. You make novel predictions to confirm them.

You should never trust your intuitions, or Revelation, or personal experiences. You should doubt them. Then test, verify, and differentiate them from imagination by making future predictions.

If our intuitions correspond to reality, we would expect to see X in the future. If they do not, we should not see X in the future. When we test for X, we can know whether we should trust our intuitions. Unlike religion, science doesn't use trust or faith. It tests things.

The underlying point in Rick's statement is, "Can an unguided process lead to true beliefs?" The answer is yes. Evolution cannot produce any belief. It cannot cause you to believe you exist and be wrong. It cannot cause you to imagine a round square. And, if having true beliefs is beneficial to survival, then evolution will select for true beliefs.

A process being guided or unguided is irrelevant to whether or not it produces true beliefs. What matters is the process itself. We know evolution produces many false beliefs, every fallacy, bias, illusion, delusion, misconceptions, hallucination, etc., including Hyperactive Agency Detection, the origin of God beliefs. This is why we test beliefs; we don't trust them.

Materialism Means No Free Will?

Rick says, "If we are material beings and nothing more, then our behavior is physically determined. Human free will is an illusion. And without free will it's hard to assign blame to wrongful actions." The first thing I want to mention is materialism doesn't preclude free will, nor is it deterministic. In fact, the consensus in philosophy is compatibilism, (there is materialist free will), and the consensus in physics is indeterminism, (physics isn't determined and has true randomness).

Compatibilism is the view that determinism is compatible with free will. This is the kind of free will the experts accept. This is very different from libertarian free will, which is the kind of free will that most theists believe in. When I use the term "free will" I am referring to the libertarian kind, as it is what is relevant to this discussion.

Anything the supernatural can do, the unknown natural can also do. Again, it doesn't matter if your free will is made of soul stuff or material stuff. It would equally be free will either way.

If we are allowed to go beyond the evidence, (Class A things), and add in or make up things, (Class B things), then we can explain anything or make anything possible under materialism that you think can be done supernaturally. So, it is false to think the supernatural/non-material has any advantage to explain anything over the unknown material.

"Intuitively, it seems in my self-awareness that I possess a mind that exists beyond my physical self and that I'm aware of other such minds around me." – Rick. That is a hypothesis. You would need a way to differentiate imagination from reality before that was justified to believe.

"I don't *seem* to be locked into predetermined choices" – Rick. Also, a hypothesis. You would need a way to differentiate imagination from reality before that was justified to believe.

"So, when a certain segment of atheist thinkers such as Tom informs me that I really don't transcend my physical self and that the exercise of my supposed free will is just an illusion, it comes as quite a surprise." – Rick. Suppose you look at an optical illusion and say, "Here I sit in my living room looking at the image. I have a strong notion that the thing I am looking at is clearly moving." The materialistic scientist looks at you with an exasperated expression and tells you, "It's not really moving, that's just your brain creating the illusion of movement."

This may come as a shock to you, but what matters isn't your personal experience. What matters is if there is a way to differentiate your imagination from reality. The scientists have done that for the optical illusion. If you want to question the scientist, simply denying what they say because it goes against your seemings isn't sufficient, and you would need a kind of evidence which can differentiate imagination from reality. Your seemings clearly cannot do this, demonstrated by the fact the optical illusion seems to be moving.

So, if there are models which have made numerous novel testable predictions that have been confirmed true, which go against your "seemings," then your "seemings" are defeated by the evidence. This is very much the case for free will.

Rick says, "The best solution is to assume substance dualism and accept free will and human responsibility. The denial of these three items leads to the absurdity of determinism. … Substance dualism could be false … I'm simply saying that its denial leads to absurdity." I find this odd as the consensus of experts in neurology, cognitive science, philosophy of mind, and every mind related field, disagree. In the PhilPapers Survey 2020 and 2022, Dualism was only accepted by 20% of academic philosophers. Physicalism is accepted by over 50%. And for good reason, libertarian free will is incoherent, (leads to absurdities).

For any choice you make, did your choice happen for reasons or for no reasons? (To clarify, this is not asking about "why did you choose chocolate." It is asking about your ability to make a choice at all. How do you go from a state of "no-choice" to "choice-made".) If it was caused by reasons, then it was determined by those reasons, (not free). If it was caused by no-reasons, then by definition it was purely random, (not free).

Whatever is allowing you to have the ability to make choices is either going to be determined, or random, or some combination of the two. There is nothing you can add that will be a new third option. It is absurd to just believe in this new kind of thing without being able to provide a coherent explanation of how it could cause a choice without being determined or random, (just saying "it's free" isn't an explanation).

Another reason libertarian free will is rejected in academia are the studies done which show that neurologists looking at your brain can know what choices you will make before you make them. This was a novel prediction made by materialism. If there is no free will, and your decision is predetermined by your physical brain before you are even aware of it, we can see your brain making the decision and predict what choice you will make, before you make it.

This study was done, and has been repeatedly reproduced many times. We are able to predict what you will choose with higher and higher accuracy and further ahead in time. None of the evidence supports libertarian free will. So again, until you provide a way to differentiate imagination from reality that indicates free will is true, it is nothing but an unsupported hypothesis. No different from fairies, or leprechauns, or God.

To use Rick's example, "Here I sit in my living room. The refrigerator is right around the corner. I have a strong notion that I have a free choice about whether to grab a snack from the fridge. I could do it or not. It's up to me. At the moment, I choose to refrain. Too many calories." The materialistic scientist looks at you with an exasperated expression and says, "If your choices are determined by your brain, then I should be able to electrically stimulate the desired portion of your brain to overpower your ability to refrain. Or, I could damage the part of your brain which houses the ability to refrain. Also, I will be able to look at your neurology with an fMRI, and know which decision you will make before you know which decision you will make." All of these novel predictions have been empirically confirmed with experiment.

Phineas Gage had that portion of his brain damaged; he lost the ability to "refrain." So, having the ability to refrain isn't a result of some supernatural soul thing or free will stuff. It's a physical part of your brain which can be damaged, removed, or overpowered, which you have no control over. If there are models which have made numerous novel testable predictions that have been confirmed true, which go against your "seemings," then your seemings are defeated by the evidence.

At this point many theists will fall back to using ad hoc and post-hoc rationalization to try and make this contradictory evidence fit their conclusion. But again, that's not evidence. Anyone can make anything fit their conclusion using post hoc reasoning. The differentiating factor that makes something evidence is which hypothesis made the predictions BEFORE we knew them, and got it right—Naturalism/Materialism did. To quote Richard Feynman, "It doesn't make any difference how beautiful your guess is, it doesn't matter how smart you are, or who made the guess, or what his name is … If it disagrees with experiment, it's wrong. That's all there is to it."

Rick says, "If materialism is true, no one is culpable, which I find unacceptable – morally, intuitively, and philosophically." I find it unacceptable – morally, intuitively, and philosophically, that my bank account doesn't have one billion dollars in it. But unfortunately, reality doesn't care what we find acceptable. Again, you would need a way to differentiate imagination from reality before that was justified to believe.

Rick says, "A man could rape a woman and *not be held responsible.* Imagine that. The man is simply sick. He needs an anti-rape pill. He doesn't pay for his crime, he merely checks in for health care. … There's a moral urgency that rises up in us that demands justice. The perpetrator is *guilty and must be held responsible."* Recall my example of the man with the brain tumor, and Phineas Gage. If a man committed rape but had a brain tumor causing those immoral desires and damaging the part of the brain required to "refrain" is he "guilty"? Must he be held responsible?

Let's attempt to make the example even more clear. Imagine I was an evil scientist and I decided to electrically damage the same parts of your brain that the tumor did in the previous example, causing you to rape someone. Are you "guilty"? Must you be held responsible? Clearly not. I would be culpable; it would be my fault. You would be another victim, and if there was no way to cure you, society may put you in prison to protect others, (the lesser evil), but you are not to blame.

To assume you were to blame would require belief that you have some mystical ability to overturn the impulses of your brain and biology. We know from the numerous studies done in the field of neurology such a superpower does not exist. If you believe there is such an ability to make novel predictions and revolutionize the entire field of neurology, (winning you a Nobel prize along with $1 million dollars.) I'll wait.

Now, imagine we discovered it wasn't a brain tumor or an evil scientist, but due to your genes, those parts of your brain were underdeveloped. Now are you "guilty"? Must you be held responsible?

Why is it that when you put it in the context of another agent causing the damage to your brain, it is so easy to see you are not to blame? But when it's nature causing the damage, many people still put the blame on the individual? I understand there is an intuitive desire to punish those who do evil. They are culpable and deserve the punishment, but simply having this feeling is not evidence it's true. It is again nothing more than a seeming. Without a way to differentiate imagination from reality, it's not reasonable to believe.

The optical illusion of "free will" causes people to feel as if they have the ability to overcome their brain chemistry and biology. Making them judgmental, in that, when they see others do immoral things, it is assumed they are evil and culpable and blame worthy, but have you done an fMRI on that person to know if they have a brain tumor? Do you have any real evidence this is the case? I doubt it.

Materialism Continued

"In the myriad interactions with atheists that I've enjoyed (mostly!) over the years, one of the constant themes I hear is that we must get past our fantasies and face the hard truths of reality. One of those is materialism – that matter and energy are all there is. There is no soul, no heaven, no angels or demons. There is no afterlife, just bodily decay. The deceased live only in the memories of the living. In a strange sense, I admire the consistency of this whole position. There is no possible emotional relief provided by a divine source, no spirits of the dead visiting their relatives with assurances of eternal peace. And for many atheist philosophers, the blunt reality of materialism has led them to deny ultimate meaning and objective ethics. Two examples are J.L. Mackie and Michael Ruse. This is a logical conclusion, in my view." – Rick As I mentioned before, anything the supernatural can do the unknown natural can also do.

Materialism can provide a material soul that survives after death, (and relatives can visit you). There can be a material heaven, material angels or demons. A material afterlife, material art, loyalty, nobility, poetry, familial love, intimacy, and compassion. There is no evidence of these things existing as more than emergent properties of material interactions. Just like there is no evidence of them existing supernaturally either. But when you are allowed to add things to your hypothesis that go beyond the evidence, (Class B things), you can add them to materialism just as you can add them to supernaturalism.

Secondly, even if art, loyalty, nobility, poetry, familial love, intimacy, and compassion are only emergent properties, that doesn't make them any less real or significant as if they are made of some supernatural essence. It makes no difference if a chair is made of metal, or wood, or supernatural essence goo. It is equally real and valuable in all cases. And, the evidence for both is equal:

- It is equally probable there is a material soul, as there is a supernatural soul.
- It is equally probable there is a material afterlife, as there is a supernatural afterlife.
- It is equally probable there is a material heaven, as there is a supernatural heaven.

All of these have equal support under materialism, as they do under supernaturalism. The difference is most materialists follow the evidence without adding in things to their hypothesis which have none. But they can, just as theists do and with equal support. So again, it is a mistake to think that the supernatural has any advantage to explain anything to the unknown natural.

How Secular Morality is "Far Superior" to Theistic Morality

I saved this section for last as I see it as the most important, and a good chance to summarize all the points I have brought forth in this book thus far. Secular morality is better because:

- It is a combination of ONLY Class A objects which have been demonstrated to exist, including no miracles, magic, minds outside of spacetime, omni properties, or any other Class B objects that have yet to be demonstrated to exist.
- It is not contingent on any thoughts, feelings, opinions, or any other subjective features of a mind, (not subjective).
- It starts with the evidence in the field, not the conclusion.
- Does not depend on subjective revelation, (which can't differentiate imagination from reality).
- Does not see adult humans as children too incompetent to make rational choices. (Unlike many religious views, my moral system considers adult humans without mental impairment, as sufficiently rational and reasonable actors to make responsible decisions for themselves, and not incompetent children who must obey some more knowledgeable enslaver who forces you to do traumatic, awful and immoral tasks to fulfill some amorphous/undefined character development which you may or may not see until after your death).
- Does not attribute morality to a God-being mass murders whomever it wishes.
- Does not falsely attribute morality to a God-being enslaving or assaulting people who do not consent.
- Does not use special pleading to say a God has a different standard and isn't immoral, even if he commits actions that would be immoral for anyone else.
- No ad hoc/post hoc reasoning to make contradictory data fit the hypothesis.
- Not grounded on a composition/division "like comes from like" fallacy.
- Can get to the conclusion by following the evidence of morality without carousel arguments requiring unrelated evidence/arguments

to justify it, (does not use an argument by extension that has no basis in properties of the phenomenon in question).

- Did not drown babies. (Genesis 7:11-12)
- Did not command wars
- Did not kill anyone, (unlike most gods).
- Does not send anyone to hell, or anywhere, if they don't consent.
- Tests beliefs, doesn't trust them, (no faith required).
- You don't need to be a perfect being to have a valid opinion or discover things.
- Accurately maps onto the fact human nature is progressing and improving rather than the defeatist, i.e. the "we need God, to improve" view.
- No preordained outcome of what is "best" for you.
- Does not require submission or worship or belief, (accepting of everyone, even Satan).
- Does not go against modern advances in neurology, falsely attributing blame without evidence.
- Offers a coherent definition of "heaven" rather than ambiguous promises of perfection with no explanation.
- Does not condone community/God forcing you to go through ordeals without your consent.
- Heaven/BPW is an instant gift to all conscious agents who are all-deserving immediately without need of some ordeal of life, and it is unconditional, not requiring belief or worship, and cannot be taken away by anyone, even a God.
- Explicitly labels slavery as immoral, (unlike Christianity).
- Does not change over time/unchanging, (eye for an eye -> turn the other cheek).
- Discoverable, makes novel, testable predictions.
- Does not hold the immoral view that a "creator" has the right to do as it wishes with its creation. (Even if you were to create another conscious being it would have full rights over itself.)
- The BPW is world truly deserving of worship, and yet it does not ask nor require it... which is a requirement for anything to be deserving of worship.

CHAPTER 2.4

Rick

I WILL TRY TO respond to Tom's points.

Morality of the physical world: Tom tells us that in the physical world, moral behavior is more efficient than immoral behavior and that this efficiency is caused by a "force or law of nature" that is similar to gravity. For example, "helping others" is more efficient and natural than "harming others." The physical world is structured for this efficiency.

But wouldn't it make sense for the author of all life and morality to make the world this way? How can the world *shape itself* into this posture of morality? Let's say the universe is 14 billion years old. It started with a "big bang" and continued evolving from there. In Tom's view, something in the natural stuff of the universe – something in its very atoms, something in the way it functions, tilts toward moral goodness. This built-in law of nature just exists on its own. It wasn't created. It just evolved that way. There is no mind or intelligence or will behind this law. It just is.

I could see myself entertaining the notion of a universe that rewards moral behavior. Back to the author/book analogy I've used previously, imagine the surprise of an author who discovers that the book she wrote *has its own morality.* It's inherent in the book. Where did the morality come from? No one knows.

Not from the author. And if, on an atheist view, you eliminate the author, it leaves the question dangling of the source of such morality. Apparently, the source is embedded in nature itself, in a "purposeless natural process." I guess nature is accidentally good, in Tom's view.

But if we start with the assumption of an author and ask if the book's morality is more likely her creation or is simply self-existent, the answer is obvious. Intelligence creates morality. The blind forces of nature, on their own, do not. But if God composed the universe in such a way as to slant it toward morality, any such "moral laws" would make sense. So, I suggest, that if the universe is "moral," it's because God made it that way.

Novel predictions. Tom writes: "All hypotheses start as figments of human imagination UNTIL they can make reliable novel predictions about the future. At which point we would be justified in believing they correspond to something in reality outside of our imagination."

"Reliable, testable, novel predictions" seems a category more suited to science than to ethics. Nonetheless, to follow the argument along, I think Tom is implying that the way we detect the presence of a moral law is to "test" for it. He says: "We look at phenomena, find a pattern, infer the cause, then make novel predictions about what we would expect to see if the proposed cause is correct."

Let's break this idea down:

We look at phenomena: I assume this means the data of human behavior and belief. Atheists and theists can both observe this data.

Find a pattern: Humans behave in certain ways under certain conditions. Atheists and theists can both study these patterns.

Infer the cause: for Tom, the cause is an undiscovered law of nature. For me, it's God.

Make novel predictions: I assume this refers to scientific experiments and studies that show how humans are likely to behave (and believe) under certain conditions. And since science is as much the tool of theism as atheism, why assume these "novel predictions" point to an undiscovered law of nature? Atheists often hijack science as a tool of naturalism while relegating theism to the realm of superstition and blind faith. Atheists seem to say, "We test reality. Reality rules over opinion, faith, and subjective judgments." Right. That's why thoughtful theists are not afraid of science and even claim that science is a gift from God to study the world he created. But unlike atheists, theists don't think of "novel predictions" as the ultimate standard of discovering truth. It's a helpful tool, yes. But other tools, such as wisdom literature, the lessons of history, the insights of art, poetry, and theater, and the admirable character of hero figures (Martin Luther King comes to mind), can be employed to discern the truth. To summarize, I'm trying to point out that observing the phenomena of morality and testing to see whether it fits "reality" is as much the domain of theism as atheism, and rather than being limited to just the observations of science, theism employs other resources as well, such as history, art, moral heroes, and literature. Any rule that excludes these resources is likely an atheist rule. But why should theists adhere to an atheist rule?

Gaps: Tom writes: "Using a God to explain anything, would be a 'gaps argument,' because God models have never successfully made novel predictions."

It seems to me this is an example of question-begging (assuming a conclusion without arguing for it). Science which is based on theism is as legitimate as science based on naturalism. So whenever science has been successful, it's due, in my view, to an orderly world created by God which science can study successfully. This is a coherent model. Where there are "gaps" in our scientific knowledge (many, of course) the theist is content to wait for the deliberations of science to fill in the gaps. And where the gaps simply can't be filled in, such as why there is a universe in the first place and why there are orderly laws of nature at all – both of which are more philosophical questions than scientific per se – the theist has an obvious progenitor: God.

But I'm afraid many atheists employ science (ironically, a tool given by God) to test whether there is a God at all. But that is not the job of science. The job of science is to study the natural realm, not the supernatural. *Science can make no pronouncements about anything beyond nature.* It's not equipped to study first causes. Nor is it equipped to study the ethics of God (though it can study human behavior that attempts to obey these ethical standards). So its "novel predictions," which are based on *naturalistic* science, will automatically exclude God. That's what I mean by question-begging.

Morality and evolution: Tom writes: "That is why the current consensus in most scientific fields is that morality is simply a by-product of evolution."

Well, of course. When God is not an option, evolution is the only possible alternative for morality.

Morality and the Bible. Tom writes: "We can't gain any knowledge of morality from reading the Bible. The Bible is a hypothesis just like any other. To get evidence of a hypothesis, you need to show it corresponds to something in the world independent of our imagination, e.g. novel predictions specifically related to the topic."

This sounds like prejudice against religion. Tom is measuring religion by the scientific method. For the umpteenth time, science is a helpful but not ultimate tool for discovering the truth. If we make science the ultimate tool, it won't pass its own test. Let's say we formulate the rule like this: "All truth is measured by the scientific method." Let's call that rule-X. But is rule-X actually scientific? How could we measure X scientifically? X is not a scientific statement at all but rather, a philosophical preference.

On the other hand, if we start with theism as a premise, we gain much knowledge of morality by reading the Bible. It's only when we assume naturalism as a starting point and employ the scientific method as an ultimate standard that the Bible would be rejected as a source of morality.

On a more literary, subjective basis, please read the Beatitudes and subsequent ethical teaching of Jesus in Luke 6:20-45. Rich wisdom can be gained from this sublime passage, and it has meant much to me over the years.

Evidence for morality: Tom writes: "I would need to know what Rick is using as evidence of morality. Because moral feelings, as far as I know, are the only candidate for moral phenomenon to investigate in the first place."

I'm not against moral feelings. They are super helpful. But who's to say whether moral feelings line up with the "reality" of either an undiscovered law of nature or of God? Feelings are one tool in the toolbox. Another tool is alignment with truth. If I fail to help a person in need because I don't *feel* like helping, my feelings have misguided me. But if I have a prior commitment to moral truth, I may turn around and assist, even if my feelings are not in it. This is a simple example of the insufficiency and unreliability of feelings (as important as they are), and the need for explicit moral truth to obey.

As for candidates of moral phenomena we might investigate, I suggest, as mentioned earlier, wisdom literature, historical exemplars, art, and poetry.

These are not guaranteed sources of "ontological truth" but they're certainly worth investigating, even if they don't meet the (artificial) standard of "testable, novel predictors."

Forcing morality part 1: Tom provides an extended section on avoiding moral coercion, and in his overall ethical system he deals with it fairly consistently. No one should be forced to do anything without their consent, and if we can use technology to mitigate the negative consequences of any given action, such an action is permissible. No one can decide what's "best" for someone else, since for Tom, "best" is not necessarily a desirable goal, and any such deciding is an imposition on the other person's freedom. I say: okay. Earlier in the book, I commended Tom for using his imagination to envision such a future for humankind, and while I wouldn't want to be part of that future, I give Tom his due in presenting it.

Christians as obedient children: Tom writes: "Many theists, especially Christians, see adult humans as nothing more than children with the responsibility to obey God because they are too incompetent to make responsible decisions for themselves. This comes in the form of the belief that it's ok for a supreme being to physically assault or enslave you, because it knows best. This is called special pleading.

Special pleading is an informal fallacy wherein one cites something as an exception to a general or universal principle."

This is a curious accusation. If I may break it down:

Adults are nothing more than children: Most thoughtful Christians experience a tremendous infusion of wisdom and maturity into their lives when they first come to faith and subsequently grow as disciples of Christ. One example among countless others is my friend, Chris. He will tell you that when he came to faith in Christ, he came to his senses. Hate and selfishness were flushed away. Wisdom, love, sobriety, and servanthood flowed in. The turnaround has been amazing to see. That doesn't make Chris perfect; he is still a work in progress, as are all Christians. But it does show the power of living in grateful obedience to a loving God.

Too incompetent to make responsible decisions for themselves: In one sense, yes. Children in a household are "too incompetent" to make their own decisions about schedule, food, nutrition, clothing, schooling, and the like.

They rely on their parents. The gap between children and parents is fabulously *less* than the gap between adult Christians and God. So yes, we Christians rely on the wisdom of God to lead our lives because we believe God's wisdom is vastly superior to ours. But Tom makes it sound as though such an appeal to higher wisdom is, itself, unwise. I suggest: like children rejecting the guidance of their parents, human rejection of the wisdom of God is truly unwise.

It's okay for a supreme being to physically assault and enslave you because it knows best: This seems to imply that I must be "okay" with God in order to believe in him and serve him; that God must justify himself to me to even exist. But the opposite is true. I believe in God and serve God because God best represents the ontological truth – the bottom line – of reality, not because "I'm okay" with God. Second, if Tom misunderstands the overall teaching of the Bible, I can't very well solve that issue here. Tom's quick summary of God as one who assaults and enslaves seems to imply that Tom has studied the Bible thoroughly, including the doctrine of God, and boiled it all down to two main (negative) attributes. One can always cherry-pick the Bible for difficult passages, but giving them a careful read in their literary, historical, and theological context is a larger project. I've given most of my life to that project, which has been a wonderful, rich process. It's disappointing when outsiders come along with minimal understanding (or so it appears) and dismiss it all in a sentence or two as if their observations are common knowledge. If I may suggest to readers: find a Bible app and follow one of the reading plans for a few months. The Bible is actually a library, not a single book. It's a compilation of 66 books (39 OT, 27 NT) written over about 1500 years in several different cultural contexts. Yet it hangs together with remarkable coherence. Sometimes it is difficult. But if we read the difficult passages in light of the clearer ones, we make progress and are rewarded with wisdom, encouragement, and strength. I know this sounds like so much religious babble to some, but describing it in plain language that goes back 2,000 years is best, I think, for the thoughtful (and open-minded) reader. I hope I've said something helpful regarding the straw God Tom has depicted.

Special pleading: I'd be committing this fallacy only if Christian morality voluntarily subscribed to the rules of secular morality but then demanded a special exemption. But Christianity *doesn't* subscribe to secular morality but instead claims to be the basis for all moral intuition. That is, we only know what morality is in the first place because God planted within us his moral sensibilities, which we can obey to our blessing or reject to our peril.

Forcing morality, part 2: Tom argues extensively that it's always wrong to force morality on others, even if we know what's best for them. He says we should explain to them the consequences of their actions, then allow them to decide on their own whether to take our advice. But what if this more hands-off approach causes harm to others? In society, the state imposes its will on the populace to protect the populace. It doesn't take the more passive approach of explaining its rules, say, about guns or building codes or taxes, then simply hope people will obey. Rather, it regulates these items and many others for the common good.

I think Tom would likely respond that this regulating (imposing) is a temporary and necessary evil until the time when technology will keep everyone safe. This is consistent with his position though in my opinion is far-fetched as a future reality.

Forcing morality, part 3: Tom writes: "However, forcing people into such a world without their consent, (as the Christian God did in the Bible), is clearly a form of slavery. It is without a doubt immoral in every sense of the word and would not be allowed in my BPW."

In a later addendum, Tom clarifies that he's talking about God forcing human beings to live in the overall "Christian world" of earth, heaven, and hell (earth representing the physical universe, I assume).

The accusation of slavery is pretty strong. In the household analogy I've used many times in these pages, my parents raised me in Marshall, Minnesota, without my consent. I don't fault them for that or think back on myself as a slave in their household. Did we all serve each other? Yes. Mostly, they served me until I developed the maturity to start contributing to the family. Then, servanthood was a two-way street, with them still carrying the lion's share of duties by providing me with food, shelter, nurture, and opportunities for growth. Calling such an arrangement of mutual service "slavery" seems a stretch. But by Tom's definition, I was a slave because, when I came of age, my parents gave me only one offer: *Live here under our roof, receive all the benefits of a loving home, grow into a productive adult under our tutelage, or strike out on your own and lose all this.*

Similarly, in the supposed slave-existence of the present world, God as parent creates a reality in which human beings benefit from the blessings and service of God and are expected to contribute to the betterment of the world. God creates us to be productive citizens in the context of human community. Serving others is how God defines a flourishing life. In a famous incident shortly before his death, Jesus gathers his disciples in a room, removes his outer clothing, and washes their feet. In the Roman world, this was the work of a slave. Then he says, "Now that I, your Lord and Teacher, have washed your feet, you also should wash one another's feet. I have set you an example that you should do as I have done for you" (John 13).

Jesus' vision for his disciples seems to be one of *development*. He wants them to grow in character to be more like their creator. Here, the creator (Jesus) models the kind of servanthood he has in mind by stooping to the lowest point in the room, voluntarily so.

I think one of the main differences between Tom and me, which we've touched on before, is this: Tom values autonomy while I value development. This is not to say Tom doesn't value development at all or that I don't value autonomy at all. But the initial impulse for human flourishing starts differently for Tom and me. It seems like Tom's starting point is the autonomous desires of each person. No one has the right to impose anything on anyone else. God doesn't have the right to impose the tri-part world of earth, heaven, and hell on the creatures he has made. He should give them the choice to live in a different world of their own imagining.

But God made only one world. There was no world at all before God instantiated this one. There was no "multiverse" of alternatives to which a local, powerful god could provide passageway to an autonomous traveler. Rather, the creator-God who is omniscient and all-wise decided to create the present world out of nothing. He invented human beings. All ethical standards in the world flow naturally from his character and being.

Tom seems to think that once we've been created by God, we possess inherent rights that supersede God's plan. But where do these rights come from? As much as God has built certain values such as autonomy and consent into human relations, why think these values suddenly rise higher than the one who invented them? The clay has no rights over the potter. And yes, autonomy and consent are important in God's world *to some degree.* But elevating them into something ultimate contradicts the developmental model God had in mind for the whole project of creation.

I realize that in Tom's BPW, values such as servanthood and development could be freely chosen. Christians could even inhabit their own little world. Aside from my belief that this BPW will never materialize, there's still a fundamental difference between self-determining human beings choosing their own adventure and God's vision for the moral evolution of his creatures. One begins with the self and its desires and preferences. The other begins with God as a loving father who desires the maximal "best" for his children – and thus, in Christian theology, his own Son modeling the servanthood most of us find difficult and would not freely choose.

Jesus says in Matthew 16, "Whoever wants to be my disciple must deny themselves and take up their cross and follow me. For whoever wants to save their life will lose it, but whoever loses their life for me will find it. What good will it be for someone to gain the whole world, yet forfeit their soul?"

I find these words convicting. Jesus is defining the good life as denying oneself and following him. And since he invented life in the first place, he should know what the good life is. But the autonomous self who seeks to establish their own life apart from Jesus will (paradoxically) lose it. They will forfeit their soul.

Forcing morality part 4: Tom states: "On Rick's theistic model the community and/or God are allowed to forcibly 'gradually mold' you, without your consent, into 'saints.' Even if you may reject it, and even if it will not work, they still have a right to impose this 'molding process' onto you."

Again, Tom is making theological judgments about the God of the Bible as if his observations are simply common knowledge and we all know they're true. This sounds more like the straw God of atheist websites than the conclusions of a careful reading of the text. In fact, the God of Scripture *invites* people into the process of development. They can refuse if they wish, just as a teenager can refuse his parents and thus live estranged from them.

The lesser evil: Tom writes: "The lesser evil is still an evil. It definitely is not representative of objective morality."

He's referring here to the temporary necessity to impose certain rules of behavior on persons until future technology enables everyone to be autonomous and free. Now deep into this book and having heard Tom's vision for this eutopia many times, I'm still trying to imagine it. First, I don't think it will ever occur. I could be wrong about that; time will tell. Second, complete freedom to do whatever one pleases, as long as it doesn't harm others, is not a Christian ideal. That doesn't mean Christians advocate for the unfettered imposition of their values on others. But the biblical vision of development into intellectual, spiritual, and relational maturity has as its goal the "image of God." This is hard to explain to those outside the church. It means, as Augustine taught, that the end-goal (*telos*) of life is union with God himself. That is, we grow into our ultimate selves of maximal development in all the categories just mentioned and more: rational, spiritual, moral, and emotional. This is a vision of one's "best possible self" and is consummated in a loving relationship with God in eternity.

So here we have two competing eutopias. One is Tom's Best Possible World of complete freedom and autonomy. The "best self" in this world is represented by unrestrained freedom of choice. You could aspire to be a druggie or a pirate or a saint or a lazy bum on the couch, as long as others are protected from any harm you'd cause. It's all up to you. The second eutopia is marked by personal growth toward an ultimate goal and requires sacrifice and love.

May the reader choose wisely.

Revelation and powerful Bob: In this section, Tom accuses Christians of falling back on revelation to believe in the existence of God and then inferring from his power that he is the basis of morality, "even though it has provided no evidence, nor explanation to verify anything related to morality or moral phenomenon."

This criticism seems to assume I've made an "a posteriori" conclusion about God's existence. That is, I developed something like a "cumulative case" (arguments added together) to first show that a powerful being exists, then extended the domain of his power to ethics. Tom compares this to a fictional, super-powerful guy named Bob who has amazing abilities but whose claims to shape the universe are unverifiable.

I think I'm saying something quite different than all this. Rather than justifying why I believe in God, I'm simply starting with God and asking the question of whether objective ethics fits best with God or with naturalism. Thus the argumentation I've provided in the book is not about God's existence; that is a separate question. But given God as the creator of all things, is there any reason to deny his creation of ethical values? None that I can think of. I can think of reasons why rocks couldn't provide morality but no reasons why God couldn't. Tom keeps poking at the existence of God as if I'm obligated to justify this belief – and specifically, a justification that satisfies (roughly) the scientific method. But again, those are atheist rules. Why should a theist play by atheist rules? In bringing God to the starting line, I'm fulfilling the purpose of this book, to test the basis for objective ethics. The book isn't about God's existence. Maybe Tom can talk me into writing *that* book with him some other time, though I'm not sure it would be very unique.

The undiscovered horse. Tom writes: "An undiscovered horse is better than an imaginary unicorn."

Tom brings a certain rhetorical flair to his writing, which I enjoy. But the logic here is flawed. He's referring to the supposed reality of the undiscovered law of nature versus the fictional status of God (the unicorn). He even says: "An undiscovered law is a kind of thing, (ex. laws of physics), which have been demonstrated to exist and make novel predictions consistently."

Let's examine that statement. The law of morality is *undiscovered*. Yet, we're sure it exists because it's like the laws of physics, and we know they exist. Again, *we know X exists even though X is undiscovered.* Common sense says no. But further, if you assume the undiscovered law and run scientific tests of verifiability, the conclusions point as much or more to God as to the law. And, as stated often above, science itself is as much the tool of theism as of atheism.

Stepping back for a moment, let's say for argument's sake that God does exist and has chosen to reveal himself in certain ways. These ways are available to everyone, though in Christian theism *there's always a way out.* You're never forced to believe in God, never required (or programmed) to return his love. Citing Blaise Pascal, Philosopher Stephen Evans calls these two ideas of invitation and free choice the Wide Accessibility Principle (WAP) and the Easy Resistibility Principle (ERP). Evans argues that God's self-disclosure through nature, history, philosophy, morality, and Scripture (etc.) is "widely accessible" to everyone (the WAP). But there are always alternative explanations available to the dissenter, such as those contained in Tom's naturalism. God is thus intellectually "resistible" (the ERP). Without these alternatives, belief would be coerced.[11] God would show up in such a way as to be undeniable – though in my experience, at least, some atheists will deny God no matter what. I once asked a local philosophy professor here in Minnesota what he would do if God showed up in person and performed miracles that were testable and repeatable. The professor's reply: "I'd find a way around it. The chances of me hallucinating during those interactions are greater than the chance of God being real."

Okay then. That's commitment.

In a famous quote, G.K. Chesterton wrote, "Somehow or other an extraordinary idea has arisen that the disbelievers in miracles consider them coldly and fairly, while believers in miracles accept them only in connection with some dogma. The fact is quite the other way. The believers in miracles accept them (rightly or wrongly) because they have evidence for them. The disbelievers in miracles deny them (rightly or wrongly) because they have a doctrine against them."[12]

Willingness to die for a belief makes it true? I think Tom and I agree that a willingness to die for a belief only shows the strength of the belief, not its truth content per se. Imagine a small minority of believers in first-century Rome that meets in a house church. They believe in the resurrection of Christ with all their hearts and gather each Sunday for a worship service. But such devotion is illegal. It detracts from worship of the emperor and the approved Roman gods who are seen as guardians of the empire. Christians are thus seen as undermining the security of the city by failing to sacrifice to the gods. Imperial soldiers break in and haul the believers to prison. There they are given the choice to recant their belief in the resurrected Christ or face a torturous

---

11 See Evans's discussion on "The Pascalian Constraints on Knowledge of God" in C. Stephen Evans, *Why Christian Faith Still Makes Sense: A Response to Contemporary Challenges* (Baker Academic, Kindle Ed., 2015), pp.23ff.

12 G.K. Chesterton, *The Collected Works of G.K. Chesterton, Vol. 1: Heretics, Orthodoxy, the Blatchford* Controversies (Classic Illustrated Edition, Heritage Illustrated Publishing. Kindle Edition), ch 9, location 4829.

death. They choose death. They are doused in flammable liquid, skewered on a pole, and lit on fire. Or, perhaps more mercifully: fed to the lions. The Roman historian Tacitus wrote, "Nero . . . punished in the utmost refinements of cruelty, a class of men, loathed for their vices . . . [called] Christians."

An excruciating death does not prove the resurrected Christ. It only shows the depth of early Christian belief in the resurrection and the unlikelihood of their falsifying the accounts of Jesus. In other words, they probably would not have sacrificed themselves for a known fabrication but only for something they believed with heart, mind, and soul.

So, while Tom misconstrues the claim about martyrdom, we both agree that "Being willing to die for one's beliefs is irrelevant to the truth." Though it does show conviction of belief.

Sermon on the Mount: I assume what Tom means here is that in the Christian worldview, humans are trapped in a troubled world made by God (not forced, in the first century, to listen to Jesus' sermon). That is, we had no choice about being created and we now face the double-jeopardy of serving God or going to hell. This reminds me of the complaint made by some of the hippies in the 1960s when I was a boy, which startled my 10 year-old mind. They said, "I didn't ask to be born."

To return to the household mentioned above, under normal circumstances kids are "trapped" in their families and must face the dilemma of accepting their parents and siblings or running away from home and living on the streets. Children never asked to be born into their families. And if we define parenting and childhood development as essentially bad (or at least not ideal), then something must be done. Household living as an institution must be criticized and broken up. Perhaps Tom's futuristic BPW will allow for any child who doesn't wish to live at home to be set free into a more autonomous existence. My 12 year-old grandson could make the choice to leave his loving family because consent (his consent, in this case) and personal autonomy are the highest values.

As mentioned earlier, in biblical theism, consent and personal autonomy, though important, are not ultimate. The triune God of Father, Son, and Holy Spirit live in eternity in loving relations. They are not in emotional or relational deficit; therefore, they have no inherent need to create. Yet, God chooses to create the world to share his love. Humans are created in God's image and are invited to grow into their maximal selves by loving and serving God. This is the arc of my own life, for which I'm deeply grateful.

Unfortunately, the world God made went off on its own, which grieves the heart of God. This was always a possibility. The world was not programmed to love but was given the choice to live in the household (so to speak) of God or live autonomously on its own – that is, to live in a reality of "not-God" called hell. In essence, heaven is the presence of God, hell the absence. Thus, while on earth, humans begin to partake in one or the other, heaven or hell, a choice instantiated and maximized, permanently, at death. Atheists have said to me many times over the years that "serve God or die" runs against their sensibilities. Why wouldn't a loving God simply give atheists and other dissenters a variety of choices of how they want to spend their days? Again, personal consent is an ultimate value.

I think the biblical response is that hell is just that. Hell is a place of personal autonomy where humans attempt to live exactly apart from their creator. God won't be around to restrain evil or provide models of community or ethical guidance. At least on earth, God works in and through nature and the church and through direct acts of healing to show his love. The rain falls and the sun shines on the just and the unjust. But in hell, the source of ultimate goodness is gone. Humans will need to figure things out on their own. C.S. Lewis depicts this existence as a place where persons shrink into their ultimate inhumane selves. The implication: we were created as children of God for the household of faith. That's how we develop into ultimate personhood. Minus God, however – and I mean completely and totally God-less in eternity – we un-develop into our primal, autonomous, self-determined non-selves. I'm sorry to state it so bleakly but if Christianity is true then something along the lines just mentioned is how things will be.

My friend Erik has ALS, also called Lou Gehrig's disease. It's one of the worst diseases you could contract because it disables your whole body. Erik is in a wheelchair and needs constant care, though his mind is sharp as ever. When I visit him in Montana, he talks to me through an amazing device controlled by his eyes. His family of five represents a vibrant learning community, a household of faith dedicated to serving God and serving others. When Erik was diagnosed with ALS a decade ago, he could have grown bitter and deserted God. Trapped in a failing body, he could have played the cards of consent and autonomy and entered his own place of not-God, of hell. But he believed that was the way of losing himself, not gaining it. So, he stayed faithful to God and is truly a blessing to everyone who knows him.

Tom seems to think otherwise. Serving God represents slavery and coercion. If God is real then we are trapped in a world not of our choosing.

I'm suggesting that hell is the way out. Do whatever you want there. I believe it was George Barnard Shaw who said, "Hell is where you must do what you want to do."

Secular versus religious ethics: Tom has entered the realm of theology and comparative religions. He criticizes Jesus for not whisking away people to the Best Possible World. He commends Jainism as a religion that is both before and superior to Christianity. And he rates secular value systems such as secular humanism and situational ethics above Christianity on questions like taking vengeance on one's opponents.

I like this section. Tom makes some good points that I'll mention below. One oddity, however, is the reference to ruthless dictators such as Stalin and Mao, whose horrible sins don't seem to cast any shadow on atheism as a worldview, apparently because they didn't create "a model of secular ethics." I'm struggling to understand what this means. Combined, Stalin and Mao were responsible for tens of millions of deaths. My response is that once God is removed from the equation, dictators are not accountable to any power higher than themselves. That's a flaw in atheism. I wonder what difference it might have made if Stalin and Mao had been faithful Christians steeped in the Sermon on the Mount and the Beatitudes. The teachings of Jesus have more practical value than Tom's dismissal suggests.

Second, Tom groups Hitler, Stalin, Mao, and Pol Pot together with "awful Christians" such as David Koresh (a true Christian?), Matthew Hale (a Jesus follower?), Marshall Applegate (leader of a suicide cult), and Charlemagne (Holy Roman Emperor in the early ninth century). Their commonality? None created a formal system of ethics. So, in a sense, none of their actions affects the credibility of their respective worldviews. Am I reading this right?

Furthermore, grouping David Koresh and Stalin together as bad guys in differing worldviews (one Christian – but not really; the other atheist) seems grossly out of proportion. As egregious as it was for Koresh to directly or indirectly take the lives of 75 people in a Waco shootout in 1993, is he really in the same "awful" category as *Joseph Stalin,* who starved ten million Ukrainians to death?

Third, Tom makes a good point by naming Charlemagne as a culprit. He was crowned Emperor of the Romans by Pope Leo III in the year 800, solidifying a union of church and state. He was known as a "warrior king," making military campaigns from France into Saxony, Italy, Bavaria, and Spain. Was Charlemagne a true Christian? A man who believed in Jesus and New Testament values? It's hard to say. But I accept the criticism that Christian leaders and "culture informed by Christianity" caused great harm in the Middle Ages and colonial period. Such harm represents an abandonment and twisting of the teaching of Jesus. And while atheists tend to disassociate themselves from the horrors of atheist dictators, they are often eager to point out the flaws of Christians in history. Again, this I accept. It's a fair critique of the faith. Christians should know better and do better, whether back then or now. One exception: "nominal Christians" (those in name only) who caused harm are a different matter. Christianity cannot be responsible for the interlopers or imposters who misuse its name.

On the good side. On the other side of the ledger, Christians played a leading role in the development of science, healthcare, education and, (eventually) the abolition of slavery in the West. These major contributions have been buried under an avalanche of criticism of colonialism in recent decades and are all but forgotten, yet remain important.

What I'm trying to say is that true Christian representatives in the world are a living commentary on the viability of the faith. I think atheists are right to point out our faults, though I wish they'd acknowledge our good points as well.

I would also insist that 90% of Christians in history (and today) serve their churches and communities in quiet, faithful obscurity. They don't make headlines. Their lives make for boring media coverage. Most are not debaters or apologists, so the atheist community may not encounter them much. But on Sunday mornings and Wednesday evenings, their vehicles fill church parking lots. They represent a truly caring citizenry, of which I've been a beneficiary these many years. Are they flawed? All would admit so. That's just one reason they seek the higher wisdom of a higher power, and do so together in community.

Jainism and Bible violence. I appreciate Tom's reference to the relatively small religion called "Jainism" and its emphasis on nonviolence. This is a contribution from another source that can inform Christians on domestic and foreign affairs, and even remind us of the long pacifist tradition of certain strains of the faith, such as that of the Mennonites. And if Jainism predates Christianity by 500 years or so, that is a happy coincidence of history. Judaism predates Jainism by 1500 years. Awesome. I'm sure Tom wants to avoid the well-known "genetic fallacy" of trying to falsify a position by showing where it came from, meaning, in this case: Christianity is no less true because of preceding religions with teachings that possibly overlap its own. And if Tom argues for a dependent relationship (Jainism to Christianity) it's hard to believe Jesus knew anything about Jainism – a continent away from Palestine – and borrowed from it. But I suppose it's possible. And if Tom commends Jainism to us while condemning Christianity, why does he wish to show Christianity's dependence on Jainism?

Biblical violence. The presence of Old Testament (OT) vengeance and violence is a great point of Tom's. Again, he has entered the world of theology and biblical studies. I wonder how much of the texts he's actually read. In any case, I'd work the same angle if I were in his shoes. That's why I drew attention to the violence of Stalin and Mao, above, who killed millions more than anything recorded in the OT. Nevertheless, tens of thousands of Egyptians, Canaanites, Philistines, and others did die at the hands of God or the people of Israel in the OT. Why? This topic deserves a full book or several books to cover. I will try to summarize a few points:

Cleansing. God was cleansing the earth of wickedness, such as the child sacrifices and ruthless wars and slave practices of the nations just mentioned. He did this by calling the Israelites to be his covenant people, then replacing – violently, when necessary – the people groups of the land of Canaan (modern-day Israel/Palestine) with his own beloved Israel.

Slow to anger. Prior to the conquest of Canaan, the Canaanites were given four centuries to come to their senses. In Genesis 15 we read, "Know for certain that for four hundred years your descendants [the Israelites] will be strangers in a country [Egypt] not their own . . . for the sin of the Amorites [Canaanites] has not yet reached its full measure." OT scholar David Lamb points out that in passage after passage in the OT, God is *slow to anger*. God is love. He leads with love. He creates the world out of love. But he doesn't tolerate evil, not in the long run. God is longsuffering but eventually gets angry. The harsh passages often quoted by critics of Christianity and Judaism (and sometimes by Christians and Jews themselves) usually represent the end of a longer story of patience and warnings on the part of God. In this case, he puts his own people, the Jews, on hold for four hundred years while he deals with the Canaanites. But their evil practices remain, so he carries out his judgment against them.[13]

The Hosea 13 passage mentioned by Tom: where God requires allegiance to himself as the only God, Samaria (northern Israel) will fall by the sword, its children will die, and its "pregnant women ripped open." The backdrop to this passage is that God saves his people, Israel. When they are unfaithful to him, a covenant ("marriage") vow is broken. God gives them multiple opportunities to repent and return to him. Eventually, after many invitations and warnings, he judges the people. That is his prerogative as creator. As for the language of the sword and children dashed to the ground and pregnant women ripped open: that's what will happen to Samaria when God removes his hand of protection, thus allowing the brutal armies of Assyria to invade Israel.

Jewish self-critique. Under the inspiration of God, the Jews compiled their history in the OT – what they call the Hebrew Bible – partly as a *self-critique*. Thus, they often present themselves in an unflattering light relative to the holiness and goodness of God. Rather than talk about God's wrath as a stand-alone topic, they talk about it in relation to their 1600-year history of unfaithfulness (mostly) to God and his covenant. They accuse themselves of ignoring the prophets who warned of the dangers of idol worship, temple prostitution, incest, bestiality, unjust treatment of slaves and widows, and many other sins. Eventually, after God's many warnings go unheeded, his wrath is carried out. Those are the headline passages. I'm suggesting we need the storyline leading

13   David Lamb, God Behaving Badly: *Is the God of the Old Testament Angry, Sexist and Racist?* (InterVarsity Press, 2011), pp.39-40.

up to God's judgments to understand them better, in context. And I'm trying to remind us that the Jewish scriptures are no self-lauding hagiography but rather a self-critical look in the ethical/spiritual mirror.

The New Testament (NT) spiritualizes the kingdom. Whereas the kingdom of God is physical in the OT and often takes place on the battlefield, in the NT the weapons of God are love and truth. So, an "eye for an eye" in the OT becomes "turn the other cheek" and "bless those who curse you" in the NT. Jesus bids his disciples to "be merciful, just as your Father is merciful." Instructions to the people were more basic and raw in the OT, but the future vision was always the same: a faithful people of diverse backgrounds loving God and loving neighbor. The OT represents the beginning of the journey, and the people are not yet ready for the Messiah. Think of God as a parent. He has "starter" instructions for his kids when they are young, but later the instructions are updated when the kids are older. God hasn't changed but the household rules have changed to reflect a new people who are in Jesus Christ. That's why we can't read the Bible "flat." Rather, it ascends from beginning to end. Many of the rules for Israel are no longer applicable. Tom criticizes this reading but this only shows his lack of familiarity with the Bible and its historic interpreters.

Does theology matter? To myself and millions of other people, theology matters much. But to the entrenched atheist, theology may be a lot of chatter about nothing. Since there is no God, there's no need for theology, which is the study of God and the big themes of the Bible. In one sense, this is of little concern for the theist. As the saying goes, "You be you and I'll be me." You ignore or reject or scoff at theology while I love it and find it meaningful and enriching. Earlier this evening as I write, I attended a Good Friday service at my church. It was an incredibly moving experience, a profound retelling of the trial and crucifixion of Christ that had many of us in tears. It was theological in that "gospel truths" were spoken. But it was also visceral, cutting me to pieces with intense inspiration. I felt as though I'd experienced the biblical equivalent of a dramatic play such as Phantom of the Opera (on a much smaller scale, of course). It was art and literature and theological truth all bound together in a sacred tapestry. I long for others to enter this world as well.

The authority of experimentation. Tom writes: To quote Richard Feynman, "It doesn't make any difference how beautiful your guess is, it doesn't matter how smart you are, or who made the guess, or what his name is … If it disagrees with experiment, it's wrong. That's all there is to it."

I think I can go along with most of this. I'd add that experimental results also need interpretation. Be careful of jumping to hasty conclusions, one way or another. The graduate students I work with in the sciences are constantly warning me (and themselves) to exercise caution and patience with the supposed "assured results of science." Today's truth is often tomorrow's fiction.

Tom also writes: "Isn't that [vying for truth using the results of science] better than giving up because we are imperfect, and resigning ourselves to being given a subjective revelation, which can't differentiate imagination from reality, and is no more accurate or reliable than a Magic 8 Ball or random guessing?"

Here, it seems Tom can't help claiming science for naturalism and straw-manning Christians into ignoring science in favor of revelation. But as I've said many times in this book, most thoughtful Christians love science and are not afraid of its discoveries. Thousands of scientists in America are Christians (or theists of other kinds). I have worked with them directly in my travels to over 85 campuses the past few years. They are highly motivated to use the gift of science to study God's creation for the betterment of humankind. One of many Christian scientific organizations is BioLogos, which features content from thoughtful philosophers and scientists about the physical world and its relation to ethics and God. I think a simple fact check about how educated Christians in general view science and how Christian scientists practice their trade would clear things up quickly. BioLogos.com is a good place to start.

Purposeful design. Tom writes: "The purposeful design hypothesis has made no novel predictions, ever, in any academic field."

Wow, that's a bold statement from an apparent omniscient vantage point. Tom seems to know about all the experiments in all the academic fields from all time and has concluded that purposeful design from a creator has never been a basis for the successful advancement of science. Ever.

Okay. I can't argue with omniscience.

Purposeful design part 2. Tom writes, "Simply do a Google Search for 'intelligent design.' Under every academic source, it will be listed as a pseudoscience. For this very reason humans have a bias to see design, purposefulness, intentionally, etc., in everything. Especially unknowns."

Again, this statement is simply prejudice against religion. Anyone who looks at the world and sees only *apparent* design is correct. Anyone such as a religious person who sees *real* design in the world suffers from bias, and any research project they conduct on the assumption of design is labeled pseudoscience. This is an ad hominem attack not much different than name-calling.

In any case, not everyone in the atheist camp agrees with Tom. Noted philosopher Thomas Nagel thinks the "empirical arguments" offered by design advocates "are of great interest," and that the "problems these iconoclasts [dissenters] pose for the orthodox scientific consensus should be taken seriously. They do not deserve the scorn with which they are commonly met. It is manifestly unfair."[14]

Nagle is worth quoting again: "The prevailing doctrine—that the appearance of life from dead matter and its evolution through accidental mutation and natural selection to its present forms has involved nothing but the operation of physical law—cannot be regarded as unassailable. It is an assumption governing the scientific project rather than a well-confirmed scientific hypothesis."[15] Apparently Tom disagrees with Nagel and has universalized his opinion to cover all science in all times and places.

If we look into the history of science, we find it was launched mostly by Christians who believed in an orderly universe created by God. I'm speaking of Galileo, Newton, Kepler, Copernicus, and others. "Orderly universe created by an orderly God" was their operating assumption, and they proceeded from there (sometimes facing resistance from the Catholic Church.[16]) Tom must

---

14   Nagel, *Mind and Cosmos*, p.10.

15   Ibid.

16   When the Catholic Church fell into certain corruptions in the Middle Ages, Martin Luther and others "protested" and were excommunicated, thus initiating the Protestant Reformation. One of the important points of the dispute was that Protestant doctrine represented a "novelty" in theology and was, by definition, unfaithful to the original understandings of the church. Protestants countered by accusing the Catholic Church of falling into its own novelties, such as the selling of indulgences. So, when Galileo made scientific claims that required a different reading of Scripture, it coincided with a period in which the Catholic Church was trigger-sensitive to theological novelty; thus, it rejected Galileo's ideas. But eventually the church came around.

not be aware of their experiments which pushed science out of the starting blocks and got it moving forward.

If I may suggest to readers: an excellent investigation into the history of science can be found in *Science & Religion* by Oxford scholar Alister McGrath. One of McGrath's observations is that "Many of the greatest names in the world of medieval natural science – such as Robert Grosseteste, Nicolas Oresme, and Henry of Langenstein – were all active theologians who did not see a contradiction between their faith and the investigation of the natural order." McGrath goes on to recount the contributions of Isaac Newton to both science and theology. Newton's "mechanical universe" proceeded from the assumption that a God of order had created a world of order, which could be studied profitably. McGrath notes that "The idea of the world as a machine immediately suggested the idea of *design*. Newton himself was supportive of this interpretation."[17]

Humanity is improving? Tom writes, "All the evidence we have is the world, and people in general, are getting better in every respect."

All the evidence? Apparently the evidence from wars in the Middle East, Africa, Ukraine, and elsewhere don't count as evidence. The deteriorating relations between the superpowers around the globe, involving Iran, China, North Korea, and Russia, all versus NATO and the West, don't count as evidence. The sinking political landscape in the U.S. doesn't count as evidence either. Record high levels of anxiety, loneliness, and mental health issues among Millennials and GenZ'ers do not provide counter-evidence. Tom did use the word "all."

But perhaps we *are* improving in certain ways. Racism in America (and elsewhere), while still a problem, seems to have improved since the Civil Rights movement. And in Tom's favor, technological improvements to automobiles, home alarms, vaccines, electrical and plumbing systems in homes, and many other advances have contributed to consumer health and safety.

Nevertheless, questions linger. When we do see improvement in human well-being and morality, is religion a contributing factor? Studies show that active Christians in America contribute more time and money to charity than any other group. I'm not suggesting that religion is the only cause of societal

---

17   Alister McGrath, *Science and Religion: An Introduction* (Wiley Blackwell, 3rd, ed., 2020), pp. 30-31.

improvement when it occurs but it's certainly a factor. Another lingering question is who gets to decide how "improvement" is defined. Is the practice of young kids deciding to have sex reassignment surgery without the consent of their parents an improvement? What about abortion, immigration, and gun control? Are we progressing or recessing on these issues? One person's yes is another's no. Perhaps Tom's undiscovered law of morality will weigh in on these questions and shed some light.

That the human condition is improving "comes as a shock to many Christians who think the opposite—that we are moving toward the end times. But that is a socially constructed belief reinforced by religious newscasters. The news has a penchant for negativity. Religious newscasters exacerbate that penchant exponentially."

They do? That is news to me, and I'm pretty sure I listen to religious newscasters more than Tom does.

Science doesn't use trust or faith? Tom writes, "Unlike religion, science doesn't use trust or faith. It tests things."

Tom knows the field of epistemology well enough to know that science "trusts" its instrumentation, trusts the laws of nature and their uniformity, trusts the reliability of the scientific method(s), trusts human perception and rationality, and trusts the written and verbal testimony of the scientific community, all without philosophical certainty (proof). This isn't news. Religious trust is somewhat parallel, though perhaps more personal. It trusts the evidence of philosophical argumentation, history, testimony, and experience. Science often plays into this trust as believers joyfully learn more about the natural world God has created.

Nicholas Wolterstorff, retired Yale philosopher, points out that most laypeople hold to their beliefs about natural science on the basis of testimony, not in a scientific way per se. Few of us have done the experiments in the lab or the field. But if we happen to attend a lecture or read a textbook by credible physicists or other scientists, we tend to believe their presentation of the relevant "facts" which are based, we trust, on careful methodology, peer-reviewed journals, etc.[18] Similarly, most Christians are not trained as theologians or philosophers,

---

18   See the helpful discussion in Nicholas Wolterstorff, *Religion in the University* (Yale University Press, 2019), pp.54-55.

so they trust in the work of professional philosophers in natural theology who tell them of the cogency of theistic arguments. Most of the criticism of these arguments comes from within the theistic community itself as the arguments are worked out. Those outside the community usually don't take the trouble to engage in a detailed way. The late Quinten Smith, a famous atheist philosopher at Western Michigan University, was an exception. After engaging the material for many years, he concluded that theists were equal to naturalists in "the most valued standards of analytic philosophy: conceptual precision, rigor of argumentation, technical erudition, and an in-depth defense of an original world-view," and that most naturalist philosophers were providing no more than "a hand waving dismissal of theism."[19]

All that to say, theistic method and belief cannot be subordinated so easily by secular method and belief.

Evolution producing true beliefs? Tom writes, "We know evolution produces many false beliefs, every fallacy, bias, illusion, delusion, misconceptions, hallucination, etc., including Hyperactive Agency Detection, the origin of God beliefs. This is why we test beliefs; we don't trust them."

We *know* that evolution produces false belief in God. We do? Who is "we"? Theistic scientists and philosophers? Likely not. Thousands hold university teaching positions. In any case, belief in God is only false *if God doesn't exist*. But if God *does* exist, belief in God would be true, whatever its origin. Again, the genetic fallacy: just because you can show the origin of a belief doesn't make it false.

Free will. I had trouble following Tom's train of thought here for a while, which may say more about me than Tom. But I'll pick up the argument where Tom says that my self-awareness of "seeming" not to be locked into predetermined choices is just a hypothesis and that I'd need a "way to differentiate imagination from reality before that was justified to believe."

This is tricky. Generally, internal, subjective states are seen as "incorrigible" by philosophers. That is, they can't be wrong. A clear example is, "My foot hurts." This statement can't be wrong. Philosopher Douglas Groothuis says, "You can't be wrong about feeling that pain." Even when feeling "phantom limb pain," it's still true that you're feeling pain. Does my sense of libertarian

---

19   Quentin Smith, "The Metaphilosophy of Naturalism" in *Philo*, Vol. 4, #2.

freedom count as an internal state that can't be wrong? Does the proposition "I feel free to choose A or B – to turn left or right – without being forced either way," fall into the same category as "My foot hurts"? I don't know. Seems like a close call. In a naturalistic world, Tom might be right. Perhaps libertarian free will is an illusion.

On the other hand, in a theistic world, it could be that God grants freedom to choose. One could be *influenced* by many factors and yet not *determined* by them. For example, I could be influenced by cold weather but not forced, circumstantially, to put on a jacket. This state of affairs follows from an all-powerful creator who gives away power to his creatures: the power to choose. In my camp, some Calvinist believers disagree with me on this. This is an intramural Christian dispute that stretches back to Augustine in the fifth century and beyond, and I've worked on it quite a bit. I'll simply say that the "compatibilist" idea that determinism and free will can work together never made a lot of sense to me.

Tom goes on to say that because materialism is true, scientists can "make" you do something by manipulating your brain and can even examine your brain to predict, successfully, what you will do next. I am skeptical of such predictions, but let's say that I grant it for the moment. In the substance dualism advocated by Christian philosophers and theologians, the mind doesn't "emerge" from the brain, it's a separate substance from the material world and therefore separate from the brain. Second, the two "substances" interact with each other. The material (brain) and immaterial (mind) interact.

So, there's a significant difference between the mind as a property of the brain and the mind as a *different substance* than the brain. A "property" of material reality is also material. In other words, the mind is somehow physical. However, it seems to act in ways that are different from all other physical objects we know of. Rocks don't love or hate. Trees don't intend actions in the future. Blades of grass are not hateful or racist. Hurricanes are not "imaginative" but are rather just carrying out their physical processes. The mind as a physical object must be very unique, relative to all other physical entities.

I'm arguing that substance dualism gives an overall better account of subjective human states and attitudes such as love and hate and intention and forming a proposition than the mind as a kind of physical property of the brain. In other words, there's an "I" about me, a soul that is not reducible to physical reality. This makes sense in Christian theism, and the Socratics held to it as well (in various ways). I'm also saying that since the mind and brain interact, it's not surprising that scientists can shape behavior by manipulating the brain. If the two substances, mind and brain, interact, then affecting one would likely affect the other. Isn't this the premise of taking drugs (physical input) for better mental health?

Back to predicting behavior, I'm skeptical that things are as cut and dried as Tom indicates. In any case, would such predictions count against God? I don't see why. The mind affects the brain; the brain affects the mind. Can we examine the brain to see what the mind will decide? Maybe. But the mind has already had input into the brain. It's a two-way street in dualism, and the materialist has no way of testing for this. For the materialist, input flows in only one direction (I assume) – from brain to mind, since the mind "emerges" from the brain. However, since the materialist is confined to the conceptual limitations of this one-way input, any experiment in which the brain *seems* to determine the mind or where an examination of the brain *seems* to predict behavior would necessarily miss the prior and ongoing *two-way input* between brain and mind.

To summarize this section, Tom and I are back to a book-length stand-off, which in some ways I regret: on the premise of naturalism you get one conclusion and on the premise of theism you get another. I don't know how to get around this. Tom keeps saying that the ability to "make predictions" is the crucial and deciding factor between us and that this factor always favors naturalism. But this only pushes the problem back a level. Any such scientific procedures employed in this testing are as much theistic as secular and, in my view, point more naturally to God than to the impersonal, non-purposeful (meaningless? Not meant as an insult) forces of raw nature. *God gave the gift of wonderment and curiosity to his creatures, and science is the result. Christians use science as an act of worship, a recognition of the beauty, glory, and orderliness of nature. The cosmos is a theater where the glory of God is put on display, and science helps us see it better.* That's my little manifesto on science and faith.

The Rape pill. Tom explains that in an ultimate sense, people are not responsible for their immoral actions if those actions are the result of brain (physical) malfunctions. I accept this to some extent, as I mentioned earlier in the book. Innocence by pleas of insanity, chemical imbalances, and disease certainly play a role. But again, materialism doesn't provide a way for the mind to affect the brain. It would take a separate substance (an immaterial substance) to do that, which theism provides. Substance dualism makes more sense of our moral outrage at injustices such as murder and rape than does materialism. Materialism softens the offense of the murderer and the rapist. And while the dualism I'm advocating can factor brain dysfunction into the equation, the entire project cannot be reduced to the material reality of the brain. For normal functioning adults, a person is rightly held responsible for their actions because the mind affects the brain (and the whole body). "You" did the action. I'm afraid in materialism there is no "you" aside from your physical self. Tom even admits that "my moral system considers adult humans without mental impairment, as sufficiently rational and reasonable actors to make responsible decisions for themselves."

Wonderful. I think we agree here. If they make "responsible decisions" then they should be "held responsible" for their actions.

I saw this played out in a courtroom, recently. There was a rapist. He was fully aware of his actions. He raped my friend. I was there to support her. There was no materialist "excuse" for the perpetrator. A society whose Best Possible World moves in the general direction of excusing the rapist is, in my view (and in the view of many victims) not "best" at all, but really bad.

Add-ons to natural, supernatural. I'm not as free to add things to my worldview as Tom seems to indicate. Christian theism has theological and doctrinal constraints. I can't make it do anything I want. I can't "add on" a property at will. Christian theism arrives on the scene just as is. Tom seems freer than I am to update his materialistic worldview to accommodate any contingency that comes along. It's as though he wants to show the absurdity of theism by "doing just anything" with materialism and thus showing theists that they're doing the same. He seems to be saying, "Two can play this game of multiplying superpowers with no constraints."

I suppose if I were constructing Christian theism on the fly, I could do just that. I could make it explain anything and everything just by building in superpowers such as omniscience and omnipresence, then call it a "worldview"

173

that represents the ultimate omni-omni. This would be a way of *defining* truth into existence. I hope I'm capturing the atheist critique fairly.

And I hope I'm doing something quite different than this. I'm applying to ethics a received tradition that makes sense of the world as a place created good, fallen into disarray, and called back to the original good and beyond by an appearance from the creator (Christ). Inherent in this creator-God is the power to make a universe that includes sentient beings. That's a lot of power but I wouldn't call it "unlimited" in an unconstrained way. In Christian theism, God can't create a square circle or ten gods bigger than himself or a rock so heavy he can't lift it. The classic understanding of God that goes back to Jesus (Christianity) and Moses (Judaism) never makes such claims. If other traditions do, that is their business. And if critics try to force Christians in that direction, we are not beholden to them.

All this to say that religion as revealed by God to which Christians and practicing Jews subscribe is a *bounded set of beliefs*. If Tom wishes to caricature it as an unbounded set of beliefs and concepts that can do just anything at the whim of a practitioner such as myself, that is his business. But that kind of power is not mine to exercise.

At this point, Tom might object that Christian theism as a worldview is not *testable.* I reply that the requirement of testability is itself not testable. Second, the kind of macro-testability that we might choose to apply to a worldview as a whole favors Christian theism over naturalism, especially in the area of ethics as shown in this book. In my view, Christian theism provides the most comprehensive explanation of reality, with the fewest problems, of any worldview. I don't know how to say that any plainer. The reader, of course, will be the judge of the success of my overall argumentation. I know that Tom will not agree with my assessment – which shows, I trust, that friends don't need to agree on everything to remain friends.

A material soul and afterlife? Tom writes:
- "It is equally probable there is a material soul, as there is a supernatural soul.
- It is equally probable there is a material afterlife, as there is a supernatural afterlife.

- It is equally probable there is a material heaven, as there is a supernatural heaven."

I'm not sure how you'd measure this probability. And it seems Tom is redefining words such as soul, afterlife, and heaven – all of which are normally thought of as nonmaterial.

How secular morality is "far superior" to theistic morality. Since I've responded to all these accusations above, I'll trust the reader to review what I've written. Tom laces his accusations with a heavy dose of rhetoric, such as a politician might do to smear his opponent. Again, I'll trust the thoughtful reader to distinguish rhetoric from cogent argumentation.

CHAPTER 2.5

Tom

I THINK IT'S ALWAYS important to remember the goal. What is the purpose of each of the arguments being presented? What started this line of reasoning was the question Rick asked, "What does Tom's model have that he does not?"

To think about this another way, if we started from a neutral perspective, not assuming either Rick or I are correct about morality, and compared the entailments of each of our models, which has more red flags and things you would not expect in a correct model of morality? And, vice versa.

I have mentioned multiple times that starting with your conclusion, e.g. "starting with God" is wrong. It's begging the question/circular reasoning—assuming your conclusion is true.

This is a problem because it makes it impossible for you to look at the evidence and compare different models to see which best fits the evidence. This is why you should always start with the evidence, never the conclusion.

In Rick's model, there are a handful of individuals who can kill millions, drown babies, command others to kill on their behalf, and not only are all such actions not-immoral, but they are in fact considered moral. This should be a clear red flag, something that should not be expected on a true model of morality. In my model, no such exceptions exist.

A model of morality in which there are some who have the ability to mass murder with impunity is a red flag. In addition, being able to do so, and have it be considered moral is clearly another red flag. But, this on its own doesn't necessarily invalidate a model of morality, as long as the individuals never actually take advantage of this impunity, and never do or command any killing. However, in many religious models, especially the Abrahamic models, their God goes one step further and actually does the killing, over and over and over again. And, not only do they kill adults who supposedly have free will, but also helpless children, (even infants such as when God flooded the world). And again, this is considered *moral* under that view. I cannot conceive of a greater red flag indicating that a model of morality is clearly wrong.

If I were speaking to a non-Christian who advocated for a model of morality grounded in a conscious agent, I would use this as the prime example of why such a model is clearly wrong.

To say that some action is right or wrong, by virtue of who is doing the action, is the embodiment of subjective morality. "It's wrong in Culture A but not in Culture B," or "Wrong to person A, but not to person B," or "It's wrong for you, but not for God."

Another red flag to consider is if a model of morality holds people with more power to a lower moral standard. It makes sense to say that those with less options have to do something which is considered immoral for someone with more options, like in the doctor analogy I use of a doctor in the 1800's justified in cutting your leg off to save your life. So, the action of cutting your leg off, which would be immoral for a modern doctor with access to antibiotics, would not be justified for a doctor with less power, such as one from the 1800's. However, a model or morality which reverses this and says the doctor with more power is justified to cut your leg off, is a red flag.

The more powerful someone is, the higher the standard to which they should be held—if they have the means to solve the problem without causing gratuitous suffering, and choose not to, that is immoral.

God is defined as being all powerful. Presumably this means he is powerful enough to do all logically possible things. That means, if there is a single logically possible way to save the world without flooding it, and the God does not do so, he is immoral.

Logically possible just means it has no contradiction or essentially, "Can you imagine it?" We cannot imagine things which have a logical contradiction, like a round square, or a married bachelor. So, if you can imagine it, it is most likely logically possible, and I'm sure you can imagine many ways God could have saved the world without drowning it.

For example, he could have teleported all of the Canaanites, or everyone in the world to their own world in my BPW, where it is impossible to force anyone to do anything they don't consent to doing. This would save all the victims, and kill no one in the process. Then God could have gone back to his earth and continued his plan, without having killed a single person and saving all the victims, without affecting anyone's free will.

To say something like, it's logically impossible for God to do anything against his nature, is self-defeating. It is simply admitting God's nature is immoral by saying the alternative options are better than the nature of God.

Another red flag to consider is when the victims are children, babies, infants, people who have a mental handicap, the elderly, etc. People who are more vulnerable. All of these types of people existed on the earth when God supposedly flooded it. Did the evil babies deserve to be drowned to death by the all-powerful God?

I can understand how Rick can see statements such as "drown babies" as rhetoric, however the goal is not to be rhetorical but to show the furthest extent of the consequences of such a model of morality.

The ability to kill with impunity is a red flag.

Actually, taking advantage of that and actually killing, is a red flag.

Killing adult humans who are supposedly culpable, is a red flag.

Killing children, infants, the mentally handicapped, is a further red flag.

My model does not have any of these red flags. (Rick does mentioned several red flags my model does have which I will discuss later.)

Adults are children red flag

"Children in a household are "too incompetent" to make their own decisions about schedule, food, nutrition, clothing, schooling, and the like. They rely on their parents. The gap between children and parents is fabulously less than the gap between adult Christians and God. So yes, we Christians rely on the wisdom of God to lead our lives because we believe God's wisdom is vastly superior to ours. But Tom makes it sound as though such an appeal to higher wisdom is, itself, unwise. I suggest: that like children rejecting the guidance of their parents, human rejection of the wisdom of God is truly unwise."–*Rick*

I'm not arguing that appeal to higher wisdom is itself unwise. The problem is, there is an inherent contradiction with giving humans "free will" and "agency" which includes the freedom to reject God, leading to eternal torment; yet, at the same time arguing that human adults are so childlike in respect to God, that he is allowed to murder or torture you and your loved ones, for your own good–because he knows better.

You have the freedom to make the most important decision ever, yet you are too incompetent/childlike to make many other smaller decisions. So, God gets to make them for you. Again, this seems like a complete inversion of logic. If we are childlike compared to God, shouldn't he protect us against making the wrong "most important" decision rather than the less important ones?

The truth is, adult humans have an adequate level of rationality to make decisions for themselves. If you know better than someone, you can explain to them the knowledge they are missing. Such as, if there is some consequence down the road they don't know about you can tell them, show them the evidence, or as an all-powerful being just show them the future. Then, let them decide for themselves.

Let us compare the two models of morality and how they address this question of what to do when humans are about to make a decision that has negative consequences they are unaware of:

Rick's model: God can torture you until you do the correct thing.

Tom's model: You can explain the consequences to them and "show them the future" so they can understand and decide for themselves.

Again, let us look from a neutral perspective without "starting with God" and assuming we are correct. Which of these is the red flag and which would you expect under a model of objective morality?

Misunderstanding the overall teaching of the Bible

"Tom's quick summary of God as one who assaults and enslaves seems to imply that Tom has studied the Bible thoroughly, including the doctrine of God, and boiled it all down to two main (negative) attributes. One can always cherry-pick the Bible for difficult passages, but giving them a careful read in their literary, historical, and theological context is a larger project. ... it's disappointing when outsiders come along with minimal understanding (or so it appears) and dismiss it all in a sentence or two."–Rick

Rick implies I may be taking the Bible out of context or don't understand the Bible. There are two problems with this claim:

First, I was a Christian for almost 20 years. I read the Bible cover to cover multiple times and have studied it extensively with the assistance of experts on the Greek, Hebrew and Aramaic texts over the course of my thousand-or-so debates on religion, (many of which are with some of the leading experts in the field).

Second, if Rick were correct, then people who have studied the Bible thoroughly would not come to the same conclusion. Yet, we see the opposite:

"If God tortures, maims, and murders people just to see how they would react – to see if they would not blame him, when in fact he is to blame – then this does not seem to me to be a God worthy of worship. Worthy of fear, yes. Of praise? No." – Bart D. Ehrman (from his article "Is the God of Job Worthy of Worship?")

Bart Ehrman has studied the Bible far more than both Rick and I combined. He is one of the world leading experts on it, especially the New Testament. It would most certainly be wrong to say he has, "a minimal understanding of the Bible," and he is not alone. There are many experts on the Bible who hold these views. In fact, I believe it is only, or predominantly, those who believe in the Abrahamic God, who do not share these views.

Which is a more likely explanation, that the world's leading experts in the field from many different ideologies are all misunderstanding the Bible in the exact same way, or that those who already believe in the God are biased and are looking for a way to try and make the text conform with their expectations? Either way, it is not correct to imply that this is a position only held by those who haven't studied the Bible or have a minimal understanding of it.

Believing that any who truly study the Bible could not conclude God is a moral monster is a common rhetorical argument that makes Christians feel secure in their faith, and is guided by their intuitions/preconceptions, but it is simply false.

This is not to say God never did anything good in the Bible, but that is irrelevant. The number of good things you do, do not overwrite the bad things you do. The reason I focus on the bad things is because, when we are debating the ground of objective morality, we want to look at the blemishes/the bad entailments that we would have to accept if we adopt a model. Rick might be arguing because there is a good consequence to the apparent "bad" actions, that makes the action by God good overall?

This may be indicative of another red flag.

If a model of morality believes that a greater number of "good" consequences can make a smaller number of "bad" consequences moral, then any atrocity can be justified by saving more lives in the end. Or in other words, the ends justifies the means. Suppose Hitler's actions in WW2 lead to a perfect utopia, would that have made his actions against the Jews, (and many others), moral? Of course not.

Doing bad things that lead to good outcomes, does not make the bad things moral. Especially when you are powerful enough to achieve the good outcomes without the bad action, (like in the doctor analogy).

Far-Fetched?

"**Forcing morality, part 2:** Tom argues extensively that it's always wrong to force morality on others, even if we know what's best for them. He says we should explain to them the consequences of their actions, then allow them to decide on their own whether to take our advice. But what if this more hands-off approach causes harm to others? In society, the state imposes its will on the populace to protect the populace. It doesn't take the more passive approach of explaining its rules, say, about guns or building codes or taxes, then simply hoping people will obey. Rather, it regulates these items and many others for the common good.

I think Tom would likely respond that this regulating (imposing) is a temporary and necessary evil until the time when technology will keep everyone safe. This is consistent with his position though in my opinion is far-fetched as a future reality."

Yes, that is a completely accurate view of what I would say, but how is this far-fetched?

Rick believes in an all-powerful being. He could literally do this in Rick's worldview, and presumably does, in a place called heaven. (Later Rick also argues that maybe Hell is like my BPW, which makes it even more strange to say it's far-fetched.)

It seems ironic to believe that such a place already exists somewhere in your own worldview, while at the same time believing it is far-fetched in another worldview. Double standard? Hypocrisy? Bias? I don't know…

I believe Rick to be saying that it is far-fetched that *humans* will ever achieve this level of technology, but that is irrelevant. The argument isn't whether humans will actually achieve this one day. The argument is which option is moral/the moral standard. Imagine there is an all-powerful being, he can choose between these two options:

A: An all powerful being, *"Imposes its will on the populace to protect the populace."*

B: An all powerful being, *"Creates the world with the technology/laws of physics, that keeps everyone safe and doesn't impose its will on the populace."*

Which option is moral/the moral standard?

Rick's model will answer that A is the moral choice.

My model will answer that B is the moral choice.

Going back to the doctor analogy, a doctor with more "power" who chooses to cause excess, unnecessary harm, is immoral. That is exactly what seems to be happening if the all-powerful being chooses A.

Whether or not humans could actually achieve this world isn't the point. The question is which answer is the red flag, and which would be expected on a correct view of objective morality?

"Forcing morality, part 3: Tom writes: Forcing people into such a world [of Christianity] without their consent, as the Christian God did in the Bible, is clearly a form of slavery and is without a doubt immoral in every sense of the word and would not be allowed in my BPW.

In a later addendum, Tom clarifies that he's talking about God forcing human beings to live in the overall "Christian world" of earth, heaven, and hell, (earth representing the physical universe, I assume).

The accusation of slavery is pretty strong. In the household analogy I've used many times in these pages, my parents raised me in Marshall, Minnesota, without my consent. I don't fault them for that or think back on myself as a slave in their household." –Rick

Imagine your parents could choose two different places to live:

A: A place with suffering, starvation, rape, murder, torture, disease, disfigurement, birth defects, etc. Many of which will definitely affect you, some have a high chance, some with a low chance.

B: A place with none of those, but all the other good and mundane things.

Both locations have the same price, same distance to resources, and your parents could easily pick either location, but they decide to pick A because they think you will gain some kind of development that you would otherwise not be able to achieve in B.

Now here is the kicker, you're born and you don't like it in A. You got cancer or a virus, you were beat up by other kids, adults harmed you, and it sucks. You decide, "Mom/Dad, I don't like it here, I'm going to B." Your parents reply, "Sorry son, you can't, you are stuck in A until you die."

Your parents, God in the analogy, has made the decision for you that you will be stuck in world A, whether you like it or not, burdened with all the turmoil of this place because they wanted you to have this "development" thing.

Is slavery not an accurate representation of this situation?

Here is what they didn't tell you. If you started in B, you can leave and visit A, then come back to B whenever you want. So, the argument that you wouldn't be able to get some development doesn't make much sense. As I mentioned earlier, in my BPW you can consensually go to a world exactly like earth, as described by the Christian worldview, but you will retain the ability to leave if you don't consent to being there.

Notice this analogy also has the red flag I mentioned earlier of treating us, adult humans, as if we are children in respect to God, and God has the right to trap us in world A without our consent.

How is this not slavery?

"Similarly, in the supposed slave-existence of the present world, God as parent creates a reality in which human beings benefit from the blessings and service of God and are expected to contribute to the betterment of the world. God creates us to be productive citizens in the context of human community. Serving others is how God defines a flourishing life."–Rick

Slavery definition Wikipedia:

"Slavery is the ownership of a person as property, especially in regards to their labour. Slavery typically involves compulsory work, with the slave's location of work and residence dictated by the party that holds them in bondage."

I only have one question; can I snap my fingers to leave and go to my BPW?

"I think the biblical response is that hell is just that. Hell is a place of personal autonomy where humans attempt to live exactly apart from their creator ... Humans will need to figure things out on their own. C.S. Lewis depicts this existence as a place where persons shrink into their ultimate inhumane selves. ... Minus God ... we un-develop into our primal, autonomous, self-determined non-selves. I'm sorry to state it so bleakly but if Christianity is true then something along the lines just mentioned is how things will be."–Rick

Maybe as Rick implies, "Hell" is my BPW. Take a moment and imagine that the Bible actually described Hell in the way I describe the BPW:

A place where it was impossible for anyone, (including God), to force anyone else to do anything they don't consent to doing, including nature— meaning no death, no aging, no disease, no hunger, etc. You can travel to any world you want, design your world the way you want. Start community worlds with others, etc.

Just imagine reading that in the Bible.

How would you feel? What would you think? How would that compare to how you felt when you first read about Hell in the KJV, (or whichever current version you prefer)?

I hope that my BPW becomes the contemporary view of Hell in Christianity.

I wouldn't want to be part of that future.

"Forcing morality part 1: Tom provides an extended section on avoiding moral coercion, and in his overall ethical system he deals with it fairly consistently. No one should be forced to do anything without their consent, and if we can use technology to mitigate the negative consequences of any given action, such an action is permissible. No one can decide what's "best" for someone else, since for Tom, "best" is not necessarily a desirable goal, and any such deciding is an imposition on the other person's freedom. I say: okay. Earlier in the book, I commended Tom for using his imagination to envision such a future for humankind, and while I wouldn't want to be part of that future, I give Tom his due in presenting it."–Rick

I have heard this argument before, so I wanted to comment on it.

In my BPW, a Christian could choose to go to the Christian world. One exactly like they believe this world to be, with heaven, hell, and earth just as God designed it. The only difference being, anyone who does not consent to be trapped in that world could snap their fingers and go to a world of their choosing.

What is there to object to in this scenario; others having the freedom to not be bound by the Christian worldview? I cannot comprehend why this would be objectionable for anyone.

The only other reason I can think of for someone not wanting to be in my BPW is if they were afraid they would make "wrong" choices.

This is a fair concern. For example you could give up your ability to go back to your own world and choose to be a slave to another. And, it is possible that the person you choose to be subservient to tortures and murders people, like the Abrahamic God.

In the BPW, you would be guaranteed a certain level of knowledge and rationality, and before signing yourself away, you would need to be made aware and have full knowledge of all the consequences, which you could know just by snapping your fingers. So, the "God" could never hide anything from you prior to the arrangement unless you knowingly consented to let them by simply not snapping your fingers and checking. So, the only way that is possible is if you knowingly allow them to conceal things from you, or you know the consequences and agree anyway. That is your right. If you want to sign away your freedom and become a servant of the Christian God, you are free to do so. Though, I think in the BPW no one would ever give up those freedoms because of the minimum level of rationality they are endowed with.

Autonomy vs. Development

"I think one of the main differences between Tom and me, which we've touched on before, is this: Tom values autonomy while I value development. This is not to say Tom doesn't value development at all or that I don't value autonomy at all. But the initial impulse for human flourishing starts differently for Tom and me."–Rick

I'm not talking about human flourishing; I'm talking about morality. Which is more moral, forcing humans to suffer in order to flourish, or giving them the choice for themselves? If the ends justifies the means, then forcing them to flourish would be considered moral.

"It seems like Tom's starting point is the autonomous desires of each person. No one has the right to impose anything on anyone else. God doesn't have the right to impose the tri-part world of earth, heaven, and hell on the creatures he has made. He should give them the choice to live in a different world of their own imagining." –Rick

AMEN!

"But God made only one world. There was no world at all before God instantiated this one. There was no "multiverse" of alternatives to which a local, powerful god could provide passageway to an autonomous traveler. Rather, the creator-God who is omniscient and all-wise decided to create the present world out of nothing."–Rick

What's telling is that God could have created those multiverses as well, but didn't.

"Tom seems to think that once we've been created by God, we possess inherent rights that supersede God's plan."–*Rick*

DOUBLE AMEN! Yes, I think any conscious agent has inherent rights to autonomy to not be forced to abide by the plans of another. Again, which is the red flag, and which would you expect of a model of morality?

"Why think these values suddenly rise higher than the one who invented them? The clay has no rights over the potter. And yes, autonomy and consent are important in God's world to some degree. But elevating them into something ultimate contradicts the developmental model God had in mind for the whole project of creation."–Rick

I believe this to be another red flag. If a conscious being has ownership rights over any other conscious being it creates, (without the other being consenting), that's just slavery.

Slavery definition Wikipedia:

"Slavery is the ownership of a person as property, especially in regards to their labour. Slavery typically involves compulsory work, with the slave's location of work and residence dictated by the party that holds them in bondage."

"There's still a fundamental difference between self-determining human beings choosing their own adventure and God's vision for the moral evolution of his creatures."–Rick

The difference is; one is slavery, and one is not. The ability to choose to abide by God's plan is fine. Forcing people to abide by it is not fine.

Some additional red flags would be:

John Rawls Veil of Ignorance

John Rawls Difference Principle

Nozick's Free Movement Society

Original Position (David Gauthier)

Principle of Equal Consideration of Interests (Peter Singer)

Fair Equality of Opportunity (Dworkin)

Principle of Non-Domination (Pettit)

Principle of Equal Moral Consideration (Regan)

Principle of Autonomy (Kant)

Principle of Subsidiarity

Principle of Fair Opportunity (Roemer)

Each of these is an example of a principle in philosophy of ethics which can be used to compare models. Each involves a test. For example, Rawls' Veil of Ignorance states that we should imagine ourselves behind a veil which prevents us from seeing where we will be placed in society. So, we can see all the members of society, the rich, the poor, healthy/unhealthy, etc. And, we know how they will be treated in society, (like if you have no healthcare will the hospitals give you the best care?). Not knowing which demographic, you will become once you enter the society, would you still choose to be a part of that society knowing you could be stuck with the least desirable position in it?

A moral model of society would be one where you would be fine with joining—not knowing in which position of society you would end up.

If we look at my model, all conscious agents get their own world, which they can do with whatever they like. So, it would literally make no difference in which position in society you were placed, as they are all identical.

In the Christian worldview, you could be placed in the position of one of the babies about to be drowned, or a member of Sodom, (about to be destroyed), or Lot's wife, (who is going to look back and be turned to salt because she decided to look in a particular direction).

Which of these passes the test of Rawls Veil of Ignorance?

Each of the principles I listed proposes a similar test to judge a moral model of society, or a model of the world in this case. In each case my model comes out as more just, and more moral, than the model of the world in the Christian's worldview as created by God.

The Red Flags of My Model

Red flag 1: Mind over matter

"Wouldn't it make sense for the author of all life and morality to make the world this way? How can the world shape itself into this posture of morality? Let's say the universe is 14 billion years old. It started with a "big bang" and continued evolving from there. In Tom's view, something in the natural stuff of the universe – something in its very atoms, something in the way it functions, tilts toward moral goodness. This built-in law of nature just exists on its own.

It wasn't created. It just evolved that way. There is no mind or intelligence or will behind this law. It just is."–Rick

Rick seems to have skipped a step. If he asks, "Wouldn't it make sense for the author of all life and morality to make the world this way?"

Well, no. The only reason that would make sense is, if you believe the creator already had some disposition or property in itself to make the world this way. Maybe God wanted an immoral world, or a world with nothing but rocks. If that's what you believed God to be like, then it would not make sense at all that he would make a world of life and morality.

So first, if you already believe God has some disposition to make a moral world with life, you have to ask how did the God shape itself to have the dispositions it has?

Or as Rick phrased it:

In [Rick's] view, something in the [God] stuff – something in its very [nature], something in the way it functions, tilts toward moral goodness. This built-in [disposition] of [God] just exists on its own. It wasn't created. It just [is] that way. There is no mind or intelligence or will behind this [disposition]. It just is.

(I replaced the word "evolved" because I would not say the moral law evolved. I would say it is a fundamental part of reality which just is.)

Presumably Rick would say, God did not design its own dispositions; they are a part of its nature. Why can't Rick see the same logic applies to a universe? Morality can be a part of reality/the universe's nature, just like God's dispositions are a part of his nature. There is not some other mind that designed God's nature. God's mind didn't design God's nature. So, "There is no mind or intelligence or will behind this [disposition]. It just is." It is no more surprising that a universe may have some moral property, than God may have the disposition to create the world in 7 days rather than 8.

Either way, whether you believe in God or nature, there is some fundamental set of properties that make up the universe and/or God, and those properties are uncreated and undesigned, they just are. In my case, I believe morality itself to be such a property. In Rick's case he believes the nature of God to create morality to be the property. So, I do not follow how Rick concludes it is more likely morality would be fundamental under the God hypothesis than the natural one. Just as nature may not have a fundamental moral property, God may not have the disposition to create morality. So, the probabilities are the same.

This applies directly to Rick's book/author analogy. Who made God in such a way he would write a reality like this? No one—it's just a part of his uncreated/undesigned nature? Then, why not skip the middleman and say morality is just a part of reality's uncreated/undesigned nature?

Red flag 2: My model rejects other forms of evidence.

"Unlike atheists, theists don't think of "novel predictions" as the ultimate standard of discovering truth. It's a helpful tool, yes. But other tools, such as wisdom literature, the lessons of history, the insights of art, poetry, and theater, and the admirable character of hero figures, (Martin Luther King comes to mind), can be employed to discern the truth. To summarize, I'm trying to point out that observing the phenomena of morality and testing to see whether it fits "reality" is as much the domain of theism as atheism, and rather than being limited to just the observations of science, theism employs other resources as well, such as history, art, moral heroes, and literature. Any rule that excludes these resources is likely an atheist rule. But why should theists adhere to an atheist rule?"–Rick

I agree. But, history, art, moral heroes, and literature are already covered in my model by "moral intuitions." Those are all examples of "feelings."

Art and literature, and examples of people expressing their "feelings" via a medium. Moral heroes are people acting based on their "moral feelings" or moral beliefs. A belief that something is morally true is also a "feeling." History is an example of people in the past documenting events or their feelings, which when you read inspire your "feelings."

I'm happy to grant these as evidence we can use to seek a pattern, as they are all examples of moral intuitions–the intuitions of the actor behind the art, literature, hero, history, and the intuitions of the experiencer—the one seeing or reading about them.

I think the difference isn't that atheists don't use these as evidence, but that theists are doing more than using them as evidence. I believe when theists experience art, literature, history, heroes, and they feel an emotional resonance between the art/artist and their own moral intuitions/beliefs, they seem to infer this emotional resonance is evidence that the beliefs and motivations of the artists and/or the experiencer are true.

"As for candidates of moral phenomena we might investigate, I suggest, as mentioned earlier, wisdom literature, historical exemplars, art, and poetry. These are not guaranteed sources of "ontological truth" but they're certainly worth investigating, even if they don't meet the (artificial) standard of "testable, novel predictors.""–Rick

I include all of these under the label of "moral intuition" or "feelings." The way we gain knowledge from these examples is by experiencing them, and reflecting on the intuition or feelings we get from them. They are essentially other people's intuitions and feelings, transformed into words or pictures, or other forms of expression. These then, we can experience and they can align or inspire or change our intuitions and feelings. So, I wouldn't disagree that we should include them as sources for learning about morality. On the contrary, I have already included all of those in my model. Literally, they are the primary examples I use as "moral progress" by comparing historical examples of the moral intuitions from people and literature from the past and present.

So, as I mentioned, the only evidence of morality we currently have is "feelings."

Where I think I would disagree is that each of these are examples of data points. Data points you can use to build a hypothesis, but they can't tell you anything about the truth on their own. They are essentially a collection of intuitions and feelings from across history and people groups. You need some way to test them—to differentiate imagination from reality, in order to filter out which are true and which are false. Without an additional way to differentiate imagination from reality, you are essentially just reflecting on your own intuitions when you read these books, articles, etc., and allowing your own imagination to determine what is true.

Red flag 3: Far-fetched

As I mentioned before, the idea my model is far-fetched is self-defeating from the Christian worldview, and any other which entails an all-powerful being who can literally create the BPW by snapping their fingers.

It would be far-fetched to assume humans will achieve this on their own anytime soon, but whether or not humans will achieve the BPW is irrelevant to whether or not it is an accurate description of a perfectly moral world.

Red flag 4: Not focused on development

Any development that can be achieved in the Christian worldview can be achieved in the BPW. The only difference is that it is optional, or can only occur to people who consent, or those who simply desire it snap their fingers. As in the BPW—if you want a certain kind of character development you can simply snap your fingers and make your consciousness that way.

Red flag 5: No culpability/rape pill

"The Rape pill. Tom explains that in an ultimate sense, people are not responsible for their immoral actions if those actions are the result of brain (physical) malfunctions. I accept this to some extent, as I mentioned earlier in the book. Innocence by pleas of insanity, chemical imbalances, and disease certainly play a role. But again, materialism doesn't provide a way for the mind to affect the brain. It would take a separate substance (an immaterial substance) to do that, which theism provides. Substance dualism makes more sense of our moral outrage at injustices such as murder and rape than does materialism. Materialism softens the offense of the murderer and the rapist. And while the dualism I'm advocating can factor brain dysfunction into the equation, the entire project cannot be reduced to the material reality of the brain. For normal functioning adults, a person is rightly held responsible for their actions because the mind affects the brain (and the whole body). "You" did the action. I'm afraid in materialism there is no "you" aside from your physical self. Tom even admits that "my moral system considers adult humans without mental impairment, as sufficiently rational and reasonable actors to make responsible decisions for themselves." Wonderful. I think we agree here. If they make "responsible decisions" then they should be "held responsible" for their actions.

I saw this played out in a courtroom this past week. There was a rapist. He was fully aware of his actions. He raped my friend. I was there to support her. There was no materialist "excuse" for the perpetrator. A society whose Best Possible World moves in the general direction of excusing the rapist is, in my view, (and in the view of many victims), not "best" at all, but really bad."

This is an understandable red flag; many people intuitively believe others are culpable and evil if they do certain actions.

If we are truly culpable for our actions, my model would agree we should hold the culprit accountable. So, this is not so much a criticism of my model as it is a criticism of following the evidence.

We have no evidence of a soul, no evidence of a "non-physical mind," no evidence of libertarian free will. We have an abundance of evidence of human brains being determined by biological and physical states completely outside our control.

Evidence supersedes our intuitions, and if it is the case that those we perceive as "evil" are in fact victims of biology, then it is immoral to treat them as perpetrators, and it seems both Rick and I agree on this point.

Comparing Red Flags

Rick's model red flags:
 The ability to kill with impunity.
 Actually, taking advantage of that and actually killing.
 Killing adult humans who are supposedly culpable.
 Killing children, infants, the mentally handicapped.
 Treating individuals with more power, as less culpable.
Tom's model red flags:

Matter over mind

Rejects other forms of evidence

Far-fetched

Not focused on development

No culpability

Even if we ignore the responses I have to each, the red flags of my model seem trivial by comparison to the red flags of Rick's model.

Other topics I wanted to address

"Stalin and Mao revisited

"Combined, Stalin and Mao were responsible for tens of millions of deaths. My response is that once God is removed from the equation, dictators are not accountable to any power higher than themselves. That's a flaw in atheism. I wonder what difference it might have made if Stalin and Mao had been faithful Christians steeped in the Sermon on the Mount and the Beatitudes. The teachings of Jesus have more practical value than Tom's dismissal suggests."–Rick

I think Rick's own words sum up why this tired argument by theists fails so miserably. Quoting Rick, with slight modifications:

"On the good side. [Atheists] played a leading role in the development of science, healthcare, education and, (eventually), the abolition of slavery in the West.

What I'm trying to say is that true [Atheist] representatives in the world are a living commentary on the viability of [non-belief].

I would also insist that 90% of [Atheists] in history (and today) serve their communities in quiet, obscurity. They don't make headlines. Their lives make for boring media coverage. Most are not debaters or apologists, so the theist community may not encounter them much. They represent a truly caring citizenry, of which I've been a beneficiary these many years. Are they flawed? All would admit so. That's just one reason they seek [a better world], and do so together in community."

I believe the core misunderstanding of theists who try to associate Stalin, Mao, Pol Pot, etc., with atheism, is that they believe that human nature is so bad it naturally leads to people like them, UNLESS you have a moral authority which inspires you. This is false, as pointed out indirectly by Rick, "90% of [Atheists] in history, (and today), serve their communities in quiet, obscurity."

Humans, both with and without a moral authority, are inspired to commit atrocities. Remember God himself is right up there with these evil individuals with the number of people he has killed, and many people obeyed his commands, (or what they perceived to be his commands), to kill many more. The vast majority of mass murderers are religious extremists who have a moral authority—the same Abrahamic God Rick believes in.

Having a moral authority isn't the cure for immoral behavior, and not having a moral authority does not increase immoral behavior.

"If I fail to help a person in need because I don't feel like helping, my feelings have misguided me. But if I have a prior commitment to moral truth, I may turn around and assist, even if my feelings are not in it. This is a simple example of the insufficiency and unreliability of feelings (as important as they are), and the need for explicit moral truth to obey."–Rick

A belief in a moral truth is also a feeling. So, this would still be an example of "moral feelings." But, the main issue here is that there are many people who believe in moral truth, but harm others—such as religious extremists. And, there are many who do not believe in moral truth, (moral subjectivists), who still turn around and help people.

You simply don't need God. You don't need a moral truth. You just need to feel it's good to help others, for any reason.

Gaps Arguments

"Tom writes: Using a God to explain anything, would be a "gaps argument" because God models have never successfully made novel predictions. It seems to me this is an example of question-begging (assuming a conclusion without arguing for it)."–Rick

I was fairly certain I gave an argument for this. A Gaps argument is when a gap is filled with something that has not previously provided evidence/successful prediction. Therefore, if you see "white goose, white goose, white goose, _____," if you say the blank will be a "Black goose" that would be a "Black goose of the gaps" as in the world of this argument, no prior evidence of Black geese exists. Therefore, if there is no prior evidence of God existing, then any use of God as a filler for any unknown would be a God of the gaps.

"Science which is based on theism is as legitimate as science based on naturalism."–Rick

Science is a methodology; it's based on the ways that work to differentiate imagination from reality. Science isn't based on what reality ultimately is—that's what we are trying to discover by using science. So, science which is based on theism is *illegitimate* just like science based on naturalism. Always start with the evidence, never the conclusion.

"The job of science is to study the natural realm, not the supernatural. Science can make no pronouncements about anything beyond nature. It's not equipped to study first causes. Nor is it equipped to study the ethics of God, (though it can study human behavior that attempts to obey these ethical standards). So, its "novel predictions," which are based on naturalistic science, will automatically exclude God. That's what I mean by question-begging."–Rick

Science/novel prediction, does this. There may be other methods, but you would have to demonstrate they can differentiate imagination from reality at a higher rate than chance, before they could be accepted as evidence.

Things which exist naturally make many... many... many... successful predictions. Things which supposedly exist supernaturally do not.

Therefore, we should be naturalists.

Noticed I did not start with any assumption of naturalism, nor did I exclude the supernatural, which Rick, (and many theists), repeatedly accuse atheists of doing. If the supernatural made successful predictions, it would be accepted by my argument. There are many natural things which don't make predictions, and those are rejected by my argument because we can't differentiate them from imagination.

Notice, the criteria for excluding certain things as evidence isn't an "atheist rule" that was meant to exclude God or the supernatural. It's a very sensible rule: if the method can't differentiate imagination from reality, it must be excluded.

Morality and Evolution

"Tom writes: That is why the current consensus in most scientific fields is that morality is simply a by-product of evolution.

Well, of course. When God is not an option, evolution is the only possible alternative for morality."–Rick

Well, no… There are many alternative ways to ground objective morality which I listed earlier. The reason evolution is the consensus is because it has the most evidence.

If you see a hoof print in the snow, what is the best explanation:

Horse (A thing with a lot of evidence that it exists and can fully explain the phenomenon.)

Unicorn (A thing with many properties which have no evidence, but could explain the data.)

Evolution is just the horse, and all the others are unicorns—including mine.

Bible Knowledge–Morality and the Bible.

"Tom writes: We can't gain any knowledge of morality from reading the Bible, the Bible is a hypothesis just like any other, and to get evidence of a hypothesis you need to show it corresponds to something in the world independent of our imagination, e.g. novel predictions specifically related to the topic.
This sounds like prejudice against religion."–Rick

This is not prejudice. It is true of all books. You can't know a book is true by reading the book. You would need to independently verify the facts in the book by testing them—by doing something in reality outside of the book.

"On the other hand, if we start with theism as a premise, we gain much knowledge of morality by reading the Bible. It's only when we assume naturalism as a starting point and employ the scientific method as an ultimate standard that the Bible would be rejected as a source of morality."–Rick

Again, you can't know if a book is true by reading the book. You would need to independently verify the facts in the book by testing them in reality. This is why you can't gain knowledge from reading the Bible. You would need some independent way to verify what it's saying is true. This has no assumption of naturalism. But I would agree the scientific method is the ultimate standard. Meaning, you need some way to differentiate imagination from reality to know if what you read in the Bible is true.

"Tom is measuring religion by the scientific method. For the umpteenth time, science is a helpful, but not ultimate tool, for discovering the truth."–Rick

What science does is differentiate imagination from reality. So yes, it is the ultimate tool for discovering truth. Any tool that can discover truth outside of your imagination is science.

"If we make science the ultimate tool, it won't pass its own test. Let's say we formulate the rule like this: "All truth is measured by the scientific method." Let's call that rule-X. But, is rule-X actually scientific? How could we measure X scientifically? X is not a scientific statement at all but rather, a philosophical preference." –Rick

This doesn't quite make sense. Rick is misinterpreting my claim. My claim isn't that ANY and ALL truth must be scientifically verified—only the claims about something that exists independent of imagination. There is a distinction between conceptual truths and empirical truths. Conceptual truths are things which are true by definition: 1+1=2, A=A, bachelors are unmarried, etc. These statements do not exist anywhere in reality. You can't find them under a rock or hold them in your hand. They are true conceptually in our minds by definition. Science doesn't claim to have any say over conceptual truths. Empirical truths are things which correspond to reality: stars are hot, the world is round, horses exist, etc. These are the things science can verify as being true or not. So, there are many true statements which science does not claim to be able to evaluate–the conceptual/imaginary statements.

This would not be what it means for science to "pass its own test." In order to put science to its own test, we would need to go back to the definition of science: science is the way(s) to differentiate imagination from reality.

So, when you apply science to itself and ask "is science imagination or reality?" the conclusion is: science is an imaginary method made up by humans. For something to "pass the test" you need to claim it exists independent of our imagination, then the scientific method can be applied to verify that it actually does. No one claims the method of science is an actually existing thing. You can't have a cup of science or hold science in your hand. So yes, science can apply to itself very easily, and when you test if it exists independent of imagination, it does not, science concludes that "science" is imaginary. Duh.

Intelligent/Purposeful Design

"Tom writes: The purposeful design hypothesis has made no novel predictions, ever, in any academic field.

Wow, that's a bold statement from an apparent omniscient vantage point. Tom seems to know about all the experiments in all the academic fields from all time and has concluded that purposeful design from a creator has never been a basis for the successful advancement of science. Ever. Okay. I can't argue with omniscience." –Rick

I'm not the one saying this, the scientific community is.

From the Wiki on Intelligent design:

"The unequivocal consensus in the scientific community is that intelligent design is not science and has no place in a science curriculum.[8] The U.S. National Academy of Sciences has stated that "creationism, intelligent design, and other claims of supernatural intervention in the origin of life or of species are not science because they are not testable by the methods of science."[98] The U.S. National Science Teachers Association and the American Association for the Advancement of Science have termed it pseudoscience.[74] Others in the scientific community have denounced its tactics, accusing the ID movement of manufacturing false attacks against evolution, of engaging in misinformation and misrepresentation about science, and marginalizing those who teach it.[99]

The failure to follow the procedures of scientific discourse and the failure to submit work to the scientific community that withstands scrutiny have weighed against intelligent design being accepted as valid science.[128] The intelligent design movement has not published a properly peer-reviewed article supporting ID in a scientific journal, and has failed to publish supporting peer-reviewed research or data.[128] The only article published in a peer-reviewed scientific journal that made a case for intelligent design was quickly withdrawn by the publisher for having circumvented the journal's peer-review standards.[129] The Discovery Institute says that a number of intelligent design articles have been published in peer-reviewed journals,[130] but critics, largely members of the scientific community, reject this claim and state intelligent design proponents have set up their own journals with peer review that lack impartiality and rigor,[n 28] consisting entirely of intelligent design supporters.[n 29]"

ID proponents can do science

"If we look into the history of science, we find it was launched mostly by Christians who believed in an orderly universe created by God. I'm speaking of Galileo, Newton, Kepler, Copernicus, and others. "Orderly universe created by an orderly God" was their operating assumption, and they proceeded from there (sometimes facing resistance from the Catholic Church.) Tom must not be aware of their experiments which pushed science out of the starting blocks and got it moving forward."–Rick

I think there are two topics Rick is conflating here. First is: whether you can believe, or be motivated by, ID and do real science. Second is: the ability for the hypothesis of ID to make predictions. I don't dispute that you can believe or be inspired by pseudoscience, but still do good science. The question is, does the hypothesis of ID make predictions… not whether people can believe it and also do science.

What we would need is an example of something we don't know yet and have not yet seen about the world, which is expected under the ID hypothesis— then discover that is correct. These don't exist, hence the quotes from the Wiki.

Prejudice against ID

"Tom writes, Simply do a google search for "intelligent design" and under every academic source it will be listed as a pseudoscience, for this very reason. Humans have a bias to see design, purposefulness, intentionally, etc. in everything especially unknowns.

Again, this statement is simply prejudice against religion. Anyone who looks at the world and sees only apparent design is correct. Anyone such as a religious person who sees real design in the world suffers from bias, and any research project they conduct on the assumption of design is labeled pseudoscience. This is an ad hominem attack not much different than name-calling." –Rick

This is not prejudice nor ad hominem. I'm not saying ID is wrong because it's silly, (that would be a prejudice and an ad hominem). The reason ID fails is listed in the Wiki, clearly outlined with rational argument and evidence:

From the wiki:

"...the phrase *intelligent design* makes use of an assumption of the quality of an observable intelligence, a concept that has no scientific consensus definition. The characteristics of intelligence are assumed by intelligent design proponents to be observable without specifying what the criteria for the measurement of intelligence should be. Critics say that the design detection methods proposed by intelligent design proponents are radically different from conventional design detection, undermining the key elements that make it possible as legitimate science. Intelligent design proponents, they say, are proposing both searching for a designer without knowing anything about that designer's abilities, parameters, or intentions (which scientists do know when searching for the results of human intelligence), as well as denying the distinction between natural/artificial design that allows scientists to compare complex designed artifacts against the background of the sorts of complexity found in nature.[n 30]"

Essentially, what this is saying is that when you look at an object there needs to be something about the object that identifies it as a designed object–information, complexity, a BMW logo, etc. The problem is no proposed definition of any such property has ever been able to work. When we test the proposed definitions with a list of known designed and non-designed things, the proposed definitions have never been able to accurately differentiate which is which. So, they fail as a means to differentiate design from non-design. This is just one example of dozens listed on the Wiki for why ID methodologically fails.

Because of these methodological failures, ID is pseudoscience and is silly.

I understand why many theists think that the ID movement is rejected because of bias. The major ID proponents have done an excellent job to make their argument look like scientific evidence. So much so, that it is very hard for people who are not experts in epistemology or science to be able to identify why the ID arguments are not the same as real scientific evidence. Because it looks as much like real scientific evidence, people who cannot tell the difference are justified in thinking the only reason it is rejected is because of bias, (and why this is a common ID argument to explain why their arguments are rejected). If there were no arguments against ID, and people simply rejected it on principle, I would agree that it was simply a bias. But, when it has been examined thoroughly, and to exhaustion, to find every flaw in the idea, (and these flaws have been presented in abundant clarity), it cannot be called a prejudice any more then there is a prejudice against flat earth or phrenology or astrology.

"In any case, not everyone in the atheist camp agrees with Tom. Noted philosopher Thomas Nagel thinks…"

Forget the atheist camp, let us look at the theist camp. Most scientists in America are Christian. The majority of biologists, physiologists, and organic chemists are Christian.

They believe in an Intelligent Designer, but they also believe the ID hypothesis is pseudoscience.

The unequivocal consensus in the scientific community is that intelligent design is not science and has no place in a science curriculum.[8]

In the Kitzmiller vs. Dover trial, (A trail on Intelligent Design), the judge, U.S. District Judge John E. Jones III, (who is a Christian), ruled not only on the smaller issue that teaching ID was unconstitutional, but also on the larger issue of whether ID was a scientific theory, and based on the testimonies and evidence presented in the courtroom he concluded it is not. These included testimonies of the leading ID proponents including William A. Dembski and Michael Behe.

If ID is only rejected because of a bias, why do the experts who also believe in an intelligent designer reject it? Why did the Christian judge reject it? Why did many of the expert witnesses in the case, who are Christian, reject it?

What is more likely—all of the Christian scientific experts in biology, chemistry, and physiology etc., who all believe in an intelligent designer… are they all being fooled by prejudice and ad hominem? Or, are the methodological flaws in ID so obvious to the experts that they do not take it seriously?

I would encourage readers to watch the lecture, "The Collapse of Intelligent Design," by Kenneth R. Miller, a Christian biologist who goes in detail through the methodological failures of ID.

"Nagel is worth quoting again: "The prevailing doctrine—that the appearance of life from dead matter and its evolution through accidental mutation and natural selection to its present forms has involved nothing but the operation of physical law—cannot be regarded as unassailable. It is an assumption governing the scientific project rather than a well-confirmed scientific hypothesis."–Rick

Nagel is correct here. If we naturalists start with our conclusion that the laws of physics alone created life, that would be begging the question. Which is why we never start with our conclusion. In my model, I clearly outline a way to overturn the natural law hypothesis and replace it with ID—make successful novel testable predictions. So, the natural hypothesis is not unassailable. And, I agree with Nagel that if it were unassailable, that would be unreasonable.

Nothing is unassailable in science, ever. Not even the laws of logic.

"The totality of our so-called knowledge or beliefs, from the most casual matters of geography and history to the profoundest laws of atomic physics or even of pure mathematics and logic, is a man-made fabric which impinges on experience only along the edges [...] no statement is immune to revision. Revision even of the logical law of the excluded middle has been proposed as a means of simplifying quantum mechanics; and what difference is there in principle between such a shift and the shift whereby Kepler superseded Ptolemy, or Einstein Newton, or Darwin Aristotle?–Quine 1951, "The Verification Theory and Reductionism", p.41"

Is the world Improving?

Many religious people believe that the world is in moral decline. I believe this is likely connected to their belief that turning away from their God, which they believe to be the source of morality and goodness, intuitively causes them to believe the world must be getting worse.

"Tom writes, 'All the evidence we have is the world, and people in general, are getting better in every respect.'

All the evidence? Apparently, the evidence from wars in the Middle East, Africa, Ukraine, and elsewhere don't count as evidence. The deteriorating relations between the superpowers around the globe, involving Iran, China, North Korea, and Russia, all versus NATO and the West, doesn't count as evidence. The sinking political landscape in the U.S. doesn't count as evidence either. Record high levels of anxiety, loneliness, and mental health issues among Millennials and GenZ'ers do not provide counter-evidence. Tom did use the word 'all.'"–Rick

Those are evidence, but they don't indicate decline. When we want to know if things are getting better or worse, we can't just look at the present. If I told you a number "57" is that evidence of the pattern going higher or lower than the previous number? You would have no idea as I haven't given you the previous number. The same applies to Rick's examples above. For those to be evidence indicating whether the world is improving or declining, we would need to compare them to previous years, and whether the same kinds of events were happening more, or less often. Let us take a look at the past to see which direction we are going.

Since most of Rick's examples are of wars, we can start with a simple statistic: violent deaths. Conflicts between large nations are at the lowest they have ever been in human history; this should give you an indication of what we are about to discover.

If we look at the 21st century, which includes all of Rick's above examples, three one-hundredths of one percent of people die from violent deaths.

If we look at the time period with the worst atrocities we can think of, including Stalin, Mao, Pol Pot, Hitler, etc., the percent of humans who died violently was 3% of all humans during that time period.

Let us include abortions. I agree abortion is immoral if the baby is conscious. Many abortions happen— about 14/1000 women of child bearing age. So, if we include abortions maybe that will drastically increase the numbers?

The most important information about the development of fetuses is when they become conscious or aware, or when they become able to feel anything. Scientific evidence suggests consciousness likely emerges, at the earliest, after the first trimester, at least three or four months into pregnancy. (To review this research, search the US National Library of Medicine at PubMed.gov for fetal pain and fetal consciousness. [1]) Consciousness develops after most abortions occur, so most abortions do not affect conscious, feeling fetuses.

https://pressbooks.pub/nathannobis/chapter/3-fetal-consciousness-facts-about-abortions/

93.5% of abortions were performed before the first trimester (before consciousness is formed).

https://www.cdc.gov/reproductive-health/data-statistics/abortion-surveillance-findings-reports.html

14–93.5% = 1. So, 1 out of every 1000 is a violent death of a conscious agent, which would be 0.1% added to the violent death count of the present year. That doesn't really affect the numbers much so let's just include all abortions, which would add 1.4%.

So, if we look at the worst atrocities you can think of and add all abortions, we get a whopping 4.4% of humans who died violently.

I bet you can guess where I'm going with this…

We have data from prehistoric skeletons, and dozens of studies have analyzed the skeletons to measure how many died from violent deaths. The average from 20 such studies ranging the prehistoric time scales, shows that on average 15% of all skeletons died from violent deaths in past eras. (Prof. Steven Pinker–The Better Angels of Our Nature: A History of Violence and Humanity)

15 is more than 4 4, therefore an improvement. Humanity is getting better.

But wait there's more.

Sweden is a country that has particularly good historical demographic data. It was the first country to establish an office for population statistics: the Tabellverket, founded in 1749. Going back to their records we can look up the child mortality at the time. During the first three decades of the existence of the statistical office — the period from 1750 to 1780 — their data tells us that 40% of children died before the age of 15.1

https://ourworldindata.org/child-mortality-in-the-past

In the 1700's, 40% of children died before the age of 14. Today, globally it's 4%.

So, in the past 15% of people died violent deaths, and 40% of children died before age 14. If we look at the worst modern atrocities of Hitler, Stalin, etc., and include ALL abortions, both stats are below 4%. That is a 10-fold decrease. Humanity is getting better.

But wait there's more.

Laws that prohibit absolutely the practice of abortion are a relatively recent development. In the early Roman Catholic church, abortion was permitted for male fetuses in the first 40 days of pregnancy and for female fetuses in the first 80-90 days. Not until 1588 did Pope Sixtus V declare all abortion murder, with excommunication as the punishment. Only 3 years later a new pope found the absolute sanction unworkable and again allowed early abortions. 300 years would pass before the Catholic church under Pius IX again declared all abortion murder.

https://pubmed.ncbi.nlm.nih.gov/12340403/

So, even in the case of abortion, the fact that more people see it as immoral now than they did in the past, is evidence of moral improvement.

And, as a fun addition, during the supposed global flood in Genesis 99.9999999% of humans died violent deaths.

And, it's not just abortion and violent deaths—every single measurable metric has the same exact pattern. Anxiety, loneliness, and mental health were all worse in past human history when most humans were starving to death, dying of the black plague, or were literally slaves. Technically, people with mental health issues died or were killed far more often in past history because there were no mental health clinics, (incidentally lowering the number of people with mental health issues relative to today). Is this evidence of decline or improvement?

So yes, ALL of the evidence including all of the examples Rick listed are examples of the world improving.

I would encourage readers to watch the lecture given by Steven Pinker:

"Prof. Steven Pinker–The Better Angels of Our Nature: A History of Violence and Humanity"

His opening line in the lecture:

"Believe it or not, and I know most people do not, violence has been in decline for long stretches of time. And today we may be living in the most peaceful era in our species existence."–Steven Pinker

He goes through a plethora of examples of all the biggest most obvious things we would consider to be significant to human well-being, and shows decisively that they are all improving exponentially.

Many Christians, (and humans in general), make the mistake of looking primarily at their personal experiences—what has happened in their life-time—,as a basis for their beliefs about the world. In the theistic worldview personal experience is given significantly more weight than it should be, both as evidence for the resurrection and other miracles, and for grounding beliefs about the world. Personal experience, (testimony), is terrible evidence. Even in a courtroom, testimony is the lowest form of evidence and only applies to extremely mundane things.

Using your personal experience of what has happened in your lifetime to judge something as immense "as whether the world is improving or declining, is like seeing the temperature drop by 2 degrees in the past hour and saying its evidence of global cooling.

Science doesn't use trust or faith?

"Tom writes, "Unlike religion, science doesn't use trust or faith, it tests things. Tom knows the field of epistemology well enough to know that science "trusts" its instrumentation, trusts the laws of nature and their uniformity, trusts the reliability of the scientific method(s), trusts human perception and rationality, and trusts the written and verbal testimony of the scientific community, all without philosophical certainty (proof). This isn't news. Religious trust is somewhat parallel, though perhaps more personal. It trusts the evidence of philosophical argumentation, history, testimony, and experience. Science often plays into this trust as believers joyfully learn more about the natural world God has created."–Rick

Rick is confusing faith and trust. You do not need certainty to have knowledge. All of the things Rick listed about science are things which have tens of thousands of confirmed empirical tests supporting them. God does not.

If by "faith" Rick means: thousands of verified empirical tests confirming the reliability of the thing in question, then you can't have faith in God, because God does not have that.

Rick is then creating a false equivalence between theists "trusting" philosophical argumentation, history, testimony, and experience, (all of which are incredibly unreliable), and equating that to the trust and reliability of the scientific method(s), which has hundreds of thousands of tests to confirm it. Rick is also making a false equivalence between the testimony of religious personal experiences and the written and verbal testimony of the scientific community. Unlike the testimony of religious experiences, we don't trust scientific testimony, we test it. And, if you find they are wrong, you are rewarded with many awards.

It is a false equivalence fallacy to claim that these are the same simply because they both lack 100% certainty. That is like saying, buying a lottery ticket and having "trust" you will win is the same as someone believing their car will start in the morning, and they also have "trust."

Science only accepts things with an extremely high level of reliability. Anyone who accepts faith accepts many methods with low and extremely-low reliability. That would never be accepted in science.

"Nicholas Wolterstorff, retired Yale philosopher, points out that most laypeople hold to their beliefs about natural science on the basis of testimony, not in a scientific way per se. Few of us have done the experiments in the lab or the field. But, if we happen to attend a lecture or read a textbook by credible physicists, we tend to believe their presentation of the relevant "facts" which are based, we trust, on careful methodology, peer-reviewed journals, etc." –Rick

As mentioned earlier, testimony is evidence for things which already have an empirical basis. However, testimony is never evidence of things without an empirical basis such as miracles, magic, mythical creatures, the paranormal, supernatural, etc. If a scientist gave a lecture that unicorns or leprechauns existed, we would not be satisfied with a lecture... we would need to see a unicorn.

"Similarly, most Christians are not trained as theologians or philosophers, so they trust in the work of professional philosophers in natural theology who tell them of the cogency of theistic arguments. Most of the criticism of these arguments comes from within the theistic community itself as the arguments are worked out. Those outside the community usually don't take the trouble to engage in a detailed way. The late Quinten Smith, a famous atheist philosopher at Western Michigan University, was an exception. After engaging the material for many years, he concluded that theists were equal to naturalists in "the most valued standards of analytic philosophy: conceptual precision, rigor of argumentation, technical erudition, and an in-depth defense of an original world-view," and that most naturalist philosophers were providing no more than "a hand waving dismissal of theism." –Rick

I agree with Quentin Smith, analytic criteria are conceptual criteria which are used to distinguish the elegance of ideas and hypothesis. Given enough time and effort, you can think any hypothesis into a very elegant theory to fit the data and meet these criteria... but science doesn't care about any of that.

"If it disagrees with experiment, it's wrong. And that simple statement is the key to science. It doesn't make any difference how beautiful your guess is, it doesn't make any difference how smart you are, who made the guess, or what his name is. If it disagrees with experiment, it's wrong. That's all there is to it." – Richard Feynman

All of the criteria Rick/Smith listed: conceptual precision, rigor of argumentation, technical erudition, and an in-depth defense of an original world-view... these all fall under the "how beautiful your guess is" line.

Evolution producing true beliefs?

"Tom writes, We know evolution produces many false beliefs, every fallacy, bias, illusion, delusion, misconceptions, hallucination, etc. Including hyperactive agency detection, the origin of God beliefs.

We know that evolution produces false belief in God. We do? Who is "we"? Theistic scientists and philosophers? Likely not. Thousands hold university teaching positions. In any case, belief in God is only false if God doesn't exist. But if God does exist, belief in God would be true, whatever its origin. Again, the genetic fallacy: just because you can show the origin of a belief doesn't make it false."–Rick

I think my point here is best explained by an excellent quote by Matt Dillahunty:

"While many Christians claim divine revelation — some even claiming that the truth has been revealed to them in such a way that there's no possibility that they could be wrong — there's hardly any points of doctrine upon which all these purported conduits of divine revelation agree. Which means that some if not all of them are wrong. And if you want to know what's wrong with Judaism, you ask a Christian. If you want to know what's wrong with Christianity, you ask a Muslim. If you want to know what's wrong with Catholicism, or Protestantism, or Calvinism, Hypercalvinism, Neocalvinism, Southern Baptists, the Church of Christ, or the First Baptist Church of Memphis, you can go to the Second Baptist Church of Memphis or any other denomination."

Other than the Universalists who believe all religion is true, everyone believes everyone else has wrong beliefs about God, and for millions of Gods they invented. So, I can't understand why Rick would find fault with my statement above.

My argument here is not that it is necessarily the case that all God beliefs were a byproduct of evolution, (though i believe that to be the case), my argument is that no matter which God you believe in, you believe all the other Gods to be invented. So, you accept the vast majority of God beliefs to be false products of fallacious, bias, illusions, delusions, etc., so there are only two options:

The vast majority of belief in God(s) are false delusions.

Or...

All beliefs in God(s) are false delusions.

Either way, we know the vast majority are false delusions produced by evolution.

Free Will

"I had trouble following Tom's train of thought here for a while, which may say more about me than Tom. But I'll pick up the argument where Tom says that my self-awareness of "seeming" not to be locked into predetermined choices is just a hypothesis and that I'd need a "way to differentiate imagination from reality before that was justified to believe.

This is tricky. Generally, internal, subjective states are seen as "incorrigible" by philosophers. That is, they can't be wrong. A clear example is, "My foot hurts." This statement can't be wrong. Philosopher Douglas Groothuis says, "You can't be wrong about feeling that pain." Even when feeling "phantom limb pain," it's still true that you're feeling pain. Does my sense of libertarian freedom count as an internal state that can't be wrong? Does the proposition "I feel free to choose A or B – to turn left or right – without being forced either way," fall into the same category as "My foot hurts"? I don't know. Seems like a close call. In a naturalistic world, Tom might be right. Perhaps libertarian free will is an illusion."–Rick

I agree it is true that Rick feels free, just like it is true Rick feels his foot hurts, and both of those are incorrigibly true. But, Rick is going a step further than what incorrigibility applies, as he is not simply stating it is true— you are having a feeling—but, also implying that the feeling is true (corresponds to reality).

Suppose I said "I feel that I am on fire." Now, it is incorrigibly true that I am having the feeling, but it is not incorrigibly true that I am actually on fire. I may feel as if I am on fire, but that could be a product of my imagination from a dream, or a chemical imbalance, or a drug, or a delusion. The same applies to feeling as if you have free will. Even if you feel as if you are free, that does not make it incorrigible that you are free.

"On the other hand, in a theistic world, it could be that God grants freedom to choose. One could be influenced by many factors and yet not determined by them. For example, I could be influenced by cold weather but not forced, circumstantially, to put on a jacket. This state of affairs follows from an all-powerful creator who gives away power to his creatures: the power to choose. In my camp, some Calvinist believers disagree with me on this. This is an intramural Christian dispute that stretches back to Augustine in the fourth century and beyond, and I've worked on it quite a bit. I'll simply say that the "compatibilist" idea that determinism and free will can work together never made a lot of sense to me."–Rick

I think Rick may be granting too much. If compatibilism is true then there is no libertarian free will. Choices are determined just as naturalism states. Meaning, God's actions are all also determined by his unconscious nature, including in regard to morality.

If that is the case, the ultimate ground for morality is the unconscious nature of God with no mind, which would be almost identical to my view of an undiscovered law of physics grounding morality, and then all of Rick's criticisms about morality requiring a mind go out the window.

Substance dualism

"I'm arguing that substance dualism gives an overall better account of subjective human states and attitudes, such as love, and hate, and intention, and forming a proposition, than the mind as a kind of physical property of the brain. In other words, there's an "I" about me, a soul that is not reducible to physical reality."–Rick

Substance dualism is rejected by the consensus of scientists, (and philosophers), in every academic field for the same reason as miracles, magic, mythical creatures, etc.

In order for substance dualism to be reasonable to accept, you would need the second substance to make novel testable predictions. Until then "the second substance" is no different from fairies, or leprechauns, or magic.

I agree that we have not yet found a way to reduce consciousness to physical states, but to argue that because we have not been able to do this, it therefore must be a new kind of thing, is an argument from ignorance:

It hasn't been solved by X, therefore it must be Y.

The inability for one model to solve a problem isn't evidence for a different model being able to solve the problem.

If you have 10 axles and the first 9 are broken, is that evidence the 10th works? No.

The same applies here. Even if physical explanation can't explain consciousness, that does not mean substance dualism can. The only difference between physicalism and dualism is that physical stuff has been discovered. So, its properties are limited by what we know about physical stuff. Dualism has not been discovered. So, it's only limited by our imagination. Even if dualism is true, and there is a second kind of stuff out there, there is no reason to believe it would be any better suited to explain consciousness than the physical stuff.

Evidence in the form of novel predictions would need to be provided for one model or the other before either can claim to explain the phenomenon of consciousness.

A Material Soul and Afterlife?

"Tom writes: 'It is equally probable that there is a material soul, as there is a supernatural soul. It is equally probable that there is a material afterlife, as there is a supernatural afterlife. It is equally probable that there is a material heaven, as there is a supernatural heaven.'

I'm not sure how you'd measure this probability. And it seems Tom is messing with the ordinary definitions of words such as soul, afterlife, and heaven – all of which are normally thought of as nonmaterial. I guess you can make anything work if you redefine the terms."–Rick

Definitions are a social construction. They are not based on evidence, nor reason; they are made up. There is no evidence, nor reason, nor argument, that there cannot be a physical soul or afterlife. It is simply the fact that we typically constrain the term physical to refer to things that already have evidence, that they exist, and we do not constrain the term supernatural in the same way.

Because of this we typically do not think of the possibility of physical souls or a physical after life, However, you can posit that they do exist. Just as Christians posit supernatural souls/afterlife exists and both have equal evidence, which is none.

There is no reason, nor evidence, we cannot have a matter or energy-based afterlife or soul. Definitions do not limit reality; they are simply how we commonly use words.

To measure how likely an immaterial afterlife vs. a material afterlife is, you would need novel predictions to show one is able to accurately predict the future more than the other. And, neither have provided any such novel predictions that have been confirmed.

Objective vs. Subjective

There is an easy way to test for special pleading, of the two terms objective and subjective. Only one is contentious.

Rick and I likely agree on the definition of subjective: stance dependent.

Now we ask, what is the antonym of subjective? Objective.

What is the definition of objective?

Now, one of our definitions will be the exact opposite of subjective, and one will have added something which is not the opposite.

My definition of objective is: stance independent.

Rick's definition of objective is: stance independent, but also any unchanging fundamental truths about reality.

Has one of these added something, which is not the opposite of something, in the definition of the antonym? If so, that's special pleading.

Let's go one step further. Let's try to make an antonym out of Rick's definition of Objective.

Subjective: stance dependent, but also changing non-fundamental truths about reality.

Now, that doesn't look too bad until you realize, the distance to the moon is 255,000 miles. This is a changing non-fundamental truth, so is it subjective? Whoopsies. All scientific facts are now subjective based on that definition.

The reason Rick and many Christians do this kind of special pleading is because they think subjectivity is bad, and to some degree it is. So, Rick wants to keep objectivity in his worldview. But also, everything in reality—both facts and morality—are contingent on God's "stances." So, Rick and many Christians add something to the definition of objective so they can keep the term in their worldview.

How Readers Can Get Involved

An invitation from Tom Jump

A Call to Embrace a New Path

As you close this book, you've journeyed through the depths of our models of objective morality and explored the profound implications for a meaningful life. If the ideas and principles I presented have resonated with you, and you find yourself inspired by this vision of a just and ethical world, I invite you to take the next step.

Join Our Community

Embrace the values and practices that can transform not only your own life, but also the lives of those around you. By joining the Church of the Best Possible World, you'll become part of a vibrant community dedicated to living out these principles and striving for a higher standard of morality.

Get Involved

Connect with us through "www.churchofthebestpossibleworld.org" to find out more about our community, events, and ways to engage. Discover how you can contribute to a collective effort that aims to foster integrity, compassion, and wisdom. You can also find information on my YouTube channel "www.youtube.com/TJump".

Be a Beacon of Change

Together, we can build a world grounded in objective morality and shared values. Your participation is not just about personal growth, but about contributing to a larger movement committed to creating a more just and harmonious society.

Thank you for exploring these ideas with us. We look forward to welcoming you on this transformative journey.

Join us today and be part of something greater.

An invitation from Rick Mattson

I appreciate Tom's efforts to build his "Church of the Best Possible World."

As for Christian churches, your local church down the street, whether Catholic, Protestant, or Orthodox, is sure to be an imperfect but loving community where you can find healing, truth, and a place of service. I invite you to check it out, especially if it's committed to teaching the Bible.

For further reading/listening about Christianity, I recommend:

- The Bible. A good place to start is the Gospel of Mark, which is the shortest of the four Gospels and gets right to the point. I find the story of Jesus in Mark's account to be very engaging and challenging.
  - If you're new to the Bible, the *New Living Translation* is helpful.
  - Biblegateway.com and the YouVersion app are both great platforms for reading Scripture.
- The "Undeceptions" podcast hosted by historian John Dixon
- "The Bible Project" podcast, which is a scholarly commentary on the Bible that is accessible for laypersons
- Tim Keller's *The Reason for God*
- Rebecca McLaughlin's *Confronting Christianity*

- Anything written by C.S. Lewis, such as *Mere Christianity* or *The Great Divorce*
- Anything written by William Lane Craig such as *Hard Questions, Real Answers (or his "Reasonable Faith" podcast and YouTube videos)*
- My own books include *Faith is Like Skydiving* (coaches your conversations with skeptics) and *Faith Unexpected* (inspiring faith stories)

You can read my blogs at www.rickmattsonoutreach.com

You can reach me at rickmattsonoutreach@gmail.com

If you wish to find purpose and hope and become a true Christian, head over to the Billy Graham website for clear instructions: https://peacewithgod.net/ Tom and I thank you for reading our book!

www.ingramcontent.com/pod-product-compliance
Lightning Source LLC
Chambersburg PA
CBHW070031100426
42740CB00013B/2655